EVOKING SOUND

G-4257

Evoking Sound

Fundamentals of Choral Conducting and Rehearsing

James Jordan
Westminster Choir College

GIA Publications, Inc.

Chicago

Library of Congress Cataloging-in-Publication Data
Jordan, James Mark.
    Evoking sound: fundamentals of choral conducting and rehearsing /
James Jordan.
        p.   cm.
    Includes bibliographical references and index.
    ISBN: 0-941050-83-1 (hardbound)
    1. Choral conducting.   I. Title.
    MT85.J63   1996   95-52071
    782.5' 145—dc20   CIP
                                                                       MN

Copyright © 1996 GIA Publications, Inc.
7404 S. Mason Ave.
Chicago, IL 60638

To my father and mother, Louis and Florence Jordan,
who always made it possible for me to live my dreams.

To Elaine Brown,
who by the way she lives and lived her life
and who through her teaching and example
taught me and many others to find music honestly
within myself and others.

In fact, a part of the function of education is to help us escape—not from our own time, for we are bound by that—but from the intellectual and emotional limitations of our own time.

—T. S. Elliot

CONTENTS

PART II

LITERATURE FOR STUDY AND SELF-EVALUATION

PART III

A PRIMER FOR REHEARSAL TECHNIQUE

APPENDIX I

APPENDIX II

BIBLIOGRAPHY AND SUGGESTED LIST FOR FURTHER READING

INDEX OF QUOTED PERSONS

TOPICAL INDEX

PREFACE

The pedagogy of conducting can be, I suppose, as elusive as the art of conduct ing itself. Many texts have been written dealing with conducting instrumental and choral ensembles. Those texts all deal with important issues of conducting technique and, to some degree, rehearsal technique. However, for those of us who have conducted, we soon find that success in conducting relies on elusive factors that go beyond the scope of beat pattern and beat symmetry and conducting technique.

Conducting technique is important. This book does not attempt to rewrite what has already been said about conducting technique. Refer to those books also as you study conducting. This book does attempt to provide valuable insights for both novice and experienced conductors concerning the relationship between choral sound and physical gesture. At times, while writing this book, I felt both challenged and foolish in attempting to write about such elusive, but important, subject matter. It would be much easier to discuss just the development of conducting technique. This book, however, tries to explore with each of you those human elements that evoke singers to sing both spontaneously and honestly. This book attempts to help you explore the relationship of gesture and sound. It also attempts to explore how the human spirit of the conductor and the singers can be shared with one another through the music. If conducting pedagogy has erred, it has erred on the side of avoiding the difficult discussion of the influence of gesture on sound.

This book will ask you examine issues about yourself. It will ask you to understand movement. It will ask you to learn about your own body. It will try to shed some light on the miraculous gift of hearing music. But most of all, I hope that this text will take a step toward you trusting your innermost musical instincts, your musical "inner voice." Until you listen to yourself and to your own gifts, you will find the art of conducting will reduce itself to artless physical mime.

This book is about conducting choral sound, a sound that, even though it has many individual sources within the choir, emanates from the same physical instrument, the voice. How this vocal instrument can be evoked to sing is an easier matter for the choral conductor than the conductor of an instrumental ensemble; as choral conductors, while we have a world of timbres available to us through inherent vocal color and the colors of languages, the instrument producing those colors is at least fundamentally same. I am often asked if instrumental conducting and choral conducting are the same. The philosophical, psychological, and gestural processes are the same, but an instrumental conductor must know how each instrument speaks so that his or her gestures mirror the mechanics of how sound is produced on each instrument. Details concerning instrumental conducting can be explored in other places and with other persons.

At the beginning of each chapter, you will find quotes from many sources. Those quotes are meant to both inspire, provoke thought, and deepen your understanding of conducting. My students have remarked that the quotes are a book unto themselves. After you have finished the book, return often to the quotes. They can be a constant source of inspiration and clarification.

The second portion of the book presents an overview of beginning rehearsal technique and the issues involved. I hope that you find it helpful.

Conducting is a blend of reaction to sound and teaching pedagogy. My respect and understanding of teaching and learning was profoundly affected by my work with Edwin E. Gordon. Special thanks for his lifelong dedication to research and tireless teaching, and his respect for idea and new thought. His influence on my viewpoints is far-reaching and can be seen throughout this book.

Finally, no book can go to press without the help of many persons. My thanks to Ed Harris at GIA for having the courage throughout his publishing life to care how we learn music. Thanks also to Alec Harris who has shepherded this project from beginning to end. Thanks to Jan Redden of the Baylor College of Medicine for her illustration expertise. Thanks also to Elizabeth Jordan for her illustrations and her unique viewpoint on the world as a five-year-old. I am convinced that that viewpoint is important for us all to have throughout our lives. Special thanks and gratitude to Neil Borgstrom at GIA for his artistic and painstaking editing of the manuscript. Finally, my deepest thanks goes to the Westminster Choir College community. My colleagues Joseph Flummerfelt, Allen Crowell, Melanie Jacobsen, Andrew Megill, and Nancianne Parrella provide both inspiration and constant insights to me about the art of conducting.

Special thanks to Barry Green for the use of his exercises contained in *The Inner Game of Music Solo Workbook for Voice*. His work concerning the Inner Game of Music has made us all better performers and better teachers.

It has often been said that one is a reflection of those who have taught him. I have been fortunate to have the opportunity to observe and study with gifted teachers who have been patient with me as I struggled to understand what conducting is and is not. Thanks to Wilhelm Ehmann, Frauke Haasemann, Volker Hempfling, Janet Yamron, Jeffrey Cornelius, and Cyril Stretansky. Special thanks to James Boeringer and Gail Poch for both teaching me and providing valuable early conducting experiences, guidance, and inspiration. Thanks to former colleagues Stanley DeRusha and Markand Thakar.

Most of what I have learned, aside from my teachers, I have learned from my incredible conducting students at Westminster and from the gifted Chapel Choirs that I have been given the privilege to conduct and teach daily. The conducting students that have allowed me to teach them and share with them go nameless here. But they know well the insights they have shared and given to me as gifts that I will always cherish. And to the Chapel Choirs . . . their spirits and their love of music are my constant inspiration. Without them, I could not experience what we all believe. To each of them, I offer my gratitude and thanks.

Princeton
27 November 1995

PART I

BUILDING A RELATIONSHIP OF GESTURE TO SOUND

Chapter 1

INTRODUCTION

Every child is an artist. The problem is how to remain an artist once he grows up. (P. 20)

> Pablo Picasso
> in *The Artist's Way*, Julia Cameron

Do not fear mistakes—There are none. (P. 194)

> Miles Davis
> in *The Artist's Way*, Julia Cameron

People love chopping wood. In this activity one immediately sees results.

> Albert Einstein

How vague the general concept of conducting is was brought home to me in a letter from a record buff who fancied himself a born *chef d'orchestre*, though he admitted never having studied music. From his resume, I visualized my correspondent spending many hours cutting a graceful figure in front of his speakers as the glorious strains poured from the magic machine. Many students have practiced baton technique in such a manner, but this gentleman had come to believe that his choreography was actually the cause of the wondrous beauty sounded forth. He was convinced, moreover, that he could produce the same results with a group of musicians on a public platform. Not for a moment did I consider the man deranged. He has merely confused cause and effect, as many do when they try to imagine the task of the musical conductor. Anyone with some musical instinct can follow the outlines of a symphony with appropriately synchronized gestures and create the illusion that the follower is the leader. (P. 167)

Erich Leinsdorf
The Composer's Advocate

There are no bad choirs, only bad conductors.

Frauke Haasemann

Only a mediocre person is always at his best.

W. Somerset Maugham

Outside noisy, inside empty.

Chinese proverb

Habit, if not resisted, soon becomes necessity.

St. Augustine

Always recognize that human individuals are ends, and do not use them as means to your end.

Immanuel Kant

The best way out is always through.

Robert Frost

You know what you are.
You are what you are.
You've done what you've done and
    you are responsible for what you have done.
What you have done is you.

Wil Roadrunner
Hopi Indian artist

Creativity requires faith. Faith requires that we relinquish control. This is frightening, and we resist it. Our resistance to our creativity is a form of self-destruction. We throw up roadblocks on our own path. Why do we do this? In order to maintain an illusion of control. Depression, like anger and anxiety, is resistance, and it creates dis-ease. This manifests itself as sluggishness, confusion, "I don't know. . . ."

The truth is, we do know, and we *know* that we know.

Each of us has an inner dream that we can unfold if we will just have the courage to admit what it is. And the faith to trust our own admission. The admitting is often very difficult. A clearing affirmation can often open the channel. One excellent one is "I know the things I know." Another is "I trust my own inner guide." Either of these will eventually yield us a sense of our own direction—which we often then promptly resist! (P. 193)

Creativity—like human life itself—begins in the darkness. We need to acknowledge this. All too often, we think only in terms of light: "And then the lightbulb went on and I got it!" It is true that insights may come to us as flashes. It is true that some of these flashes may be blinding. It is, however, also true that such bright ideas are preceded by a gestation period that is interior, murky, and completely necessary. (P. 194)

Trusting our creativity is new behavior for many of us. It may feel quite threatening initially, not only to us but to our intimates. We may feel— and look—erratic. This erraticism is a normal part of getting unstuck, pulling free from the muck that has blocked us. It is important to remember that at first flush, going sane feels just like going crazy.

There is a recognizable ebb and flow to the process of recovering our creative selves. As we gain strength, so will some of the attacks of self-doubt. This is normal, and we can deal with these stronger attacks when we see them as symptoms of recovery. (P. 40)

Julia Cameron
The Artist's Way

• • • • •

I have heard it said that conducting texts either function as crutches for the musically weak or cripple the talented. I hope that neither is the case with this text. However, there is a bit of truth to that statement. Conducting texts, for the most part, deal with the "outside" aspects of making music. That is, we tend to want to teach what, perhaps, is easiest to get at. Body position, facial expression, cueing, arm position, and conducting patterns seem to be the stuff of conducting books.

So, persons learn those "outside" things, seemingly from a book. But for those of us who have struggled in the rehearsal room, the church choir loft, the public school rehearsal room, and in the conducting classroom, conducting must be a reflection of one's musical interior and one's sense of fantasy. Conducting must relay much more to singers than just tempi and entrances. Our internal aesthetic, breath, listening skills, and trust of those who sing for us are necessary and unavoidable prerequisites for conducting.

THE APPROACH

This text probably does not resemble any of the conducting texts that you have experienced. Foolhardy as it may be, this book will attempt to develop the conductor from the *inside out* rather than from the *outside in*. This book will attempt to explain the importance of breath in conducting. It will make a concerted effort to convince the reader of the important role of listening. It will try to make the case for the power of one's humanity and honesty on the podium.

But most importantly, this text will try to make you begin to trust and listen to your own instincts, if not for the first time, then once again in your life. Whether you hold five music degrees or none at all, this book begins with the assumption that each person who has a desire to conduct and share with others can only be as good as their own inner musical voice. In fact, many wonderful conductors are at work in small churches and elementary schools around the world. The problem is that they have not been taught to listen as a conductor and to follow their intuitive, musical voice.

This book, perhaps, might more rightly be considered a hefty dose of the philosophy of conducting. So be it. A conductor's understanding and acceptance of his or her equal role with the singer is a prerequisite to great music making at any level. We, as conductors, actually do not conduct; we *evoke* sounds from our singers with our gesture, which is set into motion with our own breath, the miracle that is the musical phrase. After that, we guide our singers not with our hands, but rather with our ears. It is our responsibility as conductors to intimately understand what gestures help singers and the music and which gestures hinder singers and cause the music not to sing.

For those who are reading this text after a year or many years of conducting or conducting study, or both, enter the reading and the ideas presented with an open mind. I ask only that in debating the ideas with yourself that the music, the composer, and the sound of the music be the final arbiter. For those of you for whom this is your first conducting text, trust your musical instincts and enjoy the experience!

Whether one conducts a church choir or a professional chorus, the fundamentals of conducting are the same. Many persons remark to me that they should be in "advanced" conducting class because they have a certain number of years experience. Just as the coach of the Olympic swimmer monitors his student to make sure that the basics of swimming technique are always present, so must the conducting pedagogue constantly monitor the conducting student to make sure that the basics of conducting are always present. Regardless of the chorus that you conduct, the basics must always be present for the sound to live through the music. Actually, the fundamental precepts of artistic conducting are quite simple. But as the teaching adage states, *What is usually easiest learned is hardest taught.* So it is with the art of conducting.

TRUSTING YOUR MUSIC INSTINCTS

This text is unique because of another reason. In many ways, it asks you to rely on your musical intuition and musical experience, rather than trying to imitate the musicianship or musical ideas of those who teach you or those choral conductors you admire. My experience as a conducting teacher has proven to me that, until a student trusts themselves and their inner musical voice, virtually little progress is made. Without such confidence, conducting is often gesturing that has little or nothing to do with the sound in the room at the time, and more importantly, the persons that are making it.

For the most part, the music education system that each of us has passed through does not teach us musical independence. Improvisation, the ultimate acceptance of musical responsibility on an intuitive level, is absent from most music curricula, grade school through college. Sight reading is often the excuse for teaching hearing. A student is judged musically illiterate if they cannot read music. Assumptions are constantly made as to one's musical abilities based upon one's performance, not one's hearing. For those of us who have been through college theory classes, we are asked to learn much without an overview of our innate musical abilities, otherwise known as musical aptitude. We could, I suppose, place all the blame on curricula; however, the problem of mistrust of self pervades the world in which we live. Persons are not encouraged to think, take chances, or even trust their intuitive self. Thus, many of us don't understand what the problem is when we stand in front of a choir to conduct.

Conducting is a creative act. Musical creativity requires faith—almost blind faith in one's ear and one's inner musical voice. Implicit in that blind faith is a requirement to relinquish control of both the music and others. Regardless of your depth of musical background, the steps into a creative life as a conductor require trust in self and others. When that path is followed, profound music is made. This book will constantly ask you to rely on your "ear" and to listen. Listening to your own musical voice and the musical voice of your choir is fundamental to conducting. Do not be afraid to make "mistakes" and to take chances. Only when you do take chances will growth occur. Trust yourself enough to make a mistake.

You will notice that each chapter begins with a series of quotations. These quotations were selected to provide support for the material presented in the chapter, but more importantly, to provide further depth concerning the content in the chapter. Many persons have remarked that the quotes almost are a book unto themselves. While the book was written as a fundamentals book in choral conducting, the content goes beyond a single "course" in fundamentals. It is my hope that it will become a much used resource in your library.

This book will ask you to confront your potential, expose your weaknesses, and accept them. Not an easy task. Actually, the study of conducting, correctly pursued, asks you to explore the very nature of your own creativity. That exploration asks you to trust your musical or creative instincts. Many times, this initial inward exploration feels threatening. You may feel "out of control." But it is exactly that feeling of being "out of control" which allows one's inner musical voice to speak through one's gesture.

The learning of any art form such as conducting is to recognize your potential. For the most part, it is not a matter of *adding* to but of *developing, evolving,* and *growing,* which is connected to and limited by one's experience. Just as a person cannot learn to swim without "being in the water," he or she cannot learn to conduct without "being in the sound," or more importantly, "being the sound." I hope this book will show you that each of us contain within ourselves a world of music capabilities, of music possibilities, and that, when approached in a pedagogically correct way, music can speak through us and be manifest through the sounds made by the persons we release sound from through our gesture. Just as the young child plays, so too must we learn once again to play with the sounds within us and to discover how to release those same sounds from singers in a sensible and artistic way.

One of the mentors in my life, Frauke Haasemann, always said that "there are no bad choirs, only bad conductors." While the statement seems a bit blunt, it is very true. The spirit, breath, and consequent gesture of the conductor is so influential that the sound an ensemble produces is always a reflection of the conductor's very spirit.

Chapter II

Alignment

Creating the Inner Space for Breath

Alexander first of all discovered that the relationship of his head and neck had immediate consequences for the condition of his larynx and breathing mechanism and then that the Use of his head and neck was the prime factor in coordinating the Use of the rest of his organism. He functioned best when his stature lengthened, and this came about when he allowed a Use of his head that he described as "forward and up" in relation to his neck and torso. The reader will recall that when Alexander first tried to "put" his head forward and up he found that he could not do so. Eventually, he realized that to achieve his goal he should not "do" or "put" anything, but rather apply a process of non-interfering (inhibition) and conscious reasoned intention (direction). (P. 42)

Michael Gelb
Body Learning

Alexander's work can do much more than help overcome painful body problems for the performer. It can bring the performer's body under more conscious control and therefore increase its versatility as an instrument for artistic expression.

Conductors can get better results from their orchestras because they are more in touch with the way they use energy in their bodies. (P. 184)

> Deborah Caplan
> *Back Trouble*

I formulate Alexander's discoveries as Laws of Human Movement, laws of the Scientific sense, universal and invariable. I believe there are two.

1. Habituated tensing of the muscles of the neck results in a predictable and inevitable tensing of the whole body. Release out of the tensing of the whole must begin with release of the muscles of the neck.

2. In movement, when it's free, the head leads and the body follows. More particularly, the head leads and the spine follows in sequence. (P. 3)

But here's the rub. The pattern of tensing Alexander called downward pull interferes or opposes or counters the involuntary patterns that support us. Typically, those involuntary reflex patterns lengthen us, especially when they involve the spine. Downward pull shortens us. (P. 8–9)

The word waist dominates our mapping and therefore our moving. I say the word, and not the thing, because a waist is a fiction, a kinesthetic fantasy. Something arbitrary, and nothing anatomical, is named in the word waist. . . . The central organizing feature in the body is not horizontal, but vertical. It is the spine. (P. 44)

To add insult to injury, we call our waist our middle. It is not. Our middle is the pelvic floor. We are divided in half at the hip joint. (P. 44)

> Barbara Conable, William Conable
> *How to Learn the Alexander Technique*

For if the pupil thinks of a certain "end" as desirable and starts to pursue it directly, he will certainly take the course of action that he has been accustomed to take in like conditions. In other words, he will follow his habitual procedure in regard to it, and should that procedure happen to be a bad one for the purpose, he only strengthens the incorrect experiences in connection with it by using this procedure again. If, on the other hand, the pupil stops himself from going to work in his usual way (inhibition), and proceeds to replace his old subconscious means by the new conscious means which his teacher has given him, he will have taken the first and most important step towards breaking-down of a habit, and towards that constructive, conscious and reasoning control which tends toward a mastery of the situation. It is therefore impressed on the pupil from the beginning that, as the essential preliminary to any successful work on his part, he must refuse to work directly for his "end" and keep his attention on the means whereby this end can be achieved.

F. M. Alexander
Constructive Conscious Control of the Individual

• • • • •

The most important skill that a choral conductor must develop is the ability to open the body so that breath can fall into it. While this sounds like an easy task, you will quickly find out that the ability to allow a full, deep-seated breath to enter the body and to fall low into the body is a challenge. One's ability to open the body and to breathe directly impacts the color of the sound, the rhythmic spontaneity of the musical line or phrase, the dynamics, and the overall rhythmic style of the piece being sung.

The ability to open one's body and breathe is directly related to the learned ability to properly align one's body. Because of the pace and pressures of our daily life, the alignment of the body is adversely affected by muscle tension that begins to draw the body away from its natural alignment. In essence, one must learn to enter into a pattern of unlearning poor postural habits. Good body alignment cannot be *made* to happen; one must learn how to *allow* proper alignment to happen. The work and theories of Frederick Matthias Alexander provide a valuable tool for conductors to seek out their natural alignment.

WHAT IS THE ALEXANDER TECHNIQUE?

Frederick Matthias Alexander was born in Australia in 1869. An actor by trade, he specialized in Shakespearean monologs. In the early part of his career, he was plagued by persistent hoarseness coupled with a lack of projection. Frequent consultations with a physician provided only temporary relief. After continued frustration, Alexander reasoned that his vocal difficulties were not caused by a medical problem but were most likely caused by some factor occurring while he recited his monologs. Standing in front of a mirror, Alexander began to observe his "manner of doing." As he began to speak, he noticed three problems: (1) he stiffened his neck in such a way as to cause the head to pull backward; (2) this was accompanied by a depressed larynx and (3) sucking in the breath with a gasp.

Alexander set out to try to correct these problems. He had little success with numbers 2 and 3. However, he did meet with success in preventing his head from pulling down and back. He found that if he could prevent his head from pulling down and back, the quality of both his voice and breath improved dramatically. From this simple experiment, Alexander concluded that his "manner of doing" did directly affect his functioning. He continued his observations and discovered that by moving the head/neck unit he could affect the larynx. He also discovered that when he depressed his larynx, he also tended to lift his chest, narrow his back, and shorten his overall stature.

Those observations proved to Alexander that the functioning of the vocal mechanism was influenced not only by his head and neck, but by the muscular tensions brought upon his body. Generally, his continued experiments showed that the voice functioned at its optimum when his stature lengthened. This could only be achieved when he told himself that his head should move "forward and up," that he should *allow* the muscles of his neck to release, and that he should tell his spine to release into length and width. The interrelationship of the head, neck, and torso was termed by Alexander as the Primary Control.

Alexander continued his observational study and teaching for sixty years. His observations and teaching techniques became known as the Alexander Technique. The technique has been applied widely, such applications ranging from back pain to acting, to sports, and to musicians and music making. The work of Alexander has tremendous import for our study of conducting.

THE ALEXANDER TECHNIQUE FOR CONDUCTORS

Much of what we do as conductors is highly influenced by our body attitude. As conductors, our bodies must reflect what is necessary to produce a healthy, open, and free vocal sound, regardless of the level of the singers with which we work. Many new and experienced conductors underestimate the impact that correct alignment can have upon the ensemble that they conduct and the effects that poor posture and misalignment have upon their own performance as conductors. The ramifications of poor alignment are many. Here are a few to consider.

EFFECTS OF POOR ALIGNMENT ON THE ENSEMBLE. (1) A conductor whose body is "out of alignment" will send messages to the singers to align their bodies in the same fashion. Choral ensembles, over time, will mirror the posture of their conductor. The effect of this is obvious. The inability to allow air to enter the body, the inability to "support" the musical line, poor tone, and pitch difficulties are just a few points to be mentioned. (2) Another effect of the conductor's misalignment will be on rhythm. If the conductor is misaligned, it follows that the singers will be unable to breathe properly and unable to set the breath low enough to sing well. If free breathing is not possible by the singers, then rhythmic problems will abound. The root of inconsistent tempo problems in a choral ensemble many times rests with an improper inhalation technique fueled by poor posture.

EFFECTS OF POOR ALIGNMENT ON THE CONDUCTOR. While the effects of poor posture on the choral ensemble may be many and far reaching, those effects are compounded when poor alignment affects the functioning of the conductor. (1) If the body of the conductor is not aligned, the ability to allow breath into the body will be difficult, and without proper inhalation, the conductor is unable to relay in his impulse gesture (explained in a future chapter) the essential information that an ensemble needs to sing, i.e., the depth of inhalation, the color of sound, and the pulse and rhythmic character of the piece. A conductor's body is a chamber into which air must be allowed to enter. If the passageways are blocked or obstructed because of poor alignment, the conductor's effectiveness will be diminished. (2) Body misalignment has yet another detrimental effect on the conductor. When a body is correctly aligned, the body assumes a correct posture with a minimum of muscular "holding." That is, when the skeletal structure is aligned, the muscles of the body do not have to hold the skeleton in place. The body skeleton is a miraculously engineered structure that, when correctly aligned, can balance itself without considerable muscular interference. A misaligned body denotes that something has caused the skeletal structure to depart from its most natural, unencumbered alignment. When the natural equilibrium of the skeleton is disturbed, then the muscles of the body must enter in, and hold the skeletal structure in place. The muscles then become rigid and restrict the free movement and hence the naturally free rhythm response of the body. A conductor's gestures transmitted to the singers are rigid, angular, and tense—qualities that are then reflected in the choral sound.

THE CAUSES OF MISALIGNMENT

Now that a small case has been made for the importance of alignment, let us examine the causes of misalignment from the point of view of Alexander. Alignment difficulties can begin in several parts of the body. Because the skeletal structure is so interconnected, it is difficult at times to isolate the effect of one body part on another. The more logical approach, it seems, is to understand the interaction of all major body parts and their effects upon correct alignment.

THE PELVIS. The pelvis has a central role in the postural alignment of the conductor. The easiest way to learn about the pelvis is to experience it in correct position. Sit on a hard or firm chair, preferably one with a flat seat. Place your hands with palms upward on the seat, and then sit on your hands. Find the two bony protuberances at the bottom of your pelvis and place them directly in your hands. These are known as the *sit bones*. Once you have found the sit bones and have them placed in the palms of your hands, remove your hands and allow those sit bones to directly contact the chair. Allow your feet to rest flat on the floor. Your legs should be relaxed and should swing freely from left to right. The weight of your upper body should rest squarely on those sit bones. Feel the sensation of the pelvis, now in its correct position. Take a deep breath and allow the air to fall low into the pelvis. As an experiment, now place your hands under the sit bones. Tilt the pelvis back slightly. Inhale. Is the depth of the breath as low or free? Probably not! Now roll the pelvis forward. Inhale. Likewise, the breath will not be as low.

Return now to the correct pelvis position. Check that your feet are flat upon the floor and that your legs can swing freely from the pelvis. Once the pelvis is aligned by having the sit bones come in contact with the chair, stand. As you stand, be certain not to change the relative spacing of your feet from one another, or the position of your pelvis. When this is done correctly, your pelvis will feel wider and open. *Your knees will not be locked, and your body weight should be equally distributed between the balls of your feet and your heels.* This wide and open pelvis is necessary for the good breathing technique that is the most important tool for the conductor. Now that you have experienced the correct alignment of the pelvis, it is important for you to understand the sensations of incorrect pelvic alignment. Just as you did before, tilt the pelvis slightly forward. What happens? You will find that your knees lock and that weight shifts toward the balls of your feet. You might also feel a forward tipping sensation. Now rotate your pelvis slightly backward. You will notice that you knees again lock, your thighs may become rigid, and that your weight shifts to the heels. Now, return to your seat. Find your sit bones. Check that your feet are flat on the floor and that your legs swing freely. Stand and once again experience the pelvis in its proper position for breathing, singing, and conducting.

THE INTERRELATIONSHIP OF THE HEAD AND THE SPINE. Once you have found your appropriate pelvis alignment, your body alignment is not yet complete. We now need to consider the effect of the head on our alignment.

Many approaches to the correction of posture do not draw our attention to the integral role of the head to our overall body alignment. Consider the following. How much does your head weigh? It might be difficult for you to come up with an accurate answer because of the wonder of our body's architecture. We, as a general rule, do not "feel" the weight of our head because of the engineering of our body. No matter what the position of our head, our body compensates for the shifting of the weight of the head. It is said that the weight of the head can be from 12 to 18 pounds. To bring this into some kind of focus, the weight of the head is similar to the weight of an average bowling ball! Consider further that weight must balance precariously on the top of the spinal column which ends in the center of your head between your ears. In figure 2.1 below you can see the fragility (reduced sizing as you ascend toward the head) of the vertebrae as they move into the head.

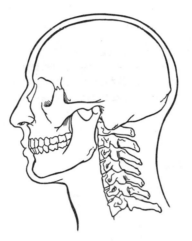

FIG. 2.1.
OUTLINE OF SKULL AND NECK VERTEBRAE

If the head (12–18 pounds!) tips slightly forward, then muscles in the back of the neck become tense and short, and attempt to counterbalance the head by taking it backward and downward on the vertebrae. This can be seen in figure 2.2.

This compression of the neck may then result in a raising of the shoulders, or a forward curving of the spine. That in turn will then cause the pelvis to roll forward and the knees to lock. When the body is so misaligned, it becomes increasingly difficult to breathe and inhibits the natural movement response to rhythm, especially in the upper body.

To begin to find your correct alignment, once again find the sit bones. Make the sit bones contact the chair. Stand as before. Now think of the suboccipital muscles (shown in the figure 2.3) at the back of the head as a hand that gently supports the back of your head off and away from your neck vertebrae.

Head misalignment in conductors is most often manifest by the shoulders appearing high and either hunched up towards the ears or pressed forward in an unnatural position. What causes this hunching is the trapezius muscle, which drapes itself downward from the back of the neck, out to the shoulders, and down

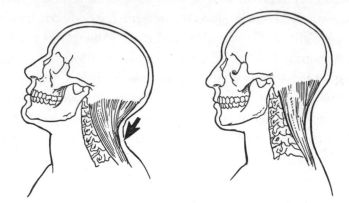

FIG. 2.2.
LEFT: NATURAL COUNTERBALANCE TENDENCY OF THE
SUBOCCIPITAL MUSCLES UNDER THE BACK
OF THE HEAD TO COMPENSATE FOR MISALIGNMENT
RIGHT: CORRECT HEAD ALIGNMENT

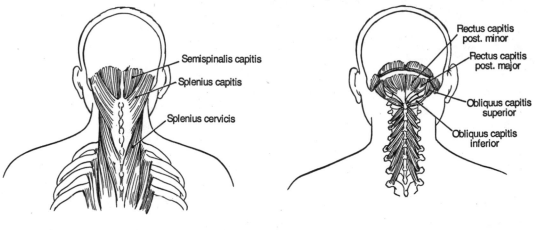

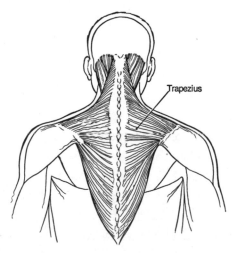

FIG. 2.3. SUBOCCIPITAL MUSCLES UNDER BACK OF THE HEAD

the back. When the head is counterbalanced by being pulled back and down, the trapezius muscle will rigidify the shoulders and greatly restrict your freedom of movement.

The perfect balancing of the head is essential to correct alignment and conducting. To achieve this balance, it is a matter of simply not interfering with the body's natural design. Because the head is heavier in the front, it will remove itself from it's backward tilt which presses upon the spinal vertebrae when the muscles in the back of the neck are allowed to *release and lengthen*. When this happens, *the spine naturally lengthens and the back widens.* How does one get the muscles in the neck to release and lengthen? You simply tell them to!

THE ALEXANDER FOUR CONCEPTS OF GOOD USE: RELEASING THE MUSCLES

The lifework of Alexander was devoted to the psychological and physiological science of removing what Alexander called postural inhibitions. Postural inhibitions are those *habits* that cause the muscles of the neck to pull the head out of its proper alignment and thus radically affect posture. What must occur, then, is a thought process that will interfere with the habitual postural response. Alexander believed that through conscious direction and correct imagery, one could tell the muscles involved to allow themselves to release so that the body could naturally find its correct alignment. Alexander also believed that the imagery must not remain localized, but instead, deal with the total body. It is not enough to focus on one part of the posture problem, i.e. the neck. The imagery must check each "danger point of the postural process." These postural checkpoints are known as the *Four Concepts of Good Use.*

THE FOUR CONCEPTS OF GOOD USE

1. Allow your neck to release so that your head can balance forward and up.
2. Allow your torso to release into length and width.
3. Allow your shoulders to release out to the sides.
4. Allow your legs to release away from your pelvis.

All of these concepts require you to be able to release your muscles. Likewise, the study of conducting will require you to understand how to release your muscles in order for the limbs to be free and able to respond to the body's inner rhythmic impulses.

RELEASE. Releasing is a term to describe how your muscles feel. If you make a fist and squeeze your fingers inward, after a while the muscles in your hand will grow tired. When this happens, slowly "let go" of the fingers so that the fingers begin to gradually relax. You may want to think of the relaxation of the muscles as the muscles becoming "quiet." Just as you can increase or decrease the tension within your hand, you can do the same thing with the larger muscle groups which support posture. Some of the following exercises will help you to feel your muscles release.

> **COFFEE CUP EXERCISE.** Pick up either a real or imaginary cup of coffee. Raise the cup of coffee to your mouth. As the cup meets your mouth, release the tension from your neck, shoulder and raised arm as is possible without moving the cup. Did you feel a decrease in the amount of muscular tension as you "told" the muscles to let go? Notice that you can still hold the cup, but with significantly less muscular tension. That reduction of muscular tension is called "release."

> **HEAD/NECK RELEASE EXERCISE.** You will need a friend to help with this exercise. Sit in a chair. Find your proper alignment. Have your friend rest her forearm on your spine and grasp your head, just below your ears, between her thumb and index finger. Have her gently move your head from side to side. Your head will probably be difficult to move. Now think of your neck muscles releasing. As you tell your neck muscles to "release" and "let go," you will find that your friend is able to move your head gently from side to side with ease.

Each of the Four Concepts of Good Use are instructions that you give to yourself. In releasing the muscles through the above statements, you do not "move" the muscles to effect the posture. What you try to approach is a state of "non-doing"; that is, the muscles become quiet and inactive so that the body can assume its natural alignment.

THE CENTRAL ROLE OF THE HEAD AND NECK: THE FOUNDATION FOR CONDUCTING. After you have found your correct sitting position by finding your sit bones, you can then move to a standing position where the pelvis maintains its same relative position as when sitting and the weight of the body is distributed equally between the balls of your feet and the heels. Now give yourself the instruction *to release your neck muscles so your head can balance forward and up.* Remember that the natural tendency of the head is to be pulled backward and downward. With this thought, you are not moving anything! You are simply trying to undo the backward pull of your neck. The word *up* always means away from the spine. The words *release your neck muscles forward and up* just enable your head to float in balance at the top of the spine, thus allowing the next Concept of Good Use to happen.

ENVISIONING THE LENGTH OF THE SPINE. After the head/neck relationship has been reestablished, you can now tell yourself *to allow your torso to release into length and width.* Your posture and the way in which you choose to carry your body is a choice that you have made either consciously or subconsciously. If you slouch in a chair, you slouch because you have "arranged" your body parts in such a manner as to shorten the actual length of the spine. This shortening, and curving, of the spine places undo pressure on the pelvis and neck to maintain the body's upright position. However, if you have released the muscles in your neck and then begin to think your spine lengthening and widening, your spine moves toward its natural lengthened position. Think of your entire torso lengthening. Another helpful image for this process is to imagine that in addition to your long spine, you also have a long tail. The image of the long tail helps to undo some additional muscle holding and lengthen the spine slightly. It is also a very helpful image to *envision your spine running up the internal center of your torso,* rather than running on the outside of your torso as is commonly envisioned (see figure 2.4).

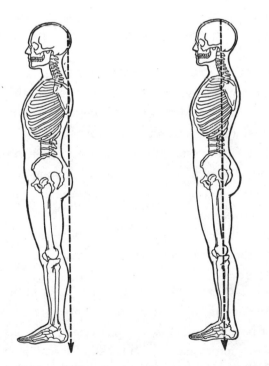

FIG. 2.4. LEFT: INCORRECT VISIONING OF ALIGNMENT
RIGHT: CORRECT VISIONING OF ALIGNMENT

It is also important to think of widening the torso at the same time your are thinking about lengthening the spine. Widening of the torso should always be envisioned with the concept of spine lengthening. If you only lengthen the spine, your lower back will likely arch. By thinking of the lower back and widening, you allow the muscles of the lower back to relax and thus eliminate the lower-back arching problem. The same widening principle should be then applied to the shoulders for the same reasons: allow your shoulders to release out to the sides.

While these first concepts were explained separately, you should ask yourself to do them concurrently by telling yourself the three concepts together:

> Let your neck release to allow your head to balance forward and up in order to let your torso and shoulders lengthen and widen.

ROLE OF THE PELVIS. The final Concept of Good Use to be discussed is to *allow your legs to release away from your pelvis.* This is used for the seated position. Simply stated, if the pelvis is resting on the sit bones, it is then unnecessary for the legs to bear any of the weight for the support of the body. By thinking that your legs release away from your pelvis, you release the muscles in the pelvis from holding the legs and thus enable the spine to lengthen. You should envision your knees moving straightforward away from your pelvis. Your legs should swing freely from the pelvis with your feet placed flat upon the floor.

ENVISIONING YOUR ALIGNMENT. Using all of the above images plus the Concepts of Good Use, you can establish the following image for correct alignment. Be seated. Find your sit bones. After you have found your sit bones, stand, maintaining the correct alignment of your pelvis. Imagine you have the feet of a duck, feet that establish a wide connection to the floor under you. Imagine energy moving out of your body through your "duck feet" to the floor. Imagine that energy is moving out your eyes, out the front of your body. Imagine that energy is also flowing out of the back of your body and directly out the top of your head. *Imagine that energy is flowing outward simultaneously via your duck feet, the front of your body, the back of your body, and the top of your head.*

PREPARING SCORES. An important point must be made that greatly effects one's conducting. If you have taken care to align your body for conducting, you must be certain that as you learn scores you also take care to align the body. Many conductors make the mistake of learning scores in a relaxed or slouching posture. The body's muscles memory is so acute that if you learn a piece of music while slouching, when that music is heard, your body's muscle memory will try to recall that posture again! Yes, that means if you have learned a piece of music slouching or lying down, your body will fight to find that posture again when the music is heard. Many postural problems with conductors begin with the body posture that was assumed when they learned the score!

UNDERSTANDING YOUR BODY ARCHITECTURE: THE ARMS

An understanding of parts of your anatomy that are central to conducting is of the utmost importance in learning to conduct. One of the most misunderstood parts of the body are the arms. When students are asked how many joints are in their arms, most usually answer three. And this is where the difficulty begins and ends with most conductors. Most persons believe that the first joint is at their shoulder, the second at their elbow, and the third at their wrist. Not only do they have the wrong number of joints, but they are located in the wrong places. There are *five* joints in each of the arms! The first joint is where the collarbone joins the sternum (breastbone). Because most persons are not even aware of where this joint is, they tighten muscles in their entire upper torso to feel like they are moving at the imagined first joint. The second and third joints are where the upper arm joins the clavicle (shoulder). The fourth joint is below what we sense as our elbow. The fifth joint is at the point where our watch usually sits; above the bony protrusion that is the joint! (See figure 2.5.) From this point onward, you should not believe that you have shoulders. Think only of the five joints that make up the arm. When you discover your true "first" joint, you will do a great deal to rid yourself of undo tension that will cause your conducting technique great difficulties.

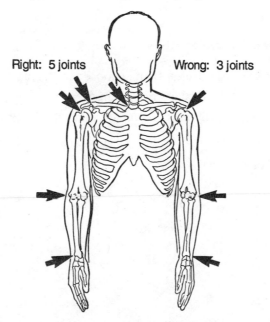

Right: 5 joints   Wrong: 3 joints

FIG. 2.5. JOINTS OF THE ARM

SUMMARY

The Four Concepts of Good Use, in order to be effective, must be used in your daily life, not just when you conduct. If you only apply them when you conduct, it will be difficult to rid yourself of your postural inhibitions (habits). The Four Concepts of Good Use must be thought of throughout your daily life: when you drive the car, walk, run, etc. Alexander's concept of the ability to *do less* with the body in order to realize your correct natural body alignment should be a lifelong goal that reaches beyond conducting into the way you live.

EXERCISES

I. Further Reading

This chapter presents only a cursory overview of some of the most important material for conductors and musicians in general. The reader is encouraged to examine books by the following authors listed in the bibliography: Alexander, Caplan, Gelb, Barker, Barlow, F. P. Jones, Maisel, and Stransky.

One of the best texts for Alexander Self-Study is the text by Barbara Conable and William Conable titled, *How to Learn The Alexander Technique: A Manual for Students.* The book is published by Andover Road Press, 1038 Harrison Avenue, Columbus, Ohio 43201. The author highly recommends this text as a companion text to this book.

II. Further Help and Alexander Study

Many students have asked, after being exposed to the material in this chapter, where can they receive individual instruction in Alexander Technique to help remedy their own individual problems. To locate a certified Alexander therapist in your area, contact the following:

The Alexander Foundation
605 West Phil-Ellena Street
Philadelphia, Pennsylvania 19119
(215) 844-0670

The American Center for Alexander Technique, Inc.
129 West 67th Street
New York, New York 10023
(212) 799-0468

The North American Society of Teachers of the Alexander Technique, Inc.
P.O. Box 806
Ansonia Station
New York, New York 10023
(212) 866-5640

The Society of Teachers of the Alexander Technique
10 London House
266 Fulham Road
London SW10 9EL
ENGLAND

CHAPTER III

UNDERSTANDING YOUR STRUCTURE

FOLLOWING GRAVITY AND RELEASING THE MUSCLES

By this time you have learned how to begin to allow your body to find it's natural alignment. Beginning any piece requires the conductor to be able to (1) breathe with and for the choir and (2) to provide a rhythmic impulse that relays both the tempo of the piece and it rhythmic character.

THE INTERACTION OF BONES AND MUSCLES

While a comprehensive understanding of anatomy is not necessary, some basic understanding of the interrelationship of bone to muscle is required. The upper limbs, obviously, are primary tools in the conducting art. Keep in mind, however, that your entire body is your conducting instrument. In fact the "core" of conducting technique is the trunk of the body. The arms and legs are necessary appendages to be dealt with! The legs, as discussed in the chapter on alignment, support the properly aligned pelvis without locking.

The shoulder blades float freely on the back, thus allowing a remarkable sense of mobility. Those shoulder blades can be elevated upward (shrugging). They can be pressed backward, they can be moved forward, they can be "squared" or "rounded." For conducting, they should remain in their relaxed position floating on the back. The area that is perceived as the shoulders is actually the shoulder blades. The conductor should have the image that they lie, without tension, on the top of the ribcage.

The upper arm attaches to the trunk of the body with a wonderful ball-and-socket joint. The shoulder is the socket while the top of the arm ends in a ball that fits into that socket. This ball-and-socket configuration allows the arm an extensive freedom of motion. The upper arm can raise and lower, move to the sides, and can rotate and twist so that the hand can assume various angles of operation. The forearm attaches to the upper arm with a hinge joint. There are two motion patterns that are possible with the forearm. First, the forearm can be raised and lowered vertically with the use of the hinge joint. A relatively wide range of motion is possible, as can be seen when one places the hands around the back. Second, the forearm can roll or rotate, as it does when you turn a doorknob.

The hand moves from the wrist. It can move up and down and side to side. While it is believed that the hand can rotate in a circular fashion, it does so only by interacting with the forearm. The fingers move through a complex arrangement of tendons. A wide range of movement for each finger is possible in addition to the movement of all the fingers as a unified, coordinated group! Moreover, the joints of each finger provide the possibility of shaping the hand.

HOLDING (LOCKING)

The term *holding*, or *locking*, is central to the conductor's understanding of how the skeletal structure interacts with the muscles to produce movement. It has been said that "bones conduct, muscles don't." While the statement seems a bit elementary, it is very true. What needs to be understood by each person studying conducting is that the way we live our lives has a tremendous impact on our muscle system, and hence, upon our skeletal system. The influence of the muscles on the skeletal system is, unfortunately, most often negative. A few examples and exercises will prove the point.

Pick up your briefcase. Better yet, choose a briefcase that belongs to someone else. Look at it, then pick it up. Now before you pick it up again, use only the minimum of muscular effort to pick up the briefcase! Pick it up again. Do you notice how much "extra" muscular effort was used when you picked up the briefcase the first time? Did your "arm" feel totally different the second time because of the dramatic change in the amount of muscle engaged to pick up the briefcase? The difference will be dramatic in most cases. If the change was not dramatic, be thankful. This means that, for some reason, you have been able to avoid the overuse of muscles that not only expends too much muscular effort, but also causes undue tension upon the skeletal system and thus reduces freedom of movement. In your daily life, you can begin to develop the proper balance of muscular exertion by just doing the minimum that is necessary to complete the movement or task. Overexerting one's muscles for every life task builds throughout the day to the point where muscular tension reigns and the freedom of the skeletal system to move is severely lessened.

Select a partner. Hold your forearm parallel to the floor. Have your partner press downward on your forearm with his or her index finger while you resist by pressing upward with your forearm. At a time unknown to you, your partner should suddenly withdraw their index finger. What happens? What happens is dependent upon the correct use of the muscle. If your arm remains in the same position when your partner's finger is pulled away suddenly, your arm is *locked* in the most dramatic fashion—that is, the muscles of the forearm and upper arm are "holding" the bones. The proper response to experience "non-holding" is, when your partner's finger is released from the top of your forearm, your arm should immediately spring in an arc *quickly* backward. Continue this drill until you can *release* the arm immediately when your partner's finger is withdrawn. When conducting, conductors must be on constant guard not to lock the movement of their arms. Locking (the muscular effort that restricts the bones from free movement) blocks the channel of rhythm impulse that was discussed above. In a conducting class, I once had a student who had experienced a severe auto accident and who required physical therapy in order to walk and move again. Her therapist gave her advice that bodes well for conductors. She instructed this patient that if she ever felt anything as she moved, there was probably something wrong! The same statement can be made for conductors. As you conduct you should *not* feel your muscles interacting with your bones. Your arms should feel light and free. Any other feeling should tell you that you are moving toward a gesture that will lock—and render the choir unable to sing.

CHAPTER IV

YOUR MOVEMENT POTENTIAL AND CONDUCTING

AN APPLICATION OF THE WORK OF RUDOLF VON LABAN FOR CONDUCTORS

Motion comes from emotion.

Children use kinesthesia to learn about their world. But Western education attempts to train the mind, and pays little attention to the kinesthetic sense.

Robert M. Abramson
Dalcroze Eurhythmics, video

While it has lately been popular in certain quarters to equate body movement with the "natural" and the "authentic" in human behavior, there is actually very little instinctive about the way we move. Due to the nature of the human brain, as mentioned earlier, voluntary movement must be learned through interaction with other human beings within a social context. Consequently, body movement is a highly structured, culturally-coded form of symbolic communication, equivalent in its sophistication to the better-known extension systems of language, music, mathematics, and so on. As part of the extended world, human movement has become an abstraction of the real, biological world. Paradoxically, body movement is at once natural *and* contrived, visceral *and* symbolic, personal *and* social, ever present *and* constantly disappearing. (P. 84–85)

> Carol-Lynne Moore, Kaoru Yamamoto
> *Beyond Words*

Looking at the whole range of innate and acquired impulses of man, one is tempted to search for a common denominator. In my opinion this denominator is not mere motion, but movement with all its spiritual implication. . . . What has to be done today— and our time seems to stand on the threshold of a new awareness of movement—is to acknowledge movement as the great integrator. This involves, of course, the conviction that movement is the vehicle which concerns the whole man with all his physical and spiritual facilities. To be able to see this great unity is not the privilege of the artist alone. Everybody, every single individual, has this unity at the basis of his natural tendencies and impulses, which can be lifted out of the treasure of forgotten truth and cultivated in all the various ramifications of life. (P. 12–13)

> Rudolf von Laban
> *The Laban Art of Movement Guild Magazine*

What one experiences through movement can never be expressed in words; in a simple step there may be a reverence of which we are scarcely aware. Yet through it something higher than just tenderness and devotion may flow into us and from us. (P. 35)

> Rudolf von Laban
> *A Life for Dance*

Of Laban's four words, weight probably is of special significance to rhythm. To perform a crusis with appropriate weight, one needs to prepare the crusis in audiation. A physical analogy may be helpful: just as there is a feeling for the shifting of weight involved in the preparation of a physical jump, so there is a feeling for the shifting of weight involved in the preparation of a crusis, that is, in the anacrusis. Unless one can jump (not hop), he will not be able to audiate or perform an anacrusis properly, because an anacrusis must incorporate the same feeling for crescendo (upward weight shift) that is characteristic of a jump. Moreover, without a feeling for relative weight and ability to shift weight at will, one will not be able to sustain movement appropriately, and without sustained movement there can be no feeling for space and flow. To engage properly in rigid (bound) sustained flow in performance, one must be audiating unbound sustained flow. (P. 155)

Edwin E. Gordon
Learning Sequences in Music, 1993

From its birth, music has registered the rhythms of the human body of which it is the complete and idealized sound image. It has been the basis of human emotion all down the ages. The successive transformations of musical rhythms, from century to century, correspond so closely to the transformations of character and temperament that, if a musical phrase of any typical composition is played, the entire mental state of the period at which was composed is revived; and, by association of ideas, there is aroused in our own bodies the muscular echo or response of the bodily movements imposed at the period in question by social conventions and necessities. If we would restore to the body all rhythms it has gradually forgotten, we must not only offer it as models the jolting, rioting rhythms of savage music, but also gradually initiate it into the successive transformations which time has given to these elementary rhythms. (P. 7)

Musical rhythmic movement consists of linking up durations, geometry consists of linking up fragments of space, while living plastic movement links up degrees of energy. (P. 10)

Economy and balance: such should be our motto. We must economize our nervous expenditure, which expresses itself in angry starts, sudden, irregular, impatient movements, depression, hypersensitiveness. We must economize our time, cease work before the point of fatigue is reached, anticipate the moment when rest becomes necessary. And we must economize our will to progress, moderate our appetites, and balance our desires of creation with the means at our command. (P. 12)

Emile Jaques-Dalcroze
Eurhythmics Art and Education

• • • • •

It goes without saying that conducting is movement and vice versa. As conductors, our movements relay our innermost rhythm, musical line, and textural colors. At times our movement courts the singers to move their sound in response to our gesture, and at other times, our conducting mimes the sound that is in our inner musical fantasy world. The ability to move freely is a prerequisite for the study of conducting. The ability to reacquaint oneself with the infinite vocabulary of movement is an essential readiness for conducting. The body must be reacquainted with its full movement potential so that through movement one can elicit, evoke, excite, awaken, mirror, court, and reflect the sound of each piece.

As children, each one of us experienced the *entire* world of movement. In our play, we ran, we jumped, we swung. We leaped and rolled and tumbled, skipped and hopped. We moved by ourselves and with others. We played circle games. Play was movement. Serious play was on the playground and in the home. Life was play and play was movement. Movement was our lives. As we grew older and more "mature," we began to move less and less. Play became a less prominent part of our life. Movement no longer "felt" natural and spontaneous. As our bodies grew, we moved less and less. The world we grew into did not encourage movement. Consequently, as we grew older, we settle upon a limited, yet efficient, movement vocabulary that will get us through our day to day life. Can that spontaneous movement of early childhood be rediscovered? Yes! Is that rediscovered movement world necessary for the development of the beginning conductor? Yes. The work of Rudolf von Laban can reawaken life movement experiences so that they can be used in conducting.

RUDOLF VON LABAN

Rudolf von Laban was born in 1879 in Bratislava, Hungary, the son of an army general. His early years were preoccupied with observing movement. As a child, he spent considerable time drawing and visualizing patterns in space. His desire to understand both physical and mental effort led him to a lengthy course of study in painting, sculpture, and stage design in Paris, Berlin, and Vienna. As part of his training, he studied various cultures, particularly the natives of Africa, the people of the Near East, and the Chinese.

In 1910 he founded his first dance group and school in Munich, where he developed one of his favorite genres, the movement choir. During World War I he lived in Switzerland and continued to develop his ideas. In 1919 he formed a stage dance group, the Tanzbuhne Laban, which specialized in expressive dance. Through that ensemble, he created many full-length dance compositions (*The Swinging Cathedral, Die Geblendeten, Gaukelei, Don Juan,* and *Die Nacht*).

In 1926, he founded the Choreographic Institute in Wurzburg, which he later moved to Berlin. That institute specialized in the development of a dance notation system, originally known as Eukinetics, which was published in 1928 as *Kinetography*. In the United States his work is known as *Labanotation*. He became director of movement at the Berlin State Opera in 1930, and subsequently was recognized as one of Europe's most famous choreographers.

Unable to continue work under the Nazi regime, Laban and some of his pupils sought sanctuary in the United Kingdom. Laban introduced Modern Educational Dance into the schools as a new creative subject. In Manchester, England, where he lived from 1942 to 1953, he helped establish the Art of Movement Studio with Lisa Ullman. Concurrently, he established the Laban-Lawrence Industrial Rhythm, which developed new approaches for the selection, training, and placing of workers, in addition to developing working processes based upon the movement of man. Through that work, Laban developed the effort graph as a means of recording the kinesthetic quality of individual performance in industry.

In 1946, the Laban Art of Movement Guild was formed. That guild supported the movement training center for movement study and educational dance based upon Laban's concepts. Laban lectured on a regular basis at his studio, and at the same time he lectured at colleges and universities.

In 1953, Laban moved to Addelstone, Surrey, where he established archives for his own work and the work of the Art of Movement Studio. In 1954, the Laban Art of Movement Centre was formed as an educational trust to perpetuate his work and to promote and provide education in the art of movement. He continued to work at Addlestone until his death in 1958.

PHILOSOPHICAL BASIS OF THE WORK OF LABAN

For Laban, the act of moving was a link between the physical and mental experiences of life. He believed that through the act of moving, one experienced an interaction of mind and body. He also believed that movement was everywhere; movement could be seen, organized, and understood in the still leaf, in the child at play, in a simple walk, and through all aspects of our daily lives.

To Laban, the central issue underlying the understanding of movement was that persons needed to visually, physically, and internally experience the energy of movement, and then develop the ability to describe those movement experiences. He believed that after helping a person to recall experiences from his "movement thinking," that person could enrich his or her movement vocabulary by experiencing similar experiences. For example, Laban believed that a person could recall movement experiences from earlier in life. The person could (a) be helped to recall the total experience of skipping, (b) be guided to make a self-analysis of his their skipping, and (c) provide a vocabulary that describes the experience of skipping in order to heighten the skipping experience. Laban believed that everyone experiences all the subtleties and complexities of movement during early childhood, but that not everyone recalls all of those movements in later life.

Part of the Laban Movement Analysis is to identify which specific movement experiences a person is not recalling, and then to provide prescriptive movement instruction to reawaken those movements in that person. Those who instruct and guide movement must have experiences in a comprehensive variety of movement themselves in order to effectively diagnose, prescribe, and teach movement. Moreover, to teach movement with meaning, movement experiences should be guided through the use of specific movement themes known as the Efforts in Combination.

THE LABAN EFFORT ELEMENTS: FLOW, WEIGHT, TIME, AND SPACE

Movement is more than a change of location of the body or a change in the position of the body limbs. There are changes in speed, changes in direction, changes in focus, and changes in the energy associated with different movements. There is consequently a constant fluctuation in levels of exertion. Laban defined exertion in movement as the interrelationship of *Flow, Weight, Time,* and *Space,* which he called the Effort Elements. For each of the four Effort Elements, Laban identified a pair of extremes that he called qualities, with the idea that the quality of each element of a given movement can be described in relation to its placement on a continuum that extends between those two extremes.

Flow is the variation in the quality of bodily tension that underlies all of the Effort Elements. The extremes of Flow are free and bound. *Free Flow* allows body energy to move through and out beyond the body boundaries without any restriction. Ideal free Flow movement is difficult to stop. A person experiencing total free Flow would be difficult to stop. A person experiencing total free Flow would be weightless and unhampered by tension. *Bound Flow* movement is restrained and can be stopped easily; it forces the mover to contain energy within the body boundary. A person experiencing extreme bound Flow would be tense to the point of motionless. Between the two extremes of free Flow and bound Flow are infinite gradations of tension.

Weight is the sensation of force or burden exerted in a movement. The extremes of Weight are light and heavy. *Light movement* can be described as delicate and overcomes the sensation of body weight. *Heavy movement* is forceful and uses the sensation of body weight to make an impact. A person must sense the quality of his or her movements as being either light or heavy. Central to one's under-standing, and consequently to one's understanding of rhythm, is the ability to sense involuntary changes in one's own body weight, as well as the ability to change Weight at will.

Time relates to the expenditure or duration of time in a movement. The extremes of Time are sustained and quick. *Sustained Time* is prolonging, lingering, or decelerating. *Quick Time* contains a sense of urgency and rapidity. For musicians, the Effort Element of Time is closely related to tempo.

Space is the manner in which energy is focused in a movement. The extremes of Space are either direct or indirect. *Indirect movement* involves a flexible but all encompassing attention to the environment. *Direct movement* involves a channeled, singularly focused awareness of the environment. The element of Space is close-ly related to the concept of focus. Is the Space in which a movement takes place focused or spread? Do all body parts focus to a central point, or are they dis-persed?

Finally, one might think of the Effort Elements of Flow, Weight, Time, and Space as the how, what, when, and where of movement.

EXPERIENCING THE EFFORTS IN COMBINATION

It is easiest to gain an understanding of the Effort Elements through their various combinations as suggested by Laban. It is difficult to experience Flow, Weight, Time, or Space separately. By adjusting the relative intensities of Flow, Weight, Time, and Space within an activity, one can relate an infinite variety of movement possibilities. Laban assigned an action verb to each combination of three Effort Elements. Central to his theory is the simultaneous concentration on the three elements of Weight, Space, and Time taking over, or predominating, changes in Flow. Laban's action verbs, which describe combinations of Effort Elements, along with movement examples for each verb, are shown in figure 4.1. The abbrevia-tions denote S = Space, W = Weight, and T = Time.

For each of the Efforts in Combination, the elements of Time, Space, and Weight interact to produce the illusion of Flow. That is, the perception of one's rhythmic and gestural flow is a byproduct of the interaction of Time, Space, and Weight. Flow cannot exist alone. It is the result of infinite combinations of Time, Weight, and Space, which produces an infinite variety of movement. The genius of Laban is the ability to observe how the combinations of Time, Space, and

Weight can be varied to produce what is perceived as Flow. These principles are important to conductors to make them aware of the infinite potential of their own movement, and to reawaken movement within themselves that may not have been used since childhood, or to reawaken movement that may not be part of their current life experience.

LABAN ACTION VERB	QUALITIES (ELEMENTS)	MOVEMENT EXAMPLES
FLOAT	indirect (S) light (W) sustained (T)	treading water at various depths
WRING	indirect (S) heavy (W) sustained (T)	wringing a beach towel
GLIDE	direct (S) light (W) sustained (T)	smoothing wrinkles in a cloth, or ice skating
PRESS	direct (S) heavy (W) sustained (T)	pushing a car
FLICK	indirect (S) light (W) quick (T)	dusting off lint from clothes
SLASH	indirect (S) heavy (W) quick (T)	fencing, or serving a tennis ball
DAB	direct (S) light (W) quick (T)	typing or tapping on a window
PUNCH	direct (S) heavy (W) quick (T)	boxing

FIG. 4.1. LABAN EFFORTS IN COMBINATION TO DESCRIBE MOVEMENT

Laban believed that to become adept with movement one should develop a daily routine of exploring the Efforts in Combination. In the initial stages of movement exploration, the "labeling" and understanding of the Effort Element content in everyday life activities provides the foundation of movement understanding because it grows out of one's personal experience. Laban believed that we have all experienced a complete spectrum of movement possibilities as children, but we have forgotten those movement experiences because the routine of our daily lives has minimized our daily movement experience. For each of the Efforts in Combination in figure 4.2, there are suggestions of life activities that would reawaken that particular Effort Combination within the conductor. Mime each of the suggestions for each category and discover how a change in one or more of the individual Effort Elements changes the movement. Add your personal experiences to each list.

FIG. 4.2. EXPERIENCES OF EFFORTS IN COMBINATION

FLOAT

INDIRECT (SPACE)
LIGHT (WEIGHT)
SUSTAINED (TIME)

tracing a picture with a pencil
floating in a pool on your back
vaulting over a high bar by means of a pole
using a bubble wand
spraying a room with air freshener
lying on a waterbed
falling into the first moments of sleep
reaching for an unfamiliar cat
staggering
swinging on a rope swing
blowing bubbles

Other: _____

_____

_____

_____

_____

WRING

INDIRECT (SPACE)
HEAVY (WEIGHT)
SUSTAINED (TIME)

twisting a washcloth dry
twisting sweater dry
twisting hair in the morning
twisting a face cloth
drying out a sponge
twisting off a bottle cap
opening a cardboard can of prepackaged cookie dough
washing socks
playing with a hula hoop
drying your hands under a blower
tightening a jar cap
turning over dirt with a trowel
squeezing juice from an orange
twisting a twist tie on a garbage bag
using a screwdriver
pulling out the stem of an apple
spinning a dreidel
opening a can of sardines
using a melon baller
opening a stuck faucet handle
massaging a muscle

Other: _____

_____

_____

_____

_____

PRESS

DIRECT (SPACE)
HEAVY (WEIGHT)
SUSTAINED (TIME)

kissing a child gently
pushing a shopping cart loaded with groceries
ironing a shirt
pressing a button on a soda machine

pushing a child on a swing
squeezing a tennis ball
pressing on the floor when doing a handstand
closing an overloaded suitcase
pushing a lawnmower in high grass
pushing a lawnmower uphill
using a paper cutter
using a hole punch
pushing in a laundromat coin cartridge
moving a piano
pedaling a mountain bike uphill
applying the brakes in a car
kneading dough for bread
removing a childproof cap
walking with an umbrella against the wind
washing a window with a squeegee
stapling papers
using a clothes pin
ringing a door bell
pushing in a thumb tack
using a screwdriver
packing trash in a filled garbage bag
using a mechanical hand drill
going through a revolving door
closing a car trunk lid when the trunk is very full
making mashed potatoes
buckling a seat belt

Other:_____

_____

_____

_____

_____

GLIDE

DIRECT (SPACE)
LIGHT (WEIGHT)
SUSTAINED (TIME)

reaching to shake hands
wiping up a spill with a paper towel

pushing off from the side of a pool and moving forward
ice-skating
erasing a blackboard
dusting or wiping off a table
drawing a violin bow across one string
spreading butter or jelly on toast
gently scratching your arm
sliding down a banister
coasting down a hill on a bicycle
roller-blading or roller-skating
throwing a paper airplane
sliding in socks on a newly polished floor
painting a wall with a roller
opening a sliding glass door
smoothing sheets when you make a bed
dusting furniture with a feather duster
putting a ring on your finger
closing a zip-lock sandwich bag
turning a page in a book
smoothing cement with a trowel
water- or snow-skiing
icing a cake
drawing a circle with a compass
playing a glissando on a piano
dusting
sliding on an icy sidewalk
shaving

Other: _____

_____

_____

_____

_____

DAB

DIRECT (SPACE)
LIGHT (WEIGHT)
QUICK (TIME)

putting the final touches on the frosting of a cake
tip-toeing

38

playing darts (moment the dart is released from the hand)
using a paint brush to make dots
poking someone's arm with a finger
dipping a cloth in a pail of water
breaking a balloon with a pin
knocking ash off a cigarette
dotting an *i*
applying antiseptic on a small cut
tap-dancing
pushing button on a remote control
typing
finger-painting
using touch-up paint
testing hot water with your finger
cleaning cob webs from the ceiling
powdering on makeup
using white glue
cleaning a child's sticky mouth
placing a cherry on a sundae

Other: _____

_____

_____

_____

_____

FLICK

INDIRECT (SPACE)
LIGHT (WEIGHT)
QUICK (TIME)

removing an insect off the table
turning a light switch on or off
leafing through the pages of a book
lightly keeping a balloon in the air
brushing debris off your desk or table
shooing a fly
wiping sweat from brow
shooting marbles
touching a hot stove
shooting marbles

throwing a frisbee
snapping your fingers
opening "flip top" toothpaste
brushing snow from a windshield
lighting a cigarette lighter
taking a basketball foul shot
striking a match
folding egg whites
throwing rice
popping soap bubbles

Other: _____

_____

_____

_____

_____

SLASH

INDIRECT (SPACE)
HEAVY (WEIGHT)
QUICK (TIME)

swinging a baseball bat
fencing
casting a fishing line
golfing
opening a cardboard carton with a utility knife
wielding a knife like a butcher
tearing a piece of paper
using an axe to chop wood
slamming a door
shaking catsup from a new bottle
employing self-defense maneuvers
sweeping a sandy floor with a push broom
beating a hanging rug clean
cutting vegetables

Other:_____

_____

_____

PUNCH

DIRECT (SPACE)
HEAVY (WEIGHT)
QUICK (TIME)

plumping a pillow
boxing
using a punching bag
applauding loudly
hammering a nail
pounding fist on a table
striking a stapler to get the staple in a hard wall
digging a hole

Other: _____

_____

_____

_____

_____

    Notice that a variation of one or more of the qualities will result in a different intensity of the movement experience. After experiencing the Efforts in Combination shown in figure 4.2, the reader is encouraged to perform the imagery exercise shown in figure 4.3. Without pause, the reader should perform quickly each pair of movements shown. If the exercises are performed correctly, the mover will feel a sudden shift of energy between the two movement experiences of each pair. Each exercise should be performed first with external body movement, and then with no external body movement, so that the mover can internalize the various combinations of movements and, more important, the changes in energy between the two movements in each combination. The quality of the Time element of each of the movements should be varied, as should the direction of each movement.

    Laban did not specifically assign names to each of the eight combinations. The names of flick, dab, etc., have grown from the wide body of Laban practitioners who have found these labels useful and in keeping with the integrity of Laban's philosophical beliefs. Laban did believe that language could be more exacting about the action than it could be for the more subtle shades of experience. Transitions occur when one moves between Effort actions by changing one of the Effort Elements. For example, one may progress from punching (direct/heavy/quick) to pressing (direct/heavy/sustained). Transitions often

PUNCH/PRESS
PUNCH/SLASH
PUNCH/DAB
SLASH/WRING
SLASH/FLICK
WRING/FLOAT
WRING/PRESS
FLOAT/FLICK
FLOAT/GLIDE
GLIDE/DAB
GLIDE/PRESS
DAB/FLICK

FIG. 4.3. MOVEMENT IMAGERY EXERCISE

involve the changing of a single component; it is possible, however, to change two or three components simultaneously.

The combinations of Elements attended to simultaneously are difficult to name. Laban referred to combinations of two factors (Elements), however, as an *incomplete Effort*. Those combinations are also referred to as *inner attitudes*, because the combination of only two Elements suggests that the movement is not yet externalized, but instead, it expresses a state of feeling Laban writes of in *The Mastery of Movement*: "It is difficult to attach names to these variations of incomplete Effort as they are concerned with pure movement experience and expression" (92). The verbal descriptions are not precise, and they are always subject to movement validation. For each combination of two factors, the mover can combine the Elements in four different ways. These combinations are known as *States*, or *Drives*. All possible combinations of the six groups are illustrated in figure 4.4. The italicized labels beneath the Elements are the commonly used labels for the States, or Drives. Remember that the descriptive terms in italics attempt to generally mirror internal feelings, not movements.

APPLICATION OF LABAN'S THEORIES TO CONDUCTING

Whether one is beginning one's study of conducting or has considerable experience conducting, the movement categorizations of Laban can be of great assistance in solving several issues. If the conductor experiences and understands the Efforts in Combination in figure 4.4, he or she begins to experience and reexperience various feelings of Weight. In order for conductors to provide gestures which evoke sound, Weight must be able to be "extracted" from their gestures at will. The feeling of weight in one's body is produced from an overexertion of the

SPACE & TIME	WEIGHT & TIME	WEIGHT & FLOW
(AWAKE)	(NEAR RHYTHM)	(DREAM)
indirect/slow	light/slow	light/free
indirect/quick	strong/slow	strong/free
direct/slow	light/quick	light/bound
direct/quick	strong/quick	strong/bound

SPACE & FLOW	FLOW & TIME	SPACE & WEIGHT
(REMOTE)	(MOBILE)	(STABILE)
indirect/free	free/slow	indirect/light
indirect/bound	free/quick	indirect/strong
direct/free	bound/slow	direct/light
direct/bound	bound/quick	direct/strong

FIG. 4.4. COMBINATIONS OF TWO EFFORT ELEMENTS INTO STATES, OR DRIVES

musculature on the bone structure. This overly muscular effort then restricts natural rhythm impulse from the conductor, and translates to retarded or impeded airflow (support) within the singers. *Most importantly, however, muscle rigidity and tenacity (weight) negatively affects one's ability to hear.* The ability to remove weight from the conducting gesture through the relaxation of muscles is a valuable tool for the conductor.

CENTERING ACTIVITIES FOR CONDUCTORS

After having become sensitized to the Efforts in Combination and to the role of Weight in conducting, several Laban exercises can assist one to find one's "gravitational," or energy, center—that is, one's "rootedness," or "grounding." Such a sense of "centeredness" in overall conducting gesture is necessary to evoke a low-seated breath from the choir. Centeredness is a feeling, a state of being. It is directly related to where one feels the weighted center of oneself. The following activities can refamiliarize conductors with their center of levity. The concept of the center of levity is the experience of shifting one's weight without a change in the strength of lightness. Heaviness, in this case, can be thought of as "giving in" to gravity.

TIPTOEING. Tiptoe around the room, making as little sound as possible. What does your body feel like? Where do you feel your center of levity? In this tiptoe activity, you most likely feel your center of levity high in your body. In order to tiptoe quietly, you actually hold back the displacement of weight as you move, or in other words, you experience lightness, which is a withholding of weight.

SKIPPING. Skipping is one of the most valuable of all movement activities because the entire body is carried by an energy continuum that is like the forward movement of a phrase or the release in the gesture that is felt during the rebound in the conducting gesture. The constant releasing of energy coupled with a dynamic inertia makes this an essential exercise to master. Perform this activity in an area that can afford the use of a large floor space. Begin skipping across the floor. Try to make it across the room with as few skips as possible, making your skips as high as possible. As you skip, make certain the upper body remains free. What image will help you to skip higher? You will find that the more that you can "hold back" your weight at the top or highest point of the skip, the higher you will be able to skip. Where do you feel your center of levity as you skip?

Another useful activity is to observe children skipping in a playground setting. Make note in your observations of their upper body alignment as they skip and the position of their heads throughout the skip.

TUG OF WAR. Engage in a tug of war with a classmate using a long, heavy bath or beach towel. Both grasp the ends of the towel, count to three and begin the tug. When done correctly, neither of you should win; it should be a standoff. Perform the tug of war again, and experiment with the positioning of your body to achieve the lowest possible center of levity. You will find that a condition of equilibrium occurs when both partners squat in an ape-like position so that their center of levity or center of weight, drops into their pelvis area. When the condition of equilibrium occurs, where to *you* feel your center? Do you feel it low in your body? You should "feel" your center of levity in that "tug-of-war" place when you conduct. If you do, you will find that when you breathe, the air will be able to drop to the same place where you feel your center of levity.

SUMMARY

For conductors, Laban's theories of movement can help a person reacquaint oneself with one's movement potential. Rhythm, which comes from a source within us, can be manifest as external movement. That external movement can be labeled to help us appreciate the infinite possibilities and experiences of rhythm manifest as movement. Rhythm is a manifestation of tension and release that provide points of reference that we commonly refer to as meter. Rhythm phrases, then, are movement manifestations of the Efforts in Combination. But more importantly, a realization of the energy of the Efforts within oneself is actually a manifestation of color through rhythm. The vocal color of a choir is directly affected by one major factor: the *breath* of the conductor. Within that breath, the rhythmic life of the piece is transferred to the choir. The rhythmicity of the breath transfers the conductor's rhythmic opinion directly to the choir. That rhythmic (movement) vocabulary can be expanded through one's facility with the Efforts in Combination.

EXERCISES

1. Watch the video *Dalcroze Eurhythmics* (GIA Publications, Inc., VHS-281) with Robert M. Abramson and answer the following questions.

a. Define and be able to demonstrate in class the differences between an arhythmic performance, an errhythmic performance, and an eurhythmic performance.

b. Discuss the difference between moving from pitch to pitch and the understanding of moving between pitches.

c. Define the word *kinesthesia*.

d. What is the relationship of affect to kinesthesia?

e. Discuss the relationship of bouncing a tennis ball to a piece of music and the art of conducting. Focus on the physics involved with the ball as you make it respond to rhythm.

2. Students should perform this exercise in pairs. One student of the pair should be blindfolded and be allowed to walk around the room for ten minutes. The other student should function as guide. The role of the guides is not to influence the path about the room by their blindfolded partner, but to merely look out for their partner's well-being. The guides should anticipate dangerous situations before they occur and steer their partner away from those situations. This activity will stress the Effort Element of Time. Without the aid of the sense of sight, the blindfolded student will experience sustained time.

3. "Mirrored mimes" is a valuable activity to perform with the entire class. The class should be asked to mirror the instructor's movements as if they are the mir-

rored image. The instructor can create various vignettes where Weight, Time, and Space are changed, in order that the students can experience changes in Flow. This activity should be performed daily as a warm-up for conducting class.

4. For the "walking mime" exercise, each student should select a partner. The exercise has more dramatic effects if the partner is either of the opposite sex or is physically different in height and/or weight. One person of the pair should be the leader, while the other should follow. The followers are instructed to imitate the gait of their partner as closely as possible. After this activity, discussions should take placed concerning how different their bodies felt as they imitated the walk of their partner.

5. Students should be asked to playact the following situations to help clarify the concepts of Weight and Flow kinesthesia.

Arm Swing. Ask the students to swing their arms. At first, ask them to use only their upper bodies. Later, ask them to employ their entire bodies into the swing. The students should discuss the importance of both lightness and strength to their arm swing.

Lightness Tasks. The students should be asked what daily tasks require lightness i.e., collating papers, picking up broken glass, fluffing a pillow, etc.

Towel Slap. Each student should bring a large, thick towel to class. Students should slap the towel against the floor in order to obtain the loudest possible sound. As they slap their towels, the students should analyze their movement patterns in order to determine which Efforts in Combination produces the loudest towel slap. The students will find that, if they grab the end of the towel and begin the activity with their hands extended backward over the head, bringing the towel directly over the top of the head and following the midline of the body will produce the loudest sound. What the students experience as the towel is slapped is a sudden use of weight. As the towel slaps to the floor, the students should feel the sudden dispersion of weight into the floor.

6. Complete your list of five life experiences for each of the Efforts in Combination in this chapter. Each of the five activities must be activities that you can perform in front of the class. The list should not include descriptions of other things that move, i.e., leaves falling, clouds floating, etc. You must be able to effectively mime each of the movements that you choose.

Chapter V

Consistent Tempo

A Prerequisite Skill
for the Conductor

The ability to recognize and to perform a consistent tempo is a prerequisite to either musical performance and conducting. The ability to recognize or to perform a consistent tempo is based upon one's ability to simultaneously hear a larger beat structure with its subdivision. An inability to recognize and to perform a consistent tempo is rooted in one's inability to move in a coordinated manner to music. Before one learns about the larger beat structure with its subdivision, fine muscle coordination of the body must be achieved

Muscle Coordination Development

This fine muscle coordination is developed separate from music listening abilities which help aurally identify larger beats and their subdivisions. Muscle coordination is usually developed using an external music stimulus, such as a record-ing. After the necessary coordination has been developed, a music learning process which internalizes rhythm pulse becomes necessary. The following coordination sequence is based upon the work of Phyllis S. Weikart (1989).

Coordination instruction moves through the following consecutive levels Level one must be achieved before level two can be attempted and so on.

MOVEMENT COORDINATION SEQUENCE

1. Single Coordinated Motion of the Arms—the movement of both arms together.
2. Single Coordinated Motion of the Legs—the movement of both legs together.
3. Alternating Single Motion of the Arms—the movement of the arms alternately.
4. Alternating Single Motion of the Legs—the movement of the legs alternately.
5. Single Coordinated Motion of the Arms and Legs—the movement of both arms together and both legs together.
6. Alternating Single Motion of the Arms and Legs Together—the movement of the arms alternately and the legs alternately.

When performing the coordination sequence above, observe the following:

a) Perform the various levels of the coordination sequence seated.
b) Until you have executed a level of the sequence accurately, no external beat should be supplied.
c) After mastering a level as evidenced by a number of successful executions, then perform that level with music. Perform each level at different tempi.

RHYTHMIC RESPONSE TO EXTERNAL MUSIC VERSUS INTERNAL MUSICAL IMPULSE

Many persons believe that if one can move to music, one has demonstrated a certain rhythmic competency. Movement to music may be an indicator of a musical rhythmic understanding. It may also be an indicator that one is able to coordinate one's movements quickly to music one hears. Until one demonstrates in solo without external music, one can never be sure of the origin or depth of one's rhythm responses. Traditional prescriptive rhythm exercises such as clapping the beat or clapping the rhythm may or may not indicate the extent to which someone hears rhythm.

How, then, can one be sure that one "hears" rhythm internally? Many rhythm pedagogies make the error of not having a consistent "input" strategy that assures that one "hears" all the component parts of the rhythm structure. The following approach attempts to do this.

THE STRUCTURE OF RHYTHM AND ITS RELATION TO RHYTHM PEDAGOGY

While most persons would agree on the importance of teaching and reinforcing rhythm skills, perhaps no aspect of music pedagogy has been subject to such confusion. Many attempts have been made to develop a pedagogy for the teaching of rhythm, but that pedagogy lags behind the pedagogy for the teaching of tonal skills. Most music curricula limit rhythm content to relatively few patterns in duple and triple meters, and even then there is confusion about whether to teach those rhythm patterns using numbers, e.g., "1-e-and-a" (for four sixteenth notes), or using mnemonic devices, e.g., "Mississippi," for the same pattern. Whatever system is used, terminology is inconsistent, leaving a chasm of illogic for conductors between what is heard and what is written. While advanced musicians have suffered through and eventually reconciled those inconsistencies of rhythm notation, children and adults who have limited experiences with music are hopelessly confused by those same inconsistencies.

NATURAL BODY RESPONSE TO RHYTHM: THE FOUNDATION FOR UNDERSTANDING RHYTHM

Between birth and age three, children learn without biases (and without notation). Their bodies move and respond to rhythm in a natural way. They play and experience rhythm and movement without inhibition. As adults, it is helpful if we learn as a child learns music.

The core of rhythm learning must be based in movement. Consider the following controversial example. Audiate (hear the sound without it being physically present) "My Country 'Tis of Thee." A music theorist might describe the tune as being in three-four time: three beats in a measure and a quarter note representing one beat. That is visually correct. However, there is a conflict between the measure signature and how the music is heard or audiated. Silently hear (audiate) "My Country 'Tis of Thee" again, but this time move to music. Do you move on each quarter note? You probably do not. Do you step or move once each measure? You probably do. Is it amusical to step to each quarter note? Yes. Would children step to each quarter note? They most likely would not.

The learning of rhythm must be organized and based upon the body's response to audiated rhythm, free of notation. Rhythm learning should be rooted not in the theory of music, but in its audiation. While the theory of music is important to the explanation of the common practice of a given period, it is not necessary for the learning of rhythm. In the same way that the reading of individual letters and of the principles of grammar is not necessary for speaking or reading a language, the knowledge of note values and of the theory of meter signatures does not directly bear upon the beginning stages of rhythm learning. However, a body that responds naturally to rhythm is a necessary prerequisite for the learning of rhythm, and for the establishment of a consistent tempo.

LAYERS OF RHYTHM AUDIATION

Rhythm, when audiated with understanding, is heard at three different levels concurrently. For the purpose of this explanation, consider the three levels as layers of audiation—that is, rhythm is audiated in relation to three separate elements. To audiate rhythm, one must organize rhythm patterns either consciously or unconsciously, but organization must take place at some level. For very talented students, the organization at more basic levels takes place unconsciously. The three elements of rhythm are pictured in figure 5.1. The *macro beat*, the largest unit of pulse to which the body can move comfortably, is at the bottom of the chart, indicating that it is fundamental to rhythm audiation. *Micro beats* are the principal subdivisions of the macro beat; the macro beat is divisible into either two or three micro beats (except in the rare case of an intact macro beat). While the macro beat is fundamental to rhythm audiation, consistent tempo cannot be established without the concurrent audiation of macro and micro beats. The macro beats and the micro beats must be audiated separately and then combined in audiation. If macro beats and micro beats are not audiated separately before being combined, each loses its fundamental character and relationship to the other; hence, inconsistent tempo is the result.

Melodic rhythm is the third layer of rhythm audiation. Melodic rhythm cannot be audiated with meaning and with consistency of tempo unless the previous two layers of rhythm are being audiated concurrent to it. Melodic rhythm is superimposed over the micro beat layer, which in turn has been superimposed over the macro beat layer. Melodic rhythms can be categorized according to one or a combination of two or more of the following descriptive terms: divisions, elongations, rests, ties, and upbeats. Combinations of those functions constitute the rhythm of the melody, which is superimposed over the audiation of macro beats and micro beats. Rhythm audiation is therefore a threefold hearing process. Of the three layers of rhythm "hearing," the most crucial, if not the most fundamental, is the middle layer. Without the ability to accurately place micro beats, one will know only unusual meter, and will never experience the feeling of a consistent tempo.

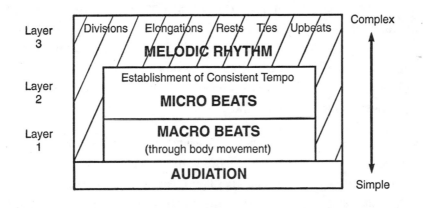

FIG. 5.1. THE FUNDAMENTAL ELEMENTS OF
RHYTHM AUDIATION: LAYERING OF THE ELEMENTS OF RHYTHM

What is the practical application toward the development of rhythm skills of the beginning conductor? Consider the performance of the following rhythm pattern in a sequence of rhythm patterns: two eighths, two eighths, four sixteenths, two eighths. You perform the rhythm, but rush the sixteenth notes. Consider now the previously suggested threefold layering of rhythm audiation. How should the rushing be corrected? First, you should move your body to macro beats at a consistent tempo while chanting micro beats (eighth notes), emphasizing an equal subdivision of the beat. You should continue that procedure until you sense a consistent tempo. When the consistent tempo has been established, the third layer of rhythm, the melodic rhythm, may be added. Remember that the strongest indicator of correct rhythm audiation is a person's sense of consistent tempo. If a consistent tempo is not present, you must remove each layer of rhythm audiation, beginning with melodic rhythm, until the problem is solved. You can then rebuild the layers back through melodic rhythm, so long as consistency of tempo is maintained. The strength of this approach to rhythm is that it separates the audiation of rhythm into three distinct layers, and reveals that melodic rhythm is superimposed over two more fundamental rhythm elements, which together provide a foundation for consistent tempo.

THE ROLE OF CONSISTENT TEMPO WHEN LEARNING A NEW PIECE

One of the problems when initially learning a new work is that when we learn the individual parts or the work as a whole, we are not persistent enough to maintain a consistent tempo. Consequently, in subsequent study sessions of the work, the tempo of the work is more subject to the flux based upon the lack of a rhythmic anchor, a consistent tempo that comes from within us. In the initial stages of learning a piece, follow the guide below·

1. *Walk the room to step and rhythmically chant the piece to find the micro beat.* Walk about the room and step the work while you chant it on a neutral syllable such as *bum, doo, pah,* etc. The pulse you most naturally step to *(regardless of the meter signature)* is the macro beat, or largest rhythm unit of the work. Remember that the unit of pulse you step to may not be the unit of pulse signified by the meter signature. Always rely on what you hear, not what you see on the printed page. If you have any difficulty doing this, perform the movement coordination sequence discussed previously in this chapter

2. *Locate the micro beat in your hands while concurrently tapping the macro beat in your feet.* After walking the piece, be seated. Tap the beat that you just stepped in your feet. While chanting the piece, determine whether the beat in your feet can be divided into twos or threes by lightly tapping your index and middle fingers of your right hand lightly onto your upturned left palm. The division of the macro beat into the next smaller subdivisions is know as the micro beat.

3. *Chant through the piece, breathing for each entrance.* Continue tapping the macro beat in your feet and the micro beat in your hands

Rhythmically chant the entire piece on a neutral syllable, taking care to breathe for each entrance. Inconsistent tempo problems are most often caused by the nonrhythmic breathing of conductors. Rhythmic breathing, key to a choir's consistent tempo, grows out of an inner consistent tempo of the conductor that is rooted in the concurrent macro and micro beat.

4. *Chant through the piece without tapping.* Remove the tapping of the macro beats in the feet and the micro beats in the hands and rhythmically chant the piece, while still breathing for each entrance. This will determine whether the consistent tempo of the piece is anchored within your audiation. If you have difficulty doing this, repeat steps 1–3 until the tempo stabilizes. Check yourself with a metronome.

EXERCISE

Using the suggestions in this chapter, prepare the following exercises from Paul Hindemith, *Elementary Training for Musicians* (New York: Schott Music Corporation, 1974)

PAGE	EXERCISE NUMBER	ACTIVITY
(a) Page 10	6.3	sing and conduct
(b) Page 10–11	6.5	sing and clap
(c) Page 14–15	9.1	sing and clap
(d) Page 16	9.3	sing and conduct
(e) Page 19–20	10.1	sing and clap
(f) Page 21–22	10.2, e–g	2-hand tapping
(g) Page 22–23	10.3	sing and conduct
(h) Page 23	10.3, d–f	speak and tap
(i) Page 36	14.3, d–e	speak and tap
(j) Page 47	17.1, c–d	2-hand tapping
(k) Page 56–57	20.2, a–d	sing and tap

(Note that there is a misprint in exercise *a*.
The last note of measure 3 should be an eighth note.)

(l) Page 60	21.2, a–e	sing and tap; sing as if key signature were printed

Chapter VI

Opening Oneself

The Aniticipatory Position—Readiness to Receive Sound and Breath

The essential problem of the sphere of the interhuman is the duality of being and seeming. . . .

We may distinguish between two types of human existence. The one proceeds from what one really is, the other from what one wishes to seem. In general, the two are found mixed together. (P. 65–66)

Whatever the meaning of the word "truth" may be in other realms, in the interhuman realm it means that men communicate themselves to one another as what they are. It does not depend on one saying to the other everything that occurs to him, but only on his letting no seeming creep in between himself and the other. It does not depend on letting himself go before another, but on his granting to the man to whom he communicates himself a share in his being. This is a question of the authenticity of the interhuman, and where this is not to be found, neither is the human element itself authentic.

Therefore, as we begin to recognize the crisis of man as the crisis of what is between man and man, we must free the concept of uprightness from the thin moralistic tones which cling to it, and let it take its tone from the concept of bodily uprightness. (P. 67)

There are two basic ways of affecting men in their views and their attitude to life. In the first a man tries to impose himself, his opinion and his attitude, on the other in such a way that the latter feels the psychical result of the action to be his own insight, which has only been freed by the influence. In the second basic way of affecting others, a man wishes to find and to further in the soul of the other the disposition toward what he has recognized as the right. Because it is the right, it must also be alive in the microcosm of the other, as one possibility. The other need only be opened out in this potentiality of his; moreover this opening out takes place not essentially by teaching, but by meeting, by existential communication between someone that is actual being and someone that is in a process of becoming. (P. 72)

> Martin Buber
> *The Knowledge of Man*

All the arts we practice are apprenticeship. The big art is our life. (P. 83)

> Mary Caroline Richards
> in *The Artist's Way*, Julia Cameron

The necessary thing is after all but this: solitude, great inner solitude. Going-into-oneself and for hours meeting no one—this one must be able to obtain. To be solitary, the way one was solitary as a child, when the grownups went around involved with things that seemed important and big because they themselves looked so busy and because one comprehended nothing of their doings.

And when one day one perceives that their occupations are paltry, their professions petrified and no longer linked with the living, why not then continue to look like a child upon it all as upon something unfamiliar, from out of the depth of one's own world, out of the expanse of one's own solitude, which is itself work and status and vocation? Why want to exchange a child's wise incomprehension for defensiveness and disdain, since incomprehension is after all being alone, while defensiveness and disdain are a sharing in that from which one wants by these means to keep apart. (P. 45–46)

> Rainer Maria Rilke
> *Letters to a Young Poet*

There is an inner and an outer music. When we are content with the outer shape of things and present them repeatedly as profound truth we are likely to be dealing with superficiality but calling it fundamentality. (P. 166–167)

Jamake Highwater
The Primal Mind

From these presuppositions there can emerge the basic relationship between choir and choir director in which the director feels himself to be an integral part of the choir. The leader must be a member of the choral body and feel at one with it. He should be the central and driving force of his group but his control should be less of an imposition from without than an implicit controlling force originating from his own person. (P. 112)

In accordance with the ideal traditional leader, the choir director should regard himself as the precentor or leading dancer who, as the best performer in his group, emerges from the group to give direction and leadership, but always withdraws again into and identifies himself with the group as *Primus inter pares.* He should cultivate and strengthen this feeling within himself. His ideal objective should be a gradual withdrawal from the choir to the point where he could on occasion be dispensable. (P. 112)

Wilhelm Ehmann
Choral Directing

The center that I cannot find is known to my unconscious mind. (P. 85)

W. H. Auden
in *The Artist's Way,* Julia Cameron

In a choral situation the greatest single obstacle to proper communication is that both parties too often are engaged in playing roles instead of attempting to live as real persons. (P. 125)

Our responsibility as choral musicians does not stop with the teaching of music. We must find time and energy for thought and study so that we can help teach people how to live. (P. 139)

Howard Swan
Conscience of a Profession

Kato Havas, the great violin teacher and author of *Stage Fright*, says that her goal in music is to "eliminate the self." "The player needs to be able to forget about himself," she writes. "This is when real communication begins. For with the elimination of the self, he is able to reach the very core of the music, and is free to transmit it." (P. 81)

Barry Green
The Inner Game of Music

I do know what I want someone to give me for Christmas. I've known since I was forty years old. Wind-up mechanical toys that make noises and go round and round and do funny things. No batteries. Toys that need me to help them out from time to time. The old fashioned painted tin ones I had as a child. That's what I want. Nobody believes me. It's what I want, I tell you.

Well, okay, that's close, but not exactly it. It's delight and simplicity that I want. Foolishness and fantasy and noise. Angels and miracles and wonder and innocence and magic. That's closer to what I want.

It's harder to talk about, but what I *really, really, really* want for Christmas is just this:

I want to be five years old again for an hour.

I want to laugh a lot and cry a lot.

I want to be picked up and rocked to sleep in someone's arms, and carried up to bed just one more time.

I know what I really want for Christmas.

I want my childhood back.

Nobody is going to give me that. I might give at least the memory of it to myself if I try. I know it doesn't make sense, but since when is Christmas about sense, anyway? It is about a child, of long ago and far away, and it is about the child of now. In you and me. Waiting behind the door of our hearts for something wonderful to happen. A child is impractical, unrealistic, simpleminded, and terribly vulnerable to joy. A child who does not need or want to understand gifts of socks or potholders. (P. 95–96)

Robert Fulghum
All I Really Need to Know I Learned in Kindergarten

I believe in man's unconscious, the deep spring from which comes his power to communicate and to love. For me, all art is a combination of these powers; art is nothing to me if it does not make contact between the creator and the perceiver on an unconscious level. Let us say that love is the way we have of communicating personally in the deepest way. What art can do is to extend this communication, magnify it, and carry it to vastly greater numbers of people. In this it needs a warm core, a hidden heating element. Without that core, art is only an exercise in techniques, a calling of attention to the artist, or a vain display. I believe in art for the warmth and love it carries within it, even if it be the lightest entertainment, or the bitterest satire, or the most shattering tragedy. For if art is cold it cannot communicate anything to anybody. (P. 141–142)

Leonard Bernstein
Findings

Psychology has been unconcerned with myth and imagination, and has shown little care for history, beauty, sensuality, or eloquence—the Renaissance themes. Its pragmatism, whether in clinic or laboratory, kills fantasy or subverts it into the service of practical goals. Love becomes a sexual problem; religion an ethnic attitude; soul a political badge. No chapters are more barren and trivial in the textbooks of psychological thought than those on imagination, emotion, and the living of life or the dying of death. Psychology has hardly been touched by anima, until recently as the soul stirs and makes claims on it for relevance and depth. (P. 220)

James Hillman
Re-Visioning Psychology

Transparency is vulnerability. It is the capacity to be open within ourselves in order that the music can flow through us—that we can be an open conduit, a free vessel. If we are not vulnerable as conductors, if we don't have the freedom to allow ourselves to be as we are, we can't take experiences offered to us by our singers and incorporate them with our own. Music does not flow through an impeded conduit. As Leonard Bernstein once said, "If the heart isn't free, the baton isn't free." How true. Thus we must work to increase the depth of our feeling function. This will lead to openness, the ability to share our inner person more freely. As we reach a deeper understanding of ourselves, we will gain deeper insights into the spirit of the music.

Vulnerability can be threatening. It is not easy to be open—to share our deepest feelings. And we have a shadow side to our lives that tries to block our transparency/vulnerability. We therefore make friends with our shadow side. The accomplishment of this is one of the great adventures of life! A strong shadow results in negative thinking while a friendly shadow results in positive thinking. How can the wonderful beauty of music come forward if our thinking is predominantly negative! (P. 12)

Weston Noble
in *The Choral Journal*, Dennis Shrock

Being open and attentive is more effective than being judgemental. This is because people naturally tend to be good and truthful when they are being received in a good and truthful manner. (P. 97)

John Heider
The Tao of Leadership

Q: What are the weaknesses you see in most young choral conductors?

A: They need to learn to study a score properly and make contact with the sound. It (making contact with the sound) is something that has to be experienced: there is a feeling that the sonority is in your hands and that the music itself goes right by your face. It would be similar to sitting right by the source of the sound when you play and having real contact with it. (P. 70)

Margaret Hillis
in *The Choral Journal*, Dennis Shrock

Let people realize clearly that every time they threaten or humiliate or hurt unnecessarily or dominate or reject another human being, they become the forces for the creation of psychotherapy, even if these be small forces. Let them recognize that every person who is kind, helpful, decent, psychologically democratic, affectionate, and warm is a psychotherapeutic force even though a small one. (p. 90)

Abraham H. Maslow
in *A Teacher Is Many Things*, Pullias and Young

Q: What is the most important thing for you in making music?

A: That the music is more important than I am. (P. 71)

Margaret Hillis
in *The Choral Journal*, Dennis Schrock

I had a terrible education. I attended school for emotionally disturbed teachers. (P. 57)

Woody Allen
in *A Teacher Affects Eternity*, Linda Sunshine

• • • • •

In the previous chapter we discussed the many aspects of alignment that need to be understood and accomplished in order to allow breath to fall effortlessly into the body and to allow the musculature of the body to relax so that the body is able to respond freely to music that is received. Just how one "opens the inside" must now be examined.

PREPARATION OF THE "INSIDE"

The *anticipatory position* is so called because it anticipates the receiving of sound from the choir. This position is not only an issue of correct alignment, but it is an issue of spiritual openness and acceptance. To many of you reading this text, this will seem to be a relatively minor point. In fact, that "openness" to the choir to receive their sound, in addition to breath coming into the body, is the part of conducting that transforms it from mere time beating to artistry. No matter whether you are a church choir director or a college conductor, the same principles apply. Many conducting texts first teach technique, i.e., the movement of the limbs to specific geometric patterns. The preparation, as it were, of the "inside" of the person is not dealt with. The preparation of the "inside" of the conductor is known only to those conductors who rise to the highest levels of the profession. The reality is that this element of "openness," of "receiving the sound," is the starting point for the development of all conducting and communication. Without opening oneself to the human beings with whom one is about to work, connection to them is impossible at the most basic of levels: person communicating with another person. Without that connection, spontaneous music making that is manifest by color, line, rhythm and spirit is impossible. From the onset, conducting must be from the inside out rather than from the outside in.

What does this "inside-out" feel like? Imagine that you have just spent many weeks shopping for a special present for the most special person in your life. You have purchased it early and have been keeping it secret for many months. The day finally arrives for you to present it to this person. What is your feeling as you present this special gift to them? What is that "inside" feeling that you feel when you are about to share and give something to another person you admire? It is not only the feeling that comes from inside you but the almost instantaneous receiving of that persons innermost feelings—all wordless and unspoken.

Imagine another life situation. You are waiting at the train station for someone you have not seen for some time and for whom you have great admiration. You wait patiently on the train platform for them. The train stops. The doors open. You quickly scan the platform for the person among hundreds of heads. You suddenly see the person and run toward them with arms outstretched. Your body opens to embrace them. What does your "inside" feel like as you welcome them? What do you feel as they, in turn, welcome you?

It would indeed be foolish to try to put into words those feelings from the above scenes. Language simply falls short in trying to express what our "inside" feels in such situations. But know that each time that you rehearse with your choir, you must be able to shed the baggage of the week, the day, or the previous hour. You must be able, prior to singing, to open your body in similar fashion to the above scenarios. The ability to do this will open the door to music making at the highest levels. To avoid openness or not to ponder its effect upon music making is to ignore one of the major tenets of artistic conducting: openness to the ensemble.

There is yet one other "state of mind" that is desirable to have in place for music making to begin. Can you recall your earliest childhood play experience? It can be an experience of playing alone or with others. Try to recall the happiest of times. You can, no doubt, recall not only the specific situation, but the "feeling" of the situation. The ideal play is that play which has no rules, no boundaries. It is timeless. One is almost virtually unaware of the world around them, for one creates a world unto itself where one is totally immersed in the activity at hand. Can you place yourself there again? To validate your experience, spend some time observing children at a local playground or daycare center. The spirit of play and spontaneity of childhood is the same spontaneity and spirit of music making. Whether it be conductor or performer that childlike, innocent state is necessary for music to speak clearly through us to others.

These two "inside" states—the welcoming, caring state and the play state—must be re-created as one begins a piece of music. To do otherwise will produce a product much less musical and much less human. It is hard to imagine a childhood without play. It is hard to imagine a life without other human beings. It should be, likewise, impossible for conductors to begin with their choir until they are able to allow their "inside" to be reflective of those qualities so that their choir can, in turn, be reflective of their conductor. Conducting, then, is very much like a mirror image of oneself, a reflection of the inside manifest in sound. That manifestation of sound begins with the preparation of the proper spirit for music making to establish itself through the attitude of the body, both physically and spiritually.

APPROPRIATE "OUTSIDE" POSITIONS AND IMAGERIES

You have been led through two processes to this point. In chapter 2 you were taught the mechanics of alignment through the theories of Alexander. That work should have laid the groundwork for "allowing" your alignment to find its correct and natural state through the proper mental imagery of posture and the role of the muscles as they interact with the skeletal system. The beginning of this chapter has established imagery for you to open your inner body so that the psychological attitude that is pivotal to spontaneous music making can be understood and refound each time one begins to make music. Now, we will discuss some imageries to assure that the arms make a logical extension from the body and, most importantly, a connection to it.

ARM POSITION. Arm and hand position always seem to be a concern to those who study conducting. Much more is made of arm position than need be made. Chances are that if you have given careful consideration to the material already presented in this book, your hand and arm position will be conducive to singing. However, it is always helpful to have some additional ideas by which to measure one's progress.

If you imagine that you are greeting a friend as was described above, what is the shape of your arms just seconds prior to the point at which you embrace them? With proper alignment in mind, your arms are probably outstretched and slightly curved. The curve of the arms is followed through the wrists and into the hands. The wrist is slightly curved, as are the fingers. The fingers of both hands are not clenched tightly, but have space between them. The fingers are relaxed and slightly rounded. Body energy is able to travel through the limbs and out the fingertips. Keep your hands *inside the line of the elbows*. At all times, however, the arms should reflect the motion of the breath in the body, that is, keep the motion of your arms consistent with your body.

HAND POSITION. To help you with hand position, imagine shaking someone's hand. What is the position of your hand? It is slightly rounded and curved, and most likely turned inward toward the center of your body. How does your hand feel during a hand shake? It feels inspirited and enlivened. The hand position for shaking hands is perhaps the one that best approximates the initial position for conducting.

INFLUENCE OF HAND POSITION UPON THE SOUND. Apart from knowing the approximate placement of the hands and arms as described above, if the conductor is aligned and listening, the body, limbs (arms), and hands accurately reflect the music. However, if the conductor has undue muscular tension, then that tension will most likely manifest itself in the hands. The shape of the hands directly influences the color of the vowel being produced by the choir—that is, if the hands are flat, with fingers held closely together, then the sound will most likely be flat, thin, and a bit edgy. If the choir is singing an *oo* vowel, and the conductor hears the *oo* color, his hands will naturally mirror a more round shape. Remember, however, that most tension problems are caused by a misalignment of the pelvis and the head, which in turn affects the head and the neck. If your hands seem to be unnatural, then focus your attention first on your alignment.

   EVALUATING ARM POSITION. Many beginning conductors, however, begin with an arm position that is too high. This occurs for many reasons which will be made obvious throughout this text. To identify the proper field for arm position, imagine this scene: You are at the checkout counter at the grocery store. The store has had a sale on canned goods, and you have decided to stock up. You ask for your canned goods to be bagged in paper bags. You have purchased enough groceries for two full paper bags. As you leave the checkout counter, you decide that you do not want to use a shopping cart to get to your car. You pick up the two bags of groceries and carry them to the car. How do you carry them so they don't fall?

   If you recreate the position of your limbs and your body, you will find that your body is aligned and tall to support the weight of the bags. You also find that your arms curve around the bags to encircle, them. The hands support the weight of the bags from underneath. This imagery is the same imagery you should strive to create in a conducting anticipatory position! Instead of the shopping bags filled with weighty canned goods, imagine that your arms encircle the sound that the choir creates, that, in fact, you are immersed in a pool of sound that is centered within the curve of your arms. Your hands need to approximate the image of supporting the sacks of groceries because your hands so "support" the sound of the choir from that low position. (Another useful image for the round spaciousness necessary between the arms and the body is to imagine holding a beach ball by encircling it with your arms, similar to the way you held the grocery bags.)

   Remember that a "kink" or angular bending at any one of the joints will tend to cause a "kink" in the choral sound that will manifest as a dull color or flatness in pitch. The roundness of the arms and the embracing body attitude is important for another reason. The gentle curving of the arms and body is sympathetic to the roundness which should be in place for the singers. The curve of the arms outward from the body encourages *both* a round and a low support. The gentle curve of the hands and wrists encourages the round interior space of the mouth and pharynx for singing. The open, relaxed fingertips have a direct influence on a tone that is open and freed.

The drawing in figure 6.1 is offered as a reference for you. Do not simply imitate these images. Arrive at your individual anticipatory position first through the imagery described above. To simply position the limbs and "mime" the photographs will not insure the proper *inward* body attitude. That inward body attitude will naturally create the appropriate arm-body attitude that will transfer directly into conducting for singers. A parallel can be seen in dance. One can certainly learn the steps for a dance by following painted footsteps on the floor, but until one feels the rhythmic "beat" of the dance inside of them, the aimless moving of the feet has no significance. Have you ever seen someone who knows the steps to a dance but has no "inside" rhythm to accompany the coordinated steps? This analogy is the same for the conductor. Body attitude and imagery about the sound must come from within. In doing so, the body will outwardly reflect what the inner body is!

It is also important to remember that the sound exists directly in front of you. While you should not reach for the sound, your hands should be in a position to touch the sound when that sound is released from the singers. This "touching" of the sound brings tremendous focus to the choral sound. Your hands should always be in the place where the sound begins.

NECK TENSION. One of the most important areas of attention and concern for the conductor is the neck. As was discussed in chapter 2, the correct alignment of the neck is essential for a natural and spontaneous gesture to be elicited from the conductor. Any neck tension or misalignment will cause the overall conducting gesture to lock. Most importantly, the natural, spontaneous impulses of rhythm and musical line will not be evoked from the choir because the neck tension creates a "blockage" of the channel through which these musical impulses are transmitted to the choir through the conductor's gesture.

WRIST TENSION. Likewise, the conductor's wrists be relaxed in the anticipatory position, just as a person's wrist is relaxed when shaking another's hand. Locking or rigidity in the wrists will produce the identical result described above concerning neck tension. Both neck and wrist must be relaxed for natural musical impulse of the conductor to be transmitted to the choir.

THE FACE. The face is a mirror of the interior of the conductor's body; that is, it relays the spirit of the conductor. It also, seemingly, opens and relaxes when the breath is taken. There should not be tension or undue facial contortions. Care must be taken to keep the face active, but muscularly relaxed, especially in the vicinity of the forehead and eyebrows. Facial tension of any type will negatively impact the choral sound.

OPENING THE CHANNEL: ARM ATTACHMENT. From the start of conducting study, it is very helpful to readjust one's concept of where the arms are attached to the body. The obvious answer is at the shoulder. Anatomically, that is

FIG. 6.1. THE ANTICIPATORY POSITION

correct; however, that image must be replaced by another one for conductors. The shoulders pose many technical challenges to both the novice and experienced conductor. If the shoulders are tense or rigid, they form a type of blockage or circuit breaker, to the rhythmic energy that comes from the "inside" of the conductor. In many cases, shoulder tension dampens or clouds the natural rhythm impulse that is within the conductor. Likewise, in many cases, the conductor is unaware that his shoulders are the culprits. He instead blames the choir for not watching, or "not being with him." If one pictures a path beginning at the point where one feels rhythm internally (at your "center" or in your abdominal area or in your chest cavity), there is a channel that must be open for the conductor's rhythm impulse to be clearly read (sensed) by the choir through the conductor's gesture. The channel begins at ones "center" (see chapter 4). The impulse for rhythm travels from that center, through the shoulders, down through the elbows, through the wrists, through the knuckles and is transmitted outward to the choir through the fingertips! The channel, then, is an open tunnel through which these basic rhythm impulses can travel without interference. The first major blockage to that rhythm channel is usually the shoulders.

To open the channel through the shoulders, the conductor should imagine that the shoulders do not exist and that his arms attach to his body in the small of the back. The shoulders should not be felt when conducting. Imagining that the arms attach at the small of the back also sets the ground work for the breath process that will be developed in chapter 7.

Exercises

1. Videotape yourself in what you believe to be a correct anticipatory position. Compare your videotape to the examples in the text.

2. Speak each of the pure vowels with your hands in an anticipatory position. As you speak each of the vowels, sustain the vowel and allow the shape and position of your hand to change. As the position of your hand changes, does the color of the vowel change?

3. One of the most important philosophical concepts that a conductor needs to develop is the concept of focus. The focus of one's musical energy and listening is central to the art of conducting. Turn to Appendix II. Take yourself through the Inner Game of Music examples and answer the questions at the end of each exercise to begin an exploration of focus and its components.

CHAPTER VII

BREATHING AND DROPPING IN

FUNDAMENTALS OF CONNECTION

Inspirit 1. To put spirit, life, or energy into; to quicken, enliven, animate, to incite, stir.

The Compact Edition of the
Oxford English Dictionary

Therefore, the basic trick is in the preparatory upbeat. It is exactly like breathing: the preparation is like an inhalation, and the music sounds like an exhalation. We all have to inhale in order to speak, for example; all verbal expression is exhaled. So it is with music: we inhale on the upbeat and sing out a phrase of music, then inhale again and breathe out the next phrase. A conductor who breathes with the music has gone far in acquiring a technique. (P. 272)

Leonard Bernstein
The Conductor's Art

For air to be in motion in or out of the bellows system a pressure difference must be created between the interior of the balloon and the atmosphere. Starting at our resting point, if the bellows are expanded and the pressure around the balloon falls and, as the balloon gets larger, the pressure within it falls and air rushes in until atmospheric pressure within the balloon is again achieved. During this process the "pleural" pressure will equal the elastic recoil of the balloon plus the pressure required to overcome the resistance to air flow. To move air more quickly, or if an added resistance to flow is applied at the mouth, a greater pressure drop is required. The reverse is true if air is to move out of this system.

Put in another way, we have a sequence of forces at work. The force moving the bellows arm is comparable to that of our breathing muscles. Its action in making the bellows larger or smaller creates a more negative or positive pressure around the balloon. In response to that pressure change the balloon grows larger or smaller. With change in the balloon volume its contained air is expanded or compressed and the pressure falls or rises. That pressure difference between the air within the balloon and the surrounding atmosphere results in a flow of air in or out through the bellows mouth until the change in volume ceases and the pressure is equal again.

Now if we leave this model and look at the breathing system in life we see that all of the above remains true; the major difference is that respiratory muscles now do the work of the force applied to the bellows arms. (P.39)

Donald F. Proctor
Breathing, Speech and Song

What happens to a body when a force does act on it is given by Newton's second law. This states that the body will accelerate, or change its speed, at a rate that is proportional to the force. (For example, the acceleration is twice as great if the force is twice as great.) The acceleration is also smaller the greater the mass (or quantity of matter) of the body. (The same force acting on a body of twice the mass will produce half the acceleration.) (P. 16)

Stephen W. Hawking
A Brief History of Time

● ● ● ● ●

Proper alignment, a clearly established anticipatory position, and the understanding of release are prerequisites for making music with a group as a conductor. The beginning of a piece of music is a wonderful simultaneity of breath and instinctive rhythm impulse made manifest through the gesture of the conductor. Once again, it is important that this "gesture" be created from the inside out rather than the outside in.

The Breathing Process

Breath is the core of all conducting gesture, all music making. The breath of the conductor and the breathing of the choir establishes the most important ingredient for spontaneous music making. The breath of the conductor establishes tempo, color, and affect of the piece. Remarkably, breath also allows the conductor to hear all of the elements of the score! There is a direct relationship between the ability to breathe and the ability to hear.

Opening the body for the breath. Many beginning conductors have trouble with the breathing process that is about to be discussed. The irony of this is that breathing is a natural process. The most important element to facilitate the breathing process is *to have the body open to receive air before the breath is taken, or initiated.* If you analyze any of the activities of life for which we take air into our bodies, you will notice that just prior to the point at which air falls into our body, a relaxation, or opening of the entire breathing tract takes place so that the airways are open in order for the air to seemingly "drop in" to our body. This opening of the body prior to the moment of inhalation is, perhaps, the single most important skill for the conductor. For example, imagine that you have just been suddenly surprised by another person. Just prior to the point when you suddenly take in air, the body instinctively opens itself to receive air quickly. This "opening" of the body is the same that takes place prior to breathing for singing and conducting singers.

The following two breathing concepts might be helpful in allowing breath to fall into the body naturally:

> Think of releasing all the muscles surrounding your torso in order to
> allow breathing.
> Think of allowing air to flow into and out of your lungs, rather than
> pulling it in or pushing it out.

Inhalation. To begin this process, we will first explore through a series of exercises ways to get air to enter the body. These exercises are designed to open the body for air acceptance and to sensitize the conductor to the sensation of air dropping into his body.

Lawnmower exercise. As a beginning exercise, imitate the activities surrounding the starting of a lawnmower. Bend over and grab the pull cord for a manually starting lawnmower. Place one leg in front of the other and grasp the pull cord. As you rapidly pull the cord toward you to start the mower, inhale rapidly and fill your lungs with as much air as is possible. Immediately exhale the air on a forceful *sshhhhhhhhhhhhhhhhhhhhh*. Repeat several times. This exercise allows you to experience large amounts of air coming into the body, while at the same time allowing you to condition the muscles around the ribs to open for breath to enter the body.

DIVING EXERCISE. This is another exercise to open the body in order for air to drop into the body. Place your hands in front of you, imagining that you are about to dive into a swimming pool. With your arms in front of you, dive into the pool, taking a "swimmer's breath," i.e., a quick, low breath. Repeat the exercise several times.

SURPRISE EXERCISE. Find your anticipatory position once again. Place your hands flat on your body below your navel. Imagine that someone has surprised you, coming up from behind you and scaring you. Your mouth drops open, and air falls into your body and drops to the level within your body where your hands rest. Do you feel the "ball of air" low in your body? If not, the muscles around that area of your lower body were sufficiently restricted to prevent the air from dropping into the body low. Getting the air to drop into the body as low as the pelvis is the goal.

FIG. 7.1. POSSIBLE HAND POSITIONS
FOR INHALATION EXERCISES

Sternum check. One of the parts of the body that many times restricts air from falling into the body is the area just below the sternum, or breastbone. Take two fingers and rest them gently on that area. Allow the air to drop into your body. Do you feel the muscles in that area as either rigid or tight ? That muscle grouping, known as the epigastrium, must be relaxed for air to drop lower into the body. It is the door to the lower body air container! Any rigidity in that area causes the inhalation process to stop at that "level" in the body. Air must be able to drop low into the body. The body must be able to open itself for air to simply drop into the body. If one watches a baby breathe, one notices the low breathing process that is naturally in place. For many reasons, the manner in which we live our daily lives causes us muscular tension, which then prohibits the body from opening spontaneously, and thus air cannot drop into the body. If there is muscular tension in that area, simply tell the muscles to relax . . . they will! Let go of all muscular "holding" and tension in that area. Place your hands again on your body below your navel and become comfortable with the "astonished" breath exercise. But this time, as you perform the exercise, check yourself in a mirror. Check your alignment. When you become "astonished," does the astonishment register on your face as well? The "astonishment" should be experienced internally and should be seen externally by others. It is not only the act of astonishment but also the energy by which one becomes astonished that is important to the conductor. Repeat the exercise with your hands in place until you can perform it without trouble.

Inspiriting the hands: connecting the hands to the breath process. Place both hands flat on your lower abdomen just below your navel. Establish your anticipatory body position once again. (Perhaps you will want to find your body anticipatory position from a seated position where you can establish your alignment from your sit bones.) Allow an "astonished" breath to fall into your body. The air should fall into your body in a fashion similar to a large ball of air falling from the sky into your body. What happens to your hands when air enters into your body? You should feel the opening of your lower body pushing outward against your hands. Exhale. Let the air drop in once again. Does your lower body *release open* as the air drops in? Pant like a dog. Can you feel the air dropping low into the body?

Now perform the exercise in figure 7.2. When performing this exercise, remember to check your alignment. Remember also that the breath should fall into the body naturally, without noise. If it does not, check to be sure that your body is open just prior to the point at which you breathe.

Listening to the breath. One of the most important skills that a conductor can develop is to be able to listen not only to his own breath, but to the breath of the choir. When conductors listen to their choir's breath, they

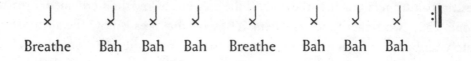

Breathe   Bah   Bah   Bah   Breathe   Bah   Bah   Bah

FIG. 7.2. INHALATION EXERCISE

instinctively synchronize and coordinate their own breath with that of their ensemble. When heard, the sound of the inhalation signals to the conductors when the choir should release sounds from their bodies. The aural sensitivity to the breath provides conductors with the opportunity to "set the sound" of the choir and insure a proper "attack."

Repeat the exercise in figure 7.2. Open your body for the breath. Allow breath to fall into your body. Listen to the breath as it comes into the body. Imagine your hands "supporting" the breath mechanism as the air falls into the body. Feel as if your hands actually hold the breath apparatus in your hands as you perform the exercise. Be sure to voice the *buh* consonants with lips lightly held together and teeth slightly apart. Continue the exercise, but begin to slowly move your arms and hands into the anticipatory position away from your body, still recreating in your hands the image that your hands mirror the actual movement of the breath apparatus as the breath falls into the body. *Imagine that your arms are attached to your body at the small of your back, not at your shoulders.* You should not feel your shoulders or your elbows as your perform this exercise. What you should "feel" is the roundness of your arms as they embrace the sound. That is, your hands mirror and recreate what is actually happening with the breath mechanism as the air comes into the body and as sound is created on *buh*. The hands will gently undulate outward as the breath falls into the body and inward as the sound *buh* is produced. Imagine that, in addition to reflecting the exact action of the breath mechanism, you can hold the sound in your hands and that you can touch that sound with your fingertips. This exercise should be performed with your eyes closed to further heighten the sensitivity of the hands to the breath process.

COORDINATING THE INSPIRITING OF THE HANDS. The above exercise should be performed until it becomes almost second nature. The exercise will likely pose a challenge because it is difficult for most of us to release the muscles in our lower body so that air falls low into the body. Continued practice will allow the opening to occur. While practicing this exercise, it is important not to move the hands independently of the breath activity. Remember that the hands are merely an extension of the breath process and that they are connected to the breath process in the most intimate of ways. Your hands are the breath and your breath is your hands! That is to say that your hands never move independently of the breath process. *The breath always initiates the motion of the hands.* Your hands do not act alone but always in unison with the breath action of your body. Remember, your breath mechanism is the genesis for all music making. Your hands do not begin the breath process; your breath mechanism does. The hands simply mirror in quick succession the activity of your body's breath process. *Your hands can act in unison with the breath because you listen to the breath as it comes into the body. Your hands (palms inward, similar to a handshake) and arms move slightly outward and upward with each inhalation.* The following exercise might be an additional help to firmly establish this concept.

STRING IMAGERY EXERCISE. Imagine that you have just had a length of string surgically implanted within your body. The surgeon began the implant on the end of each of your third fingers. He then took the string and threaded it inside your arm, through your armpit, along the inside of your shoulder body cavity, down the center of your body outside your esophagus, going around the outside of your stomach and arriving at the diaphragm muscle. He threads the string through that muscle, and then brings it outside your body through a small incision. He knots the string and attaches a large button to it. Now that the surgery is completed and you are healed, your can pull the button. As you pull the button, your arm raises! Perform this drill several times. You must pull the button (which is attached to the diaphragm) first before your hand moves! The movement of your hand is inspirited and set into motion by the activity of the diaphragm and the breath mechanism Your hands never move independently of the dropping of the breath mechanism. When the breath falls into the body and the diaphragm drops, the hands and arms instinctively follow by moving outward and turning slightly upward.

GROCERY BAG EXERCISE. As one practices the above exercises to sensitize oneself to the tandem movement of the breath and the hands, many beginning conductors tend to raise the arms too high. To avoid this pitfall, recall the image of carrying grocery bags. Imagine as you perform the *huh* exercise that you are holding two large paper grocery bags filled with heavy canned goods, one in each arm. How would you hold these bags if you wanted to carry them from the grocery store to your car without a cart? You would probably grasp the bags in such a manner as to *support* the weight of the bags from underneath while encircling the outer circumference of the bags with your arms. As you perform the above exercises, substitute sound for the grocery bags! Imagine that your arms encircle and hold the sound while your hands support and touch it! This exercise completes the "polish" for a desirable anticipatory conducting body posture and attitude that both reflects and supports sound.

INFLUENCING VOCAL COLOR THROUGH THE BREATH

Once you have begun to understand the process by which breath enters the body and how that breath manifests the rhythmic spirit, articulation, and tempo of the work, there is another factor of vocal color to consider. If you as conductor simply take a rhythmic breath, you will notice that the choir responds in a vocal tone that always seems the same. In fact, many conductors have difficulties with different styles of music because the color of their choir always remains the same. They then resort to vocal "tricks" to change the resonance of the sound by asking the choir to sing "brighter" or "darker." Certainly, adjustments such as "brighter" or "darker" may be used to further enhance a choral sound, but the initial influence upon the color of the sound is through the quality of the breath of the conductor.

Vocal color is developed "in the ear" of the conductor through her or his aural musical life experience. Listening to recordings and performances and singing in choirs contributes to one's choral color palette. But how is a conductor's sense of color transmitted to the choir, and how that ability be developed?

The ability to hear color (or perhaps more rightly labeled timbre) is one of over forty music aptitudes. Aptitudes are potentials that may or may not have been realized through training. Unfortunately, we have begun to acquire information concerning the functioning of two of those aptitudes (tonal and rhythm) but know very little about the remaining forty or so! However, just as there are no persons without any intelligence, there is some degree of the aptitude to hear colors in each of us. The challenge, then, is to awaken and develop that part of our musical aptitude which hears musical colors.

For conductors, this valuable and necessary tool can be unlocked developed through two initial processes. In the first process, you simply assign to a phrase or a section or an entire piece a physical color, such as light blue, azure, marigold, garnet, etc. Once you arrive at a color "decision," you should "breathe" the color as you inhale. Color changes within a piece can be influenced by selecting another color, and breathing that color. You should be able to hear the color change in the sound. Why does this work? There are several possible reasons. First, by imagining a section of a piece in a particular color, you are awakening your musical fantasy by going beyond the simple rhythm and pitch. Second, by fantasizing about a color or colors, and breathing that color, you directly influence the *quality* of your breath. Quality of breath refers to the *inner* space of your body when the breath is taken. By intuiting colors, you directly affect the type of breath you take, and in turn, that breath directly connects with the singers.

The second process also involves another type of fantasy. In chapter 4, the Laban Effort Elements and Efforts in Combination of Laban were discussed. By being able to remember through your "movement memory" various types of flicks, dabs, floats, presses, etc., you activate the kinesthetic, or movement, side of your fantasy, which adds another "color" dimension to your musical ideas. Specifically, by associating with an Effort combination, you make subconscious decisions concerning the Weight, Time, and Space requirements of the music, which is manifest in the forward movement of the music line, or, as Laban calls it, the Flow of the work.

GUIDELINES FOR CONDUCTING PRACTICE

One of the difficulties of studying the art of conducting is that, unlike study on the voice or and instrument, you cannot practice on the instrument that you are studying. The absence of an ensemble with which to practice conducting issues is a distinct problem! While there is no substitute for conducting an ensemble, there are certain techniques that can be used to maintain a connection between gesture and sound. Throughout this text it is important to keep the following practice principles in mind.

1. *Always practice conducting from the same body alignment position that you will be using when you conduct. There is an intimate, direct, and powerful connection between body posture and the music learning-conducting process.* You must realize that because music speaks through our entire being, every time a piece of music is performed or prepared for conducting, the body's "muscle memory" will recreate the exact body posture, body attitude and spirit that existed as the music was being learned. From the beginning of the study of conducting, the student should view score preparation as both an aural and kinesthetic exercise. The kinesthetic attitude of the body is established simultaneously when the initial learning of the score takes place; that is, if one learns a score in a slouched seated position, it is very likely that the major aspects of that posture will return subconsciously when the music is sounded. Many times it is difficult to establish a correct body alignment when posture and music learning have been unknowingly associated in this fashion.

2. *Make certain that you breathe as if you were conducting; inhale for the "preparation" to start the piece and exhale (release your breath into the sound) while you are conducting.*

3. *Never practice conducting gesture that is not intimately connected to sound.*

4. *At the very least, practice conducting with a partner to experience the music-making with another person.* It is important after the initial preparation of materials has been accomplished through singing and conducting that one conducts at least one other person to experience the human connection that occurs as one participates in the music making process as conductor-singer. By using a partner, you can also gain valuable feedback concerning effectiveness in achieving the desired music result.

5. *When you conduct other persons, let the sound be your teacher.* As you conduct your partner or a group of persons, remember that the sounds you hear are directly reflective of your body and gesture. It is important to establish a high level of honesty with regard to this aspect of conducting practice. If the sound coming back to you is not what you want, you must be willing to accept that the sound is a mirror image of your conducting. When the sound is not "good," try to change it toward your ideal by understanding the interrelationship of gesture to sound. (Ultimately, the goal of any conducting teacher is to move the students to the point where they can teach themselves through listening to the sounds that are shared with them and through them by the choir.)

6. *Listen to the breath of those you conduct.* The most basic of connections to the choir is established at the moment when inhalation takes place in both the conductor and the choir. The moment at which sound is released from the singers can only be forecast through listening to the breath of the ensemble. Not only must the conductor listen to the breath in the choir, but choir members must listen to each other breathe so as to establish an ensemble sense. That sense of ensemble begins in the communal breath.

7. *Sing and conduct when preparing musical materials for conducting class.* The feeling of what it is to sing a phrase, the feeling of sound being released from the body, is the "feeling," the "body attitude," that needs to be relayed and reinforced to the singers. Conducting gesture is reflective of what we feel as a singer as the phrase is being recreated; that is, gesture comes from the inside out. If one "plans" the geometry of one's conducting, it will never allow for spontaneous music making. Sing each part in the music. Experience what it feels like to sing that phrase. Next, conduct while singing. Then conduct without singing and maintain the same body feel-

ing that you had when you were singing. If you do this, you will find that learning conducting "technique" can be an effortless process when pursued in this way.

EXERCISE

Deborah Caplan, in her book, *Back Trouble*, suggests the following breathing exercise based upon Alexander Technique.

> Lie on your back—on the floor or in bed, whichever is more comfortable—with a small pillow under your head and a large one under your knees. Let your legs relax on the pillow. Close your eyes and visualize your rib cage as an empty cylinder, and give the cylinder a flexible floor (the diaphragm muscle). Imagine yourself as a tiny speck of consciousness floating in the center of the cylinder. As you breathe in, watch the walls and floor gently move away from you, and as you breathe out, watch them gently move toward you.
>
> Hold onto this image for a few moments. You will begin to be aware of the gentle in-and-out motion of your rib cage. If you place a hand just below your ribs in front, you will feel a slight rise (when you breathe in) and fall (when you breathe out) of your body that lets you know that the diaphragm is working freely. (P. 101)

Chapter VIII

Initiating Sound

Impulse Gesture, Ictus, the Freedom of Dropping In, Release, and Ictus Locations

Ictus [=blow, stroke, thrust.] 1. Stress on a particular syllable of a foot or verse; rhythmical or metrical stress. 2. The beat of the pulse. First use: 1707 Flover Physic Pulse-Watch 153 The Pulse is most likely consider'd ın its Ictus, which shews the Vigor of the spirits, and the Intervallum which shews the Heat of the Blood.

> The Compact Edition of the
> *Oxford English Dictionary*

All real living is meeting. (P. 11)

> Martin Buber
> *I and Thou*

The impulse behind the creation of music is not expressional in the Western psychological sense but is brought into existence by a dynamic process which is inclusive rather than exclusive, which, so to speak, is natural rather than rational. (P. 159)

> Jamake Highwater
> *The Primal Mind*

Well, and what is freedom? First of all, freedom seems to mean the absence of external restraint, the freedom to play. When we are free from external tyrannies, we seek freedom from our inner limitations. We find that in order to play we must be nimble and flexible and imaginative, we must be able to have fun, we must feel enjoyment, and sometimes long imprisonment has made us numb and sluggish. And then we find out that there are, paradoxically, disciplines which create in us capacities which allow us to seek our freedom. We learn how to rid ourselves of boredom, of stiffness, our repressed anger, our anxiety. We become brighter, more energy flows through us, our limbs rise, our spirit comes alive in our tissues. (p.22)

> Mary Caroline Richards
> *Centering*

I always found it (conducting technique) deceptively simple, functional, completely appropriate in every moment to the music played, and exactly what he needed. (P. 54)

> George Szell
> *Toscanini in the History of Orchestral Performance*

There is a vitality, a life force, an energy, a quickening, that is translated through you into action, and because there is only one of you in all time, this expression is unique. And if you block it, it will never exist through any other medium and will be lost. (P. 75)

> Martha Graham
> in *The Artist's Way*, Julia Cameron

• • • • •

In previous chapters, we learned the process by which our hands could be inspirited in order to sympathetically relay to singers the activity of the breath mechanism. We also learned the process by which we could align our bodies so that air could naturally drop into our bodies. Now that we have learned to breathe and to coordinate our hands to mirror and support the breath process, we can now study the gesture which will evoke an initial sound from the choir.

HAND POSITION

You will notice that little particular attention has been drawn to the position of the hands. In chapter 6, the anticipatory position was introduced:

> If you imagine that you are greeting a friend [in a warm embrace], what is the shape of your arms just seconds prior to the point at which you embrace them? With proper alignment in mind, your arms are probably outstretched and slightly curved. The curve of the arms is followed through the wrists and into the hands. The wrist is slightly curved, as are the fingers. The fingers of both hands are not clenched tightly, but have air space between them. The fingers are relaxed and slightly rounded. Body energy is able to travel through the limbs and out the fingertips.

A hand position that relays a welcoming and inviting gesture will work best as a starting position for a conductor. When one goes to shake the hand of another person, the "handshake" position is perhaps the one that best approximates the starting hand position for the conductor. If one thinks about the hand position during the *buh* exercise in chapter 7, it will probably approximate a handshake position. The handshake position places the palm of the hand at approximately a 45- to 60-degree angle to the floor.

THE BASIC DROP
DOWN-UP PATTERN

Find your anticipatory body position, using both arms. (Note: Many introductory conducting books begin instruction with only the right arm. This approach advocates the use of both arms, in many texts referred to as mirroring. This is done so that conducting students, from the beginning of their study, become accustomed to breathing with and for the choir with a balanced gesture that will, in turn, encourage a deep-seated breath from the choir.) Allow the breath to fall into your body and allow your hands to mirror that activity as in the *buh* exercise. Listen to the breath and let the sound of the breath guide your arms. Imagine a table placed approximately at the level of your navel. At the point when the inhalation has reached it's greatest depth in your body, allow your arms to drop (fall) downward onto the imaginary table, as close toward the center or midline of your body as possible without your hands colliding, keeping your forearms relatively parallel with the floor. If your forearms remain relatively parallel with the floor, there will be a point at which your forearm will *gently* spring straight upward. A fast or energetic upward spring in relation to the descent denotes a *non-releasing* gesture. The rebound from the ictus is a light feeling; it should not feel weighted. At the peak of the upward spring, allow the arms to drop straight downward again. The point at which the arm changes direction and bounds upward, naturally and without weight, is known as the *ictus*. The rebound upward should be free and filled with both springing buoyancy and energy but will be slightly slower in speed than the descent. You should *exhale* as the arms lightly spring upward from the imaginary table placed at your navel. The drop downward after the inhalation should be a downward free fall of the forearm. The shoulders should not participate in this activity. Remember that your arms are attached to the small of your back, not your shoulders! You should not feel muscles moving bones in this down-up movement; you should feel only the bones! When done correctly, your arms will feel light and weightless, almost like hollow tubing. You should also be totally unaware of your elbow and your shoulders. If you feel your shoulders, elbows, or your musculature, you are "holding," or "locking."

Holding was described in chapter 3. It would, perhaps, be good to review the concept of holding by revisiting the analogies presented there.

HOLDING (LOCKING). The term *holding*, or *locking*, is central to the conductor's understanding of how the skeletal structure interacts with the muscles to produce movement. It has been said that "bones conduct, muscles don't." While the statement seems a bit elementary, it is very true. What needs to be understood by each person studying conducting is that the way we live our lives has a tremendous impact on our muscle system, and hence, upon our skeletal system. The influence of the muscles on the skeletal system is, unfortunately, most often negative. A few examples and exercises will prove the point.

Pick up your briefcase. Better yet, choose a briefcase that belongs to someone else. Look at it, then pick it up. Now before you pick it up again, use only the minimum of muscular effort to pick up the brief case! Pick it up again. Do you notice how much "extra" muscular effort was used when you picked up the briefcase the first time? Did your "arm" feel totally different the second time because of the dramatic change in the amount of muscle engaged to pick up the briefcase? The difference will be dramatic in most cases. If the change was not dramatic, be thankful. This means that, for some reason, you have been able to avoid the overuse of muscles that not only expends too much muscular effort, but also causes undue tension upon the skeletal system and thus reduces freedom of movement. In your daily life, you can begin to develop the proper balance of muscular exertion by just doing the minimum that is necessary to complete the movement or task. Overexerting one's muscles for every life task builds throughout the day to the point where muscular tension reigns and the freedom of the skeletal system to move is severely lessened.

Select a partner. Hold your forearm parallel to the floor. Have your partner press downward on your forearm with his or her index finger while you resist by pressing upward with your forearm. At a time unknown to you, your partner should suddenly withdraw their index finger. What happens? What happens is dependent upon the correct use of the muscle. If your arm remains in the same position when your partner's finger is pulled away suddenly, your arm is *locked* in the most dramatic fashion—that is, the muscles of the forearm and upper arm are "holding" the bones. The proper response to experience "non-holding" is, when your partner's finger is released from the top of your forearm, your arm should immediately spring in an arc *quickly* backward. Continue this drill until you can *release* the arm immediately when your partner's finger is withdrawn. When conducting, conductors must be on constant guard not to lock the movement of their arms. Locking (the muscular effort that restricts the bones from free movement) blocks the channel of rhythm impulse that was discussed above. In a conducting class, I once had a student who had experienced a severe auto accident and who required physical therapy in order to walk and move again. Her therapist gave her advice that bodes well for conductors. She instructed this patient that if she ever felt anything as she moved, there was probably something wrong! The same statement can be made for conductors. As you conduct you should *not* feel your muscles interacting with your bones. Your arms should feel light and free. Any other feeling should tell you that you are moving toward a gesture that will lock—and render the choir unable to sing.

FULCRUM IMAGERY TO AVOID HOLDING IN THE GESTURAL VOCABULARY

If you find that you are still holding (locking) your conducting gesture, the following fulcrum imagery may help you to release your gesture (rebound) after the ictus. Many beginning conductors attempt to gain a range of motion in their arms by initiating motion in their elbow and in their shoulder. By initiating motion in the elbow and shoulder, they unknowingly create a restriction for movement, and thus holding, or locking, occurs in the gesture. Instead of imagining that motion is initiated in the joints, it is very helpful to imagine the forearm as a seesaw. The fulcrum, or center point of the seesaw, is at the midpoint of the forearm for the dropping gesture. Imagining the fulcrum point at the center of the forearm "distributes" the weight of the arm evenly, and thus allows the arm to drop in a free fall without holding. For stronger marcato gestures, it is helpful to think of the fulcrum at the elbow with the forearm being one-half of the seesaw and the other imaginary half of the seesaw extending backwards into the air. This imagery, once again, tends to allow the forearm to move more freely because of the imaginary counterbalance of the other half of the seesaw. The imaginary half of the seesaw that begins with the forearm and passes through the elbow (fulcrum) provides the arm with freedom of movement without weight.

CONSTANT EXHALATION FOR CONDUCTORS

Two examples from other fields support the arguement for constant exhalation by conductors. In the field of dance, dancers are taught to inhale as they begin to move and to exhale as they move. Exhalation occurs constantly as they move. If exhalation does not occur, the movements of the dancer become rigid and less fluid, and it then becomes increasingly more difficult to allow the body to move in a natural and unencumbered response to rhythm. Without the body air exchange, muscles begin to lock, and spontaneous movement becomes more difficult. The same is true for conductors. Since conducting is body movement, conductors should constantly exhale and release their own breath into the choral sound of the choir in a fashion that resembles the musical line of the piece. To do so will "connect" the gesture to the bodily experience of the musical line. As a practice technique, one can hum or "moan" through a piece of music while conducting. Such an activity makes the essential elements of the line and gesture act in unison, rather than the gesture becoming a disconnected geometric exercise of "drawing in the air."

In the field of medicine, the remarkable coordination of the respiratory system to the cardiopulmonary system is a source of fascination. The rate of respiration impacts the heart rate. There is an unseen connection between the human heart beat and the rhythmic pulse within our musical bodies. Breath influences heart rate, and heart rate directly influences rhythm pulse, and rhythm pulse is then manifest in our conducting gesture through the released ictus. Consequently, the breath becomes the beginning and the end of music making because it connects us to our bodies, and our bodies connect us to music, and it is that connection, shared with others, that then allows us to connect with them and make music together.

It follows then, that as one conducts, one should constantly exhale and exchange air to insure freedom of movement and natural rhythm response. A failure to exhale while conducting will most likely result in a "locking" of the muscles and lead to a tense, arhythmic conducting gesture that will not allow the choir to sing.

LOCATION OF THE ICTUS

A CLEAR RHYTHM IMPULSE. Repeat again the above activity of dropping and rebounding. Drop and rebound several times. When the arm drops downward, allowing gravity to pull it downward without any holding (or resistance) by the muscles in the arms, the ictus is the external manifestation of internal rhythmic pulse that courses through the body and releases through the fingertips at the point of ictus. That energy, or point of the beat (or pulse), exits through the tip of the third finger of one or both hands the body and is transmitted to the singers. The beginning conductor should be careful that the ictus does not "migrate" into the heel of the hand, wrist, elbow, bobbing head, neck, bobbing body, or bending knees. *For most conductors, the problem area is the neck. When alignment is correct, the neck is released and the natural rhythm impulse of the conductor can speak.* All of the natural and primal rhythm impulse of the body must be released through the third finger of the hand. When this is achieved, a clear rhythm impulse can be perceived instantaneously by the singers.

THE LINE OF ICTUS. In addition to correct alignment, another anatomical issue needs to be understood in order for the ictus to be elicited clearly to the ensemble. *As one's arms drop, the forearms should always remain parallel to the floor.* If the forearms do not remain parallel to the floor, it will be difficult for a rebound to occur. *Also, the hands should remain inside the elbows.* If the body architecture is used in this way, a clear ictus will be visible to the choir. To do otherwise is to cause the hand to "skim" or avoid a clear ictus.

GEOMETRY OF THE DROPPED DOWN-UP PATTERN

THE BASIC PATTERN. Repeat again the above activity of dropping and rebounding. Drop and rebound several times. What is the geometric pattern that results from this activity? The "pattern" that naturally occurs as a result of the structure of the body can be referred to as a basic down-up pattern, which resembles the letter *v*, but narrower, depending upon both the tempo and the style of the music. This basic natural physical response is the point from which conducting patterns are generated. See the figure 8.1.

FIG. 8.1. THE BASIC DROP DOWN-UP, OR VEE, PATTERN

THE LINE OF ICTUS. Find the anticipatory position again. Drop the hands downward and imagine that there is an imaginary table placed approximately at your navel. When your hand drops downward, your forearm is parallel to the floor. This is known as the line of ictus. If the forearm is approximately parallel to the floor, and if you imagine that table plane at your navel, there will be a point at which the arm will naturally bounce upward. *Remember that the farther away your hands are from the ictus, or breath impulse point, the slower your gesture becomes.* If the forearm is kept relatively parallel to the floor, a line of ictus is created where the natural reaction of the arm to downward free-fall motion converts to an upward motion naturally. That point at which downward motion changes to a reactive upward motion, the bottom of the vee pattern, is known as the ictus. In any piece, the initial ictus signals the point at which the choir should breathe. This impulse gesture elicits a spontaneous breath from the choir at the same moment that the conductor breathes and opens his body. This immediate communication of breath between conductor and choir establishes what can be called connection. The connection between conductor and singers is the most important aspect of conducting and music making.

ICTUS LOCATIONS

CONDUCTING PATTERNS. The use of conducting patterns evolved throughout music history. The earliest form of conducting was known as chironomy, or the conducting of chant. Chironomy emphasizes horizontal motion as a means of allowing the music to move forward. Vertical motion or vertical gestures are almost never employed. During the Middle Ages and Renaissance, singers reading part books were "conducted" by one of the singers pulsing the tactus, or primary unit of pulse, with a simple up-down motion. When the Classical period orchestra came into existence, the larger number of players seemed to demand more direction than had previously been provided by either the continuo player or the principal violinist or cellist. It is during this time that it was deemed necessary to not only indicate tactus, but to indicate spatial locations for the beats. For example, in a triple meter, beat 1 was directly in the center, beat 2 was to the right, and beat 3 was located very close to the original first beat. With the advent of texts on conducting, it seemed helpful to diagram not only beat locations, but to draw the path of the hand between those beat locations. While this seems like a helpful idea, the advent of such pattern "maps" made conductors inadvertently rely on rigid patterns that were not able to spontaneously reflect the realities of music. More serious, however, conducting pedagogy and the learning of conducting became a visual, rather than an aural, art. Conducting study became more preoccupied with the correct pattern, rather than teaching students to listen and respond to their instincts. Without conducting students being taught the valuable skill of listening, the sound could not be their teacher. They did not learn in many cases to discover for themselves, the impact of their gesture on the sound that they conducted. Rather, they relied on the conducting text for answers instead of relying on their instincts and the sound being produced from their ensemble.

This book presents a different approach to conducting patterns. Patterns *are* important, but they must reflect the sound of the music. The accepted directions and geometry of all beat patterns are endorsed in this text. The evolution of conducting patterns of motion reflect the forward movement of the phrase as manifested on the body. As one learns the patterns—or "beat locations," as they are referred to in this book—try to learn these patterns in relationship to the inner dynamic of the meters that they represent.

THE RELEASED REBOUND GESTURE. An axiom of physics states that for every action there is an equal and opposite reaction. As the arm drops to the point at which an ictus is manifested (at waist level), *it is important that the forearm is parallel to the floor* and that the forearm is never at a higher level than the upper arm. After the ictus, the arm instantaneously rebounds in the opposite direction and toward the outside. What must be understood, however, is that the rebound upward is not at the same speed as the descent of the hand-arm unit. *Moreover, the hand on the rebound never reaches the full height from which it dropped.* In reality, the conductor must *wait* for the rebound to occur. The sensation of a correct rebound is that it moves slower than the descent to the point of ictus.

Some comparisons to real life experiences might be helpful at this point. When you throw a rubber ball to the ground, the force of your downward throw gains momentum because the ball is moving with gravity. When the ball hits the ground (similar to an ictus), the ball changes direction and bounces upward. The ascent of the ball is *slower* than its descent because it is now moving against gravity. *The ball also does not return to the level from which it was dropped.* The action (throwing) and reaction (bouncing) of the ball are identical to the approach to the ictus and the rebound. When the hand-arm drops toward the point of ictus, the muscles should be released in the arm so that it engages in a free fall. When the ictus occurs, many novice conductors *make* their arms rebound upward at the same rate of speed as the descent, and the same distance is covered in both directions. In actuality, just like the bouncing ball, *the rebound or ascent will be slower than the descent.* The conductor must wait and allow the rebound to occur naturally. The correct sensation is that the rebound is *slower* than the descent to the ictus. To do other-wise creates an upward motion that is equal in intensity to the downward motion through muscular involvement of the forearm. This upward moving gesture runs the risk of becoming a subdivision, which will in turn slow the tempo and impede the natural forward movement of the line. The seemingly slower rebound is known as a released gesture because the musculature of the arm does not inhibit the natural upward motion of the arm.

CHAINING OF DROPPED-VEE PATTERNS AT ICTUS LOCA-TIONS. If one chains, or connects, a series of the down-up patterns presented above, assigning a spatial location to each ictus location, various conducting "patterns" emerge. It is most important that the conductor understand the theory by which patterns are generated as a personal response to sound, rather than legis-lated patterns by outside authorities. This text does not present patterns in the tra-ditional method; it does not present a series of spatial diagrams, or maps, along which the hands must travel. Rather, ictus locations, or locations of arrival, are identified. The way one arrives at those ictus locations is dependent on what one hears. The path to each location will be determined by the color, nature of the musical line, tempo, and rhythmic style of the piece, as well as the historical style of the work and the particular composer.

To begin learning conducting patterns, simply perform the dropped-vee pattern in figure 8.1 at each of the numbered locations or beat locations; for example, two continuous down-up patterns result in a two-beat "pattern" (figures 8.2 and 8.3). The boldface beat locations indicate the locations of drops.

FIG. 8.2. TWO-BEAT MARCATO ICTUS LOCATION

FIG. 8.3. TWO-BEAT LEGATO ICTUS LOCATION

Three continuous down-up patterns result in a three-beat marcato pattern (figure 8.4). However, notice that in the three-beat legato pattern, a drop occurs on beats 1 and 3 (figure 8.5).

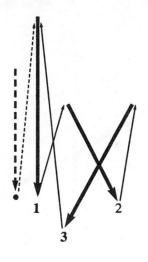

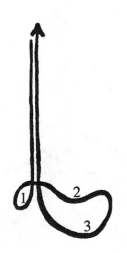

FIG. 8.4. THREE-BEAT MARCATO ICTUS LOCATION

FIG. 8.5. THREE-BEAT LEGATO ICTUS LOCATION

Four continuous down-up patterns result in a four-beat marcato pattern. In both the marcato and legato pattern, drops actually occur on beats 1 and 3 (figures 8.6 and 8.7). *It is very important that in the three-beat, beat 2 is kept down and the hands remain inside the elbows. It is also very important that in the four-beat the drop into beat 3 be kept directly down and the hands remain inside the elbows.* The boldface beat locations indicate the locations of the beats with a dropped gesture. The effect of those dropped beats on the singers is important: the low, dropped beat assists the singers to keep the breath seated low in their bodies.

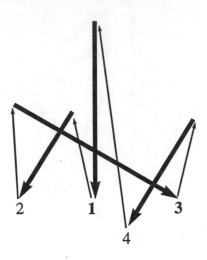

FIG. 8.6. FOUR-BEAT MARCATO ICTUS LOCATION

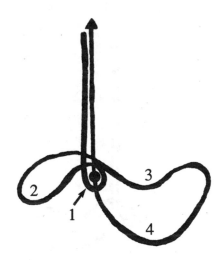

FIG. 8.7. FOUR-BEAT LEGATO ICTUS LOCATION

Five continuous down-up patterns at the beat locations shown in figure 8.8 result in various five-beat patterns. Notice that in these patterns a drop occurs either on beat 3 in a two-plus-three or on beat 4 in a three-plus-two. As mentioned previously, pay particular attention that those drops on 3 and 4 stay down and that the hands stay *inside* the elbow line. Again, the boldface numbers indicate the beats where drops occur.

FIG. 8.8. SIX-BEAT ICTUS LOCATION

FIVE-BEAT DIVIDED INTO TWO-PLUS-THREE

FIVE-BEAT DIVIDED INTO THREE-PLUS-TWO

FIG. 8.9. FIVE-BEAT ICTUS LOCATIONS

Seven continuous down-up patterns at the beat locations shown in figure 8.10 result in various seven-beat patterns. Drop occur at beats indicated by boldface numbers.

DRILL AND PRACTICE OF BEAT LOCATIONS

Because conducting gestures involve, for the most part, large muscle coordination, it will take extended amounts of practice to work these "patterns" into mus-

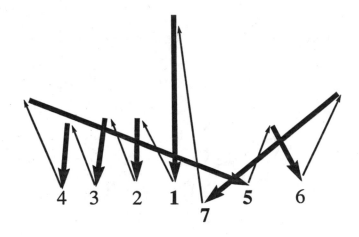

SEVEN-BEAT DIVIDED INTO TWO-PLUS-TWO-PLUS-THREE

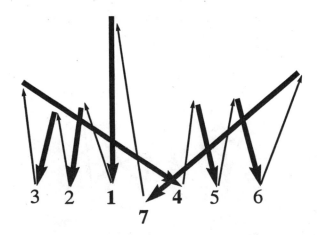

SEVEN-BEAT DIVIDED INTO THREE-PLUS-TWO-PLUS-TWO

FIG. 8.10. SEVEN-BEAT ICTUS LOCATIONS

cle memory. Hours of practice time should be spent on these patterns. Remember that as you practice these patterns, you should always make a continuous humming or moaning sound. The patterns must become automatic, almost reflexive muscle patterns of movement. If they do not become automatic, you will not be able to listen to the choir because you will be thinking of and focusing on the pattern, exclusive of the music being sounded at the time. Remember to concentrate on those beats where it is important to drop into the beat.

In the execution of all the legato conducting patterns be certain there is no forward roll of the hands or reaching forward as you move through the patterns. In the marcato patterns, be certain that there is no forward roll and that the rebound is a straight line upward from the ictus.

1. All horizontal beats must be on the *same horizontal level* as beat 1.
2. Beat 1 must always be high; when conducting, it should always rise to the top of the breastbone and be close to being centered on the body.
3. The outside beats of the pattern must be equidistant, that is, beats 2 and 3 must be equidistant from beat 1.
4. In all legato patterns, the change of direction that is accompanied by the turning of the hand through and around the first beat should be kept smaller rather than larger.
5. The final beat of the pattern should be brought as close to beat 1 as is possible.
6. Draw the patterns many times to learn them before conducting them. When drawing the pattern, overall symmetry and balance are of the utmost importance. If the pattern is sloppy and not symmetrical, it will be that way when you conduct it.

THE BREATH IMPULSE GESTURE

THE FIRST ICTUS. The first ictus in this approach to conducting is known as the breath impulse gesture. The first ictus, or the breath impulse gesture, relays the tempo, affect, color, dynamic, and line of the piece to be sung. All these necessary performance elements are relayed in the breath of the conductor.

The breath impulse gesture is, perhaps, one of the most valuable tools at the disposal of the conductor. The breath impulse gesture, as its name implies, spontaneously tells the choir to "breathe now." In many conducting texts, this is often called the preparation gesture, or simply the preparation. This gesture is often done without a direct connection to the breathing mechanism. The breath impulse gesture signals to the choir to open their bodies so that air may fall in. The easiest route to understanding the breath impulse gesture is to experience it.

Recall the anticipatory position introduced in chapter 6. Find that position. Make sure your body is open to receive air. Drop your hands straight down, and when they hit "bottom" (somewhere in the vicinity of your navel at the line of ictus), allow air to fall into your body. You may want to think of the sensation of breathing you experience when suddenly scared by a friend. When spontaneously startled, the body instinctively drops open so that breath falls into it quickly and silently. The breath seemingly drops low into the body. At the point at which the gesture hits bottom, and air enters into the body, the hands instinctively move in the opposite direction, upward and slightly outward, creating a vee pattern shown in figure 8.11.

FIG. 8.11. THE VEE PATTERN

Another way of thinking about the breath impulse gesture is to know where the hands should be located to begin a work. *Your hand position represents a point of departure for the sound.* That is, your hands should be located where the sound of the piece is to begin. For example, for a piano dynamic, your hands may be in a higher position. For a more forte dynamic, your hands will be in a lower position. The initial sound from the choir, sometimes called the attack, is a two-step process. Each time the choir begins to sing or an entrance is "cued," you need to be able to execute a two-way release: (1) you must be able to open the body, or release the body, so that air can spontaneously drop into the lungs, and (2) you must release the air from your body as the sound begins and physically let go of the sound when it begins. Most students when learning this process focus on "breathing." The breath is the most natural part of this process; we all breathe! Most students are unable to release the body so that it can open so that the breath can fall in, and then exhale, or release air, into the choral sound as the choir begins to sing. For each entrance of a voice part, you should breath cue the part that is about to enter. That is, you open your body for *each* entrance.

A REVIEW OF HOLDING (LOCKING) AND THE LINE OF ICTUS. It is important at this point in your study to be vigilant about holding and the line of ictus. These concepts can be best demonstrated by the following example. Stand up and pick up a briefcase. Place it back on the floor and pick it up a second time. As you pick it up the second time, be sensitive to the sensation in your arms and upper body. Pick up the briefcase a third time, but this time use only the minimum of muscular effort necessary. Notice that you can pick up the same briefcase with much less muscular effort! The difference between the first time you picked up the briefcase and the last time amounts to an excess of muscular involvement. This overexertion and excess muscle activity can be labeled as holding, or locking. When performing the vee pattern drills above to feel the impulse gesture in conjunction with the breath, you should not "feel" your arms, elbows or shoulders. The fingertips of the third finger of both of your hands should "feel" an imaginary dabbing sensation, but your arms should not be felt Free, unweighted, and continuous motion of the arms is the goal. This, perhaps, might be more helpful if a "map" were provided, as in figure 8.12, to orient you to the gestural directions necessary to evoke a sound from the choir.

When your body is in the anticipatory position, your hands are above the actual location of your ictus. Remembering to keep your forearms parallel to the floor, allow your body to open and breathe, releasing your arms into a free fall. Again, the line of ictus must be maintained; your breath should then fall into your body at the point of ictus. The breath impulse gesture is always at the same relative position as the first beat of the pattern. If you are experiencing difficulty, spend time with the drumstick and practice pad exercises and the rattle exercises presented later in this chapter.

INITIATING SOUND

In essence, this chapter has thus far outlined and detailed the learning of the gesture that initiates sound. The art of conducting rests almost totally with one's ability to initiate sound through breath that is reflected in the gesture. If a conductor is unable to initiate sound, then conducting degenerates into an unspontaneous act of steering the choir through physically tense gesture. Such conducting technique causes the musical line to slow its forward motion, which in turns leads to monochromatic, out-of-tune singing. The art of initiating a sound through the impulse gesture allows the choir to sing freely and allows a musical line to blossom spontaneously and appropriately colored.

FIG. 8.12. PATH OF THE BREATH IMPULSE GESTURE

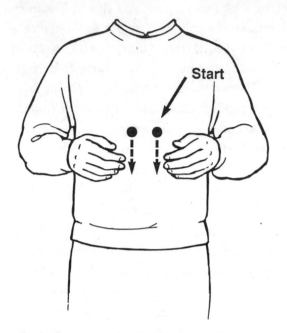

A. BEGINNING ANTICIPATORY POSITION WITH BODY "OPEN" TO ACCEPT AIR

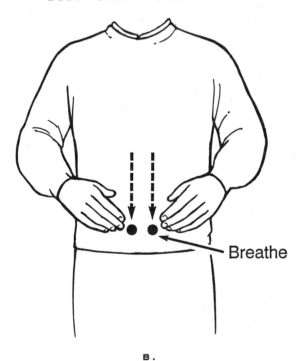

B.

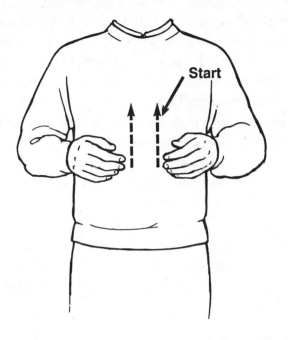

c.

CONNECTING SOUND TO GESTURE

As stated earlier, one of the difficulties regarding conducting pedagogy is that many approaches teach gesture separated from the sounds that are evoked by the gesture. Conducting is often taught as geometric gesturing in air, devoid of sound. Taught in this manner, gesture takes on a meaningless and detached role to the music making process. Gesture learned and acquired in that fashion exhibits undue rhythmic and color restrictions upon the choir because of its lack of connection to what conductors hear within themselves.

As you prepare all exercises and music examples, you must not think about gesture, nor think about how your arms move, nor for that matter, think about anything other than the sound in the room at the time it is being created. If you have practiced the patterns as suggested, they will be in your large muscle memory and should be almost reflexive in nature. You should not think about your hands or your body. The side of the brain that houses our cognitive or thinking abilities can override the other side of our brain—the intuitive, creative, and spontaneous side, which houses the gift of song. As one "conducts," or rather gestures, what is a spontaneous reaction to both the sounds within and the sounds being released from the singers bodies, one should *not* think about anything. One should not think "That sound is flat," "Wrong pitch in the bass section," and so on.

instead, one should allow the sounds to enter one's being through listening to everything with no opinion or prejudgment. When the performance (in or outside of the rehearsal) is finished, the intuitive, creative side of the brain instantaneously plays back to the cognitive side of the brain for a musical analysis (i.e., that is flat, that is sharp, the vowel color is wrong, and so on). To try to hear those problems while the music is being performed severely limits the scope of what you are able to hear. Thinking while conducting limits what you hear and, most importantly, restricts your singers from spontaneously singing because your gesture becomes unspontaneous. By thinking while you conduct, an unspoken language is communicated to the choir through an unspontaneous gesture that basically does not allow them to sing. This message is most often carried in an unreleased rebound gesture, which tries to be more to the conducting gesture than a simple release of energy from the ictus. Throughout all the exercises in this book, challenge yourself to listen and not think, and to find the music voice within yourself

THE USE OF A PERCUSSION PRACTICE PAD AND DRUMSTICKS TO EXPERIENCE DROPPING IN AND BREATH

The use of a drum practice pad and drumsticks can facilitate the experience of staccato, marcato, and legato sounds, resulting in a gesture that uses both a drop and consequent release (rebound). Drumsticks (size 2B) and a practice pad with a floor stand are needed. (You can substitute drumpad practice putty for the drumpad.) Before beginning the following suggested exercises, some instruction concerning drumstick grip and the stroke of the drumsticks is needed.[1]

INSTRUCTIONS FOR HOLDING THE STICKS. A *matched grip* is recommended. When using the matched grip, the position for both hands is the same. The stick is held between the first joint of the index finger and the thumb, about one-third of the distance from the end of the stick. The thumb should rest flat on the stick with the index finger slightly curved along the opposite side. This grip forms a pivot point. The other three fingers curl around the stick and rest lightly on the back of the stick. The drumstick lies diagonally across the palm with the palm facing the floor when performing on the practice pad. The practice pad should be adjusted to approximately waist level. The sticks should be held at about a 70-degree angle to each other.

---

[1] The author is indebted to a Westminster student, Matthew Koller, for the suggestion of this technique.

THE DRUMSTICK STROKE. The *stroke* of the sticks is primarily a wrist-arm motion moving the tip of the stick straight up and down. The arms should be comfortably at the side. A single stroke motion is similar to waving the hand up and down; then, with a lifting motion, the hand follows the natural rebound of the stroke back up to the starting position. Think of "pulling" the sound out of the practice pad as the sticks contact the pad. Thinking that the sound is being "pulled" from the practice pad elicits a released rebound. *Remember, the farther away your rebound is from the practice pad, the slower your rebound will travel.* Begin first by using the stick in one hand to contact the drum pad in order to develop the technique that will allow the drumstick to strike the pad and rebound freely, producing a staccato articulation. Once the technique has been developed in one hand, add the other hand.

PRACTICE PAD EXERCISES

EXPERIENCING STACCATO. You will first speak the staccato sound *tee* at a forte dynamic. With your sticks positioned 6–8 inches above the practice pad, allow the sticks to drop to the pad in the exact style and dynamic of the staccato and breathe in. On the next stroke and all those that follow, speak the syllable *tee* in repetition. Remember to maintain the forte dynamic. If this exercise is done correctly, the sound of the drumstick hitting the practice pad when you take your breath should be exactly the same as the sound of the drumstick when it contacts the practice pad when you speak the forte *tee*s. Stop and start this exercise over and over again. Make sure that the breath you take has the same energy your spoken *tee* possesses. After you have spoken *tee*s in repetition, it would be helpful to have a few friends perform the *tee*s for you as you initiate the sound with the drumsticks.

What do you hear as the sticks drops to the pad and your small "chorus" speaks *tee*? Notice that the striking of the practice pad always occurs *ahead* of the chorus speaking their *tee* sounds. This is correct. Beginning conductors must begin to understand from the beginning of their study *that their gesture stays slightly ahead of the performed sound if the phrase line and forward motion of the line is to be maintained.* What do you feel as you perform this exercise? Do you feel your shoulders? Are you conscious of your neck? You will not feel anything except the sensation of the stick contacting the practice pad.

Now, perform the same exercise again, but this time substitute a constant hiss on the syllable *sh* for the sound *tee*. Breathe, however, as if you were breathing in order to perform a forte staccato *tee* sound. Your breath should be identical to the one taken in the previous exercise, except that instead of performing staccato *tee* sounds, you will be performing a constant exhalation. Exhale for seven counts and breathe once again in the style of a staccato *tee* sound. Make sure that your breath is in coordination with the striking of the drum pad.

EXPERIENCING LEGATO. You will first speak the legato sound *noo* at a mezzo forte dynamic. With your sticks positioned 6–8 inches above the practice pad, allow the sticks to drop to the pad in the exact style and dynamic of the legato and breathe. On the next stroke and all those that follow, speak the syllable *noo* in repetition. Remember to maintain the mezzo forte dynamic. If this exercise is done correctly, the sound of the drumstick hitting the practice pad when you take your breath should be exactly the same as the sound of the drumstick when it contacts the practice pad when you speak the mezzo forte *noo*s. Stop and start this exercise over and over again. Make sure that the breath that you take has the same energy that your spoken *noo* possesses. After you have spoken *noo*s in repetition, again, it would be helpful to have a few friends perform the *noo*s for you as you initiate the sound with the drumsticks. What you experience will be very similar to the experience of the staccato *tee* sound, but within a mezzo forte *noo* sound.

Now, perform the same exercise again, but this time substitute a hiss on the syllable *sh* for the sound *noo*. Breathe, however, as if you were breathing in order to perform a mezzo forte *noo* sound. Your breath should be identical to the one taken in the exercise above, except that instead of performing mezzo forte *noo* sounds, you will be performing a constant exhalation. Exhale for seven counts and breathe once again in the style of a mezzo forte *noo* sound. Make sure that your breath is in coordination with the striking of the drum pad.

EXPERIENCING MARCATO. Once again, position a single drumstick approximately 6–8 inches above the surface of the practice pad. Speak the marcato sound *dah* at a forte dynamic. Now allow the sticks to drop to the pad in the exact style of the marcato syllable and breathe. On the next stroke and all those that follow, speak the syllable *dah* in repetition. Remember to maintain the forte dynamic. If this exercise is done correctly, the sound of the drumstick hitting the practice pad when you take your breath should be exactly the same as the sound of the drumstick when it contacts the practice pad when you speak the forte *dah*s. Stop and start this exercise over and over again. Make sure that the breath that you take has the same energy that your spoken forte *dah* possesses. Again, after you have spoken *dah*s in repetition, again, it would be helpful to have a few friends perform the *dah*s for you as you initiate the sound with the drumsticks. What you experience will be very similar to the experience of the staccato *tee* sound, but within a forte *dah* sound.

Now, perform the same exercise again, but this time substitute a hiss on the syllable *sh* for the sound *dah*. Breathe, however, as if you were breathing in order to perform a forte *dah* sound. Your breath should be identical to the one taken in the exercise above, except that instead of performing forte *dah* sounds, you will be performing a constant exhalation. Exhale for seven counts and breathe once again in the style of a forte *dah* sound. Make sure that your breath is in coordination with the striking of the drum pad.

In the above exercises, just after you were in your anticipatory position and before you spoke the sound of *tee, noo,* or *dah,* what occurred? *(Your hands dropped downward, and as you took your breath, they rebounded in an upward direction).* The gesture that signals inhalation to the choir is known as the impulse gesture. If you did not breathe with your hands mirroring the breath activity, reexperience the process again.

You will notice that when the breath is not properly taken—that is, with the rhythmic energy, tempo, and dynamic of what is to follow—the drumstick does not produce a clear and resonant sound.

EXERCISES WITHOUT THE DRUM PAD

EXPERIENCING STACCATO SOUNDS. After being able to produce the same sound synchronously with both hands, put the sticks down and assume an anticipatory conducting position. Begin by opening your body for the breath, breathe, and then immediately speak the forte staccato sound *tee* in repetition and move your hand to the sound you produce. As you begin, imagine your body as very open and wide, and breathe with the energy of the articulation of the word *tee* that you imagine. The energy of the breath should be behind the sound that you produce. *Listen to the sound of the syllable* tee. Perform seven *tees* in succession and breathe with energy on beat 8 and repeat the pattern. The sound *tee* should be imagined squarely between the eyes, and your entire body should feel rooted and grounded to the floor. *Listen to the sound* tee *as you produce it.* Remember to breathe without repositioning your mouth from the spoken *tee* embouchure. Keep your throat very open, wide and free, during this process. The entire body should be energized throughout the speaking of the *tee* syllable.

Move your hand to the place where you would initiate a staccato sound. Breathe and speak the word *tee.* Where and how does your hand move? Your hand, most likely, moves as if you were throwing a dart toward a dart board. That gesture could be characterized as having a great amount of energy that is focused into a staccato motion. Another helpful drill to discover the staccato sound and its corresponding gesture is to speak a staccato *ee* repeatedly. Speak an *ee* that is supported by the breath stream from deep within the body and not glottally. How does your hand reflect this staccato? Place your hands on your lower abdomen and speak the staccato *ee* again. What is the action of your body? Now raise your hands to the anticipatory position and speak the staccato *ee*. The staccato gesture must be connected to the line of breath that produces the staccato.

Your hand should have an instantaneous reaction to what is happening within your body; that is, your hand is a reflection of what your body is experiencing in producing the staccato *tee* sound. *The sound tee should feel as if it lives in your third fingertip at the point at which the sound is initiated.* Your hand should rebound after the *tee* sound at its own rate. Remember that the rebound is not a subdivision; it is a release. The rebound, when correct, feels as if you have to wait for your hand to move upward after the sound is spoken. Remember that the farther your hand is from the ictus, the slower it moves. Also notice that between the seven *tees*, when the breath is taken, it falls into the body with energy and in the rhythmic spirit of the articulation of *tee*.

RATTLE EXERCISE FOR STACCATO. Both beginning and advanced students many times have difficulty with exhibiting a clear ictus. Gestural problems are manifest, from avoiding the ictus to muscular locking after the ictus. In most cases, if the body alignment is correct, and if the arm is dropping straight down and up (keeping in mind the line of ictus), the ictus may not speak because the muscles in the arm are overinvolved with the rebound gesture. A drill to remove unnecessary muscular tension from the rebound (and also from the drop to the ictus) is to find either a small, traditional baby rattle with a round top and straight handle that is approximately three inches in length or a set of maracas available in most toy stores. Grasp the rattle with your thumb, index finger, and third finger. Shake the rattle and get it to speak in a clean, staccato sound. The rattle will only speak when excess muscular effort is removed from the arm. *Be certain that there is space between your upper arm and body.* A lack of space will inhibit the natural movement of the arm. If there is muscular effort in the arm, the sound producing beads in the rattle will either double the sound or not sound at all. After you have discovered how to make the rattle speak in a staccato fashion, hold the rattle and speak the repeated *tee* drill. You will find that when the drop and rebound are correct, the rattle speaks effortlessly.

EXPERIENCING MARCATO SOUNDS. Perform the same exercise as above, this time substituting the forte word *dah* for the forte word *tee*. Breathe and speak seven forte *dahs* When you breathe, the breath should go deep into your pelvis, well below your navel. *Listen to sound that you produce.* Describe the intensity and quality of that forte marcato sound. The marcato sound is characterized by a rhythmic thrust behind the sound followed by a decay of the sound Perform the marcato *dah* exercise again, this time making note of the thrust and decay of the sound that defines a marcato articulation. As you now breathe with the energy of a marcato and conduct the marcato, notice that your arm moves upward on the breath, with the predominant motion moving straight upward from your elbow hinge. Your arm then drops straight down in a free fall without any muscular holding. At the point at which you speak *dah*, your hand, led by your third finger, sinks clearly and decisively into the center of the beat. That hand does not slide forward or swing away from the beat. The hand falls straight down and rebounds straight up. Also notice that the marcato syllable *dah* cannot sound like the staccato syllable *tee*. With a marcato, you thrust into the "gut," or center, of sound for the marcato articulation, which is then followed immediately by a decay of the sound

If you find yourself skimming the beat (avoiding the ictus or bypassing the ictus), hold your left forearm out in front of you. Speak the word *dah* and drop your right forearm on your left forearm. In marcato, you will notice that your right forearm thrusts into your left forearm. Feel the release of your arms straight upward after the marcato is articulated.

Also check your arm position. For a forte marcato sound, your arms should reflect the quality and depth of the sound that you body desires as reflected in the breath. If the arms are held too high, then a forte marcato character of sound cannot be achieved by the choir. Remember to maintain the line of ictus with forearms parallel to the floor. If you imagine that you are carrying two large paper sacks of groceries, your arms will assume a lower, and rounder, arm position. When conducting a forte marcato, your arms should similarly reflect a lower, rounder sound seated low in the body.

SIZE OF BEAT FOR FORTE SOUNDS. In the above two exercises, you need to monitor the relationship of the size of beat to the quantity of sound. A large beat pattern does not necessarily produce a large sound. *It is the intensity of the breath and its corresponding gesture that imparts the character of the dynamic to the singer.* Dynamics are not merely a question of volume; they are changes of intensity borne *out* of the breath.

> Note: It is important that staccato and marcato articulations stay in motion at all times for the sound to continue forward! The further you move gesturally away from the impulse gesture or ictus, the slower the velocity of the gesture.

EXPERIENCING LEGATO SOUNDS. Take both arms and move them horizontally, and exhaling as you are moving them. Imagine mixing bubble bath into the water before a bath. Now do the same gesture vertically while you continue to sigh an *oo* sound. Lift your hands upward as you breathe (imagine a marionetteer working your hands with strings) and release your *oo* sound when you are full of air at the appropriate time at the top of the upward gesture. You knew when the sound should begin because you felt it within your body. You can feel the release of the sound within your body. Now, instead of the large external vertical movement outside of your body, minimize the large vertical gesture and place most of the movement *inside* your body. Do only as much gesturing as will help facilitate and evoke the sound. Concentrate on the movement of air inside your body and relax the muscularity of the gesture so that it reflects the sound your choir is to produce. Now sing *noo*. Make sure the gesture stays ahead of the sound. As you take the breath, be certain that you take the breath in the tempo you want and do not slow down. Make sure the intention of the breath is legato and that it also indicates the dynamic that you desire. In legato passages, it is often the tendency to take slower and slower breaths, thereby impacting the tempo dramatically. As you move your hands on *noo*, begin to move them more horizontally than vertically and mirror the sound. Imagine you are a cellist bowing this legato sound.

MARIONETTE IMAGERY IN LEGATO. It is often a challenge to remove the muscle tension from the gesture when experiencing a legato. A very helpful exercise is to imagine being a marionette being controlled by a puppeteer. Imagine that you have strings attached to your limbs at the *midpoints* of your forearms and upper arms and in the middle of the top of your hands, not at your joints. As you conduct the legato exercise above, imagine that someone else (the puppeteer) is moving your arms and hands. You should feel no control over your movement; instead, feel as if the puppeteer is moving you.

This exercise is extremely helpful in readjusting your mental attitude toward gesture, especially if you have studied conducting previously. By giving up control to the imaginary puppeteer, you give up the muscular control that in turn restricts the choir's ability to sing freely. By readjusting your mental attitude concerning who or what "controls" your gesture, you return the responsibility for singing to the singers, which in turn allows them to sing with a free, spontaneous tone. A gesture that does not exhibit any type of control allows singers to realize the free spontaneous voice, while a restricted, muscularly controlled and held gesture causes singers to become restricted and less musically spontaneous.

COMBINING THE EXPERIENCES OF STACCATO, MARCATO, AND LEGATO. Now that you have experienced the separate sensations of staccato, marcato, and legato, you need to experience them in combination with each other. Conduct two measures, four beats each, of staccato, two measures of legato, and two measures of marcato. Each articulation style should take place for seven counts, with count 8 being the *breath preparation* for the next articulation style (see figure 8.13). Remember, the breath preparation should be in the style of the next articulation, not the articulation that was just experienced. Further, the change in the quality of the breath for the next articulation style can only be accomplished by letting the muscles of the body release as the new breath for the new articulation is taken. For example, in moving from staccato to legato, the breath preparation on beat 8 of two bars of staccato should be a legato breath preparation in the style of what is to come, foreshadowed by a release of the body musculature just prior to the breath. As you perform the articulations of these exercises in combination, feel your ribcage moving outward as the breath is moving through your body to perform the articulations. It is this feeling of the ribcage moving outward which insures a connection between the outward gesture and the actual sound of the choir.

The objective for this exercise is to change the quality of articulation first in your own breath, thereby influencing the sound that is to follow. Perform this exercise with a few friends serving as your "choir." Listen to the color of the vowels and the effect that your breath has upon their sound. Hear how your change of intention, manifest in the breath, positively (or negatively) influences the

STACCATO	LEGATO	MARCATO

tee-tee-tee-tee-tee-tee-tee-BREATH noo-noo-noo-noo-noo-noo-noo-BREATH dah-dah-dah etc.

FIG. 8.13. COMBINING THE EXPERIENCES OF STACCATO, MARCATO, AND LEGATO

sound of your singers. Conducting is not an out-of-the-body experience. Gesture is simply a reflection of your inner body attitude as established through the breath. If you are able to accomplish the above changes in color and articulation through your breath preparation and intention, you are on your way to being able to use your breath to relay to singers changes in tempo, style, color, and dynamics. In fact, you have begun to learn one of the most valuable tools for the choral conductor: the use of the breath to evoke sound from singers in a spontaneous and free manner!

EXERCISES

1. Chant the word *bahp* in a repeating pattern of quarter notes. For each *bahp*, drop your arms downward so that the ictus and the word *bahp* occur simultaneously. Be certain that you "wait" for the rebound to occur after the ictus coinciding with *bahp*.

2. Repeat the above exercise. However, for this repetition, have the ictus occur slightly before the *bahp* sound. As with the exercise above, be certain that the

rebound from the ictus is allowed to travel at its natural upward speed. Remember that the farther your hands get away from the impulse, or ictus, the slower the velocity of the gesture.

3. Perform the staccato, marcato, and legato drills described in this chapter. Work to breathe the quality of articulation that is desired for each exercise. Discover how your internal breath space changes with each articulation, that is, how your internal body feels different for each articulation. Study the energy of the body and the relationship of body energy to the articulation.

4. For each of the rhythmic styles discussed in this chapter, make a list of life activities that effectively relay the sound of that articulation style. For example, for staccato: throwing darts, poking holes in a pin cushion with a pin; for legato: moving your hand in water at varying levels; for marcato: dabbing paint on a wall. After you make your list, perform the ideas with sound. Does the gesture that you associate with the articulation style actually reflect the quality of sound that you want?

5. Practice both with a rattle and with drumsticks and practice pad for a considerable length of time. Develop the technique of dropping with the consequent released rebound that both of these practice devices must have in order to speak cleanly. After practicing with the rattle or the drumsticks, move immediately to speaking either staccato, marcato, or legato sounds and connect gesture to the sounds that you make.

6. In practicing the patterns presented in this chapter, learn the patterns in duple and triple meters concurrently; that is, practice duple patterns interspersed with triple patterns. If one learns, for example, only a three-beat pattern, the muscle memory developed may make the learning of a four-beat pattern more difficult.

7. It is often helpful to conduct a friend when learning these patterns. Have your friend chant either legato or marcato syllables as you conduct.

8. Review the elements of correct alignment presented in chapter 11. Be sure to continually focus your attention on two elements: (1) imagine your shoulders moving toward the walls so that there is maximum space between your shoulder blades and (2) imagine your spine is long and you have a tail.

9. Revisit chapter 4 on Laban. Review the Efforts in Combination exercises that pertain to punching and dabbing. Do punching and dabbing involve dropping?

Perform those exercises again (reprinted below) and pay particular attention to the drop, if any, in each. What Laban Effort Element directly affects the drop? (Weight.)

DAB

DIRECT (SPACE)
LIGHT (WEIGHT)
QUICK (TIME)

putting the final touches on the frosting of a cake
tip-toeing
playing darts (moment the dart is released from the hand)
using a paint brush to make dots
poking someone's arm with a finger
dipping a cloth in a pail of water
breaking a balloon with a pin
knocking an ash off a cigarette
dotting an *i*
applying antiseptic on a small cut
tap-dancing
pushing button on a remote control
typing
finger-painting
using touch-up paint
testing hot water with your finger
cleaning cob webs from the ceiling
powdering on makeup
using white glue
cleaning a child's sticky mouth
placing a cherry on a sundae

Other: _____

_____

_____

_____

_____

PUNCH

DIRECT (SPACE)
HEAVY (WEIGHT)
QUICK (TIME)

plumping a pillow
boxing
using a punching bag
applauding loudly
hammering a nail
pounding your fist on a table
striking a stapler to get the staple in a hard wall
digging a hole

Other: _____

_____

_____

_____

_____

10. When practicing patterns, always do so by chanting a neutral syllable that reflects the rhythmic style of the pattern—i.e., staccato, marcato, legato—in a rhythmic subdivision. You should also close your eyes while chanting.

11. By closing your eyes you develop a kinesthetic connection to the pattern Some persons, whose eyes remain open as they practice, watch their hands instead of becoming aware of the kinesthetic feeling of the pattern and its relationship to their internal rhythmic pulse

12. Test yourself on patterns with a paper and pencil test. There is a dramatic connection between the clarity and symmetry of conducting patterns and a person's ability to draw that pattern on paper or on a blackboard. The "cognitive map" that one develops concerning the approximate path of the hand is a vital step in the conducting process. You should be able to quickly write out patterns without hesitation. You patterns should resemble the ones in the text. If they are not, practice drawing the patterns until they are accurate.

13. Videotape yourself conducting all of the patterns. Use the rating scales that follow to help identify areas that are in need of improvement. 4 = high, 2 = aver-

age. Be sure to rerun the videotape several times so that you can evaluate all of the categories carefully.

STACCATO PATTERNS

4 = high 0 = low	Trial 1	Trial 2
Your alignment is correct	4 3 2 1 0	4 3 2 1 0
There is spaciousness across the chest	4 3 2 1 0	4 3 2 1 0
There is spaciousness under the arms throughout the pattern	4 3 2 1 0	4 3 2 1 0
The arms seem to encircle or surround the sound throughout the pattern (i.e., shopping bags)	4 3 2 1 0	4 3 2 1 0
The body is open for the breath	4 3 2 1 0	4 3 2 1 0
You breathe with a clear breath impulse gesture at the start of each exercise	4 3 2 1 0	4 3 2 1 0
The breath that you take at the beginning of each passage is in the spirit of the dynamic	4 3 2 1 0	4 3 2 1 0
The gesture *follows* the breath	4 3 2 1 0	4 3 2 1 0
Beat 1 is always in the center of your body	4 3 2 1 0	4 3 2 1 0
The pattern is symmetrical	4 3 2 1 0	4 3 2 1 0
The pattern is low on the body so that it encourages low breathing	4 3 2 1 0	4 3 2 1 0
On the outside beats, your hands always stay down and around the sound	4 3 2 1 0	4 3 2 1 0
For all beats, the hand drops straight down and rebounds straight up with no "loops" or "scoops"	4 3 2 1 0	4 3 2 1 0
Wrists are not overly "loose" and "floppy"	4 3 2 1 0	4 3 2 1 0
The horizontal portion of the beat expands	4 3 2 1 0	4 3 2 1 0
Beat 1 remains high after the last beat of the measure	4 3 2 1 0	4 3 2 1 0
The hand position is not cramped or tight	4 3 2 1 0	4 3 2 1 0
There is no forward "looping" in the pattern	4 3 2 1 0	4 3 2 1 0
The ictus is apparent in the third fingertip only	4 3 2 1 0	4 3 2 1 0
The last beat of each measure is "tucked in" and close to beat 1	4 3 2 1 0	4 3 2 1 0
The rebound is released and without tension	4 3 2 1 0	4 3 2 1 0
The hand is always ahead of the sound	4 3 2 1 0	4 3 2 1 0
There is a center and focus to the entire pattern	4 3 2 1 0	4 3 2 1 0
There is a rhythmic energy emitted by the conductor	4 3 2 1 0	4 3 2 1 0

Overall Evaluation   _____   _____

MARCATO PATTERNS

4 = high 0 = low	Trial 1	Trial 2
Your alignment is correct	4 3 2 1 0	4 3 2 1 0
There is spaciousness across the chest	4 3 2 1 0	4 3 2 1 0
There is spaciousness under the arms throughout the pattern	4 3 2 1 0	4 3 2 1 0
The arms seem to encircle or surround the sound throughout the pattern (i.e., shopping bags)	4 3 2 1 0	4 3 2 1 0
The body is open for the breath	4 3 2 1 0	4 3 2 1 0
You breathe with a clear breath impulse gesture at the start of each exercise	4 3 2 1 0	4 3 2 1 0
The breath that you take at the beginning of each passage is in the spirit of the dynamic	4 3 2 1 0	4 3 2 1 0
The gesture *follows* the breath	4 3 2 1 0	4 3 2 1 0
Beat 1 is always in the center of your body	4 3 2 1 0	4 3 2 1 0
The pattern is symmetrical	4 3 2 1 0	4 3 2 1 0
The pattern is low on the body so that it encourages low breathing	4 3 2 1 0	4 3 2 1 0
On the outside beats, your hands always stay down and around the sound	4 3 2 1 0	4 3 2 1 0
For all beats, the hand drops straight down and rebounds straight up with no "loops" or "scoops"	4 3 2 1 0	4 3 2 1 0
Wrists are not overly "loose" and "floppy"	4 3 2 1 0	4 3 2 1 0
The horizontal portion of the beat expands	4 3 2 1 0	4 3 2 1 0
Beat 1 remains high after the last beat of the measure	4 3 2 1 0	4 3 2 1 0
The hand position is not cramped or tight	4 3 2 1 0	4 3 2 1 0
There is no forward "looping" in the pattern	4 3 2 1 0	4 3 2 1 0
The ictus is apparent in the third fingertip only	4 3 2 1 0	4 3 2 1 0
The last beat of each measure is "tucked in" and close to beat 1	4 3 2 1 0	4 3 2 1 0
The rebound is released and without tension	4 3 2 1 0	4 3 2 1 0
The hand is always ahead of the sound	4 3 2 1 0	4 3 2 1 0
There is a center and focus to the entire pattern	4 3 2 1 0	4 3 2 1 0
There is a rhythmic energy emitted by the conductor	4 3 2 1 0	4 3 2 1 0
Overall Evaluation	_____	_____

LEGATO PATTERNS

4 = high 0 = low	Trial 1	Trial 2
Your alignment is correct	4 3 2 1 0	4 3 2 1 0
There is spaciousness across the chest	4 3 2 1 0	4 3 2 1 0
There is spaciousness under the arms throughout the pattern	4 3 2 1 0	4 3 2 1 0
The arms seem to encircle or surround the sound throughout the pattern (i.e., shopping bags)	4 3 2 1 0	4 3 2 1 0
The body is open for the breath	4 3 2 1 0	4 3 2 1 0
You breathe with a clear breath impulse gesture at the start of each exercise	4 3 2 1 0	4 3 2 1 0
The breath that you take at the beginning of each passage is in the spirit of the dynamic	4 3 2 1 0	4 3 2 1 0
The gesture *follows* the breath	4 3 2 1 0	4 3 2 1 0
Beat 1 is always in the center of your body	4 3 2 1 0	4 3 2 1 0
The pattern is symmetrical	4 3 2 1 0	4 3 2 1 0
The pattern is low on the body so that it encourages low breathing	4 3 2 1 0	4 3 2 1 0
On the outside beats, your hands always stay down and around the sound	4 3 2 1 0	4 3 2 1 0
Your hand is not always parallel to the floor; it turns according to the direction of the pattern	4 3 2 1 0	4 3 2 1 0
Wrists are not overly "loose" and "floppy"	4 3 2 1 0	4 3 2 1 0
The horizontal portion of the beat expands	4 3 2 1 0	4 3 2 1 0
Beat 1 remains high after the last beat of the measure	4 3 2 1 0	4 3 2 1 0
The hand position is not cramped or tight	4 3 2 1 0	4 3 2 1 0
There is no forward "looping" in the pattern	4 3 2 1 0	4 3 2 1 0
The ictus is apparent in the third fingertip only	4 3 2 1 0	4 3 2 1 0
The last beat of each measure is "tucked in" and close to beat 1	4 3 2 1 0	4 3 2 1 0
The turn around beat 1 is not too large	4 3 2 1 0	4 3 2 1 0
The rebound is released and without tension	4 3 2 1 0	4 3 2 1 0
The hand is always ahead of the sound	4 3 2 1 0	4 3 2 1 0
There is a center and focus to the entire pattern	4 3 2 1 0	4 3 2 1 0
There is a rhythmic energy emitted by the conductor	4 3 2 1 0	4 3 2 1 0
Overall Evaluation	_____	_____

CHAPTER IX

GESTURAL
VOCABULARY

ALLOWING THE BODY
TO TEACH THE BODY

I feel there's something almost unfair about trying to teach a skill by putting it into words. We learn so much more when we learn through our senses and our experience. Maybe there are "information" subjects where verbal instruction works best, but music is something the body is going to have to perform and it's best learned by the body that's going to do the performing. (P. 132)

> Barry Green
> *The Inner Game of Music*

It follows, then, that the orchestral beat patterns produced by forearm and stick movement when transferred to movements of the arms in choral directing must be rounded off and be made to swing more to the outside; and instead of the predominant vertical movements the director should strive for more horizontal movement. The director and singers should think of an imaginary plane at the level of the solar plexus, and imagine that the music moves back and forth on this plane. This concept should be constantly maintained by both director and choir. (P. 115)

In accordance with the traditional leader, the choir director should regard himself as a precentor or leading dancer who, as the best performer in his group, emerges from the group to give direction and leadership, but always withdraws again into and identifies himself with the group as *Primus inter pares*. He should cultivate and strengthen this feeling within himself. His ideal objective should be a gradual withdrawal from the choir to the point where he could on occasion be dispensable. (P. 112)

The choir director must feel somewhat like an extremely skilled glass-blower, who with his highly trained hands and fingers forms with greatest dexterity, the stream of hot liquid glass while it is being poured into a work of art. (P. 116)

The mere application of a time-beating technique to the choir can, metaphorically and musically speaking, "beat the music to pieces." With all the need for a sound conducting technique, we must do our best to free the choir and the music from a straight-jacketed conducting format and to allow the free unfolding of the essence and life of the music. (P. 110)

It remains to be one of the functions of the director's left hand to stimulate and support the awareness of the suspended horizontal plane by areas of appropriate gestures. Each beat which is made with the right hand must be compensated for by an equivalent amount of sustained effort by the left hand; to stretch the point one could say: "What the right hand destroys (with its beats) the left hand must constantly sustain and support." (P. 115)

> Wilhelm Ehmann
> *Choral Directing*

Forcing yourself to use restricted means is the sort of restraint that liberates invention. It obliges you to make a kind of progress that you can't even imagine in advance. (P. 54)

> Pablo Picasso
> in *Picasso: In His Words*, Hiro Clark

• • • • •

In chapter 8, an initial case was made for the misplaced priority placed upon the learning of "conducting patterns" devoid of sound. As was stated earlier, it is important to understand the sound origin of the pattern rather than learning a stock pattern for every piece of music in triple meter. If conducting students understand the origin of the pattern, they find out very quickly that they, in fact, already know the patterns. For patterns that they do not know, they can intuit what the pattern should be based upon the music, given the beat locations provided in the previous chapter. The biggest dilemma concerning conducting patterns is that they are most often taught devoid of sound; they are taught as geometric exercises of sketching patterns in the air without sound being present. Patterns should be a reflection of sound in all its dimensions, i.e., color, line, rhythmic characteristics, and overall phrase shapes. The path and shape of the hand are as important as the movement of the arm. Conducting patterns must at all times be able to evoke and encourage sound from the singers. Conducting patterns should never restrict the spontaneous nature of singing.

The Nature of the Choral Instrument

Many of the patterns employed by choral conductors have grown out of the instrumental music tradition. If one believes that the sound that is being evoked and influenced should be a reflection of the conducting gesture, then patterns for conducting in the choral genre may take a different path from those patterns that are used to communicate with instrumentalists. The difference between the two genres is in how the sound producing instruments of the two genres speak. For instrumental conductors, their conducting technique must take into account how sound is produced on the attack by a wide variety of instrumental colors. They must understand how the oboe makes a sound. They must also understand the clarinet, trumpet, French horn, trombone, bassoon, flute, violin, viola, cello, string bass, and an entire battery of percussion instruments. Their study of instrumental conducting involves itself with gesture that makes those instruments speak as clearly and cleanly as possible. Depending on the instrumental ensemble that sits before the conductor, the way that they sound music will vary depending upon the orchestration of the score.

Choral ensembles are unique because sound speaks through one, natural instrument: the voice. The voice is connected directly to a human spirit and life-giving breath mechanism. Just as it is important for the instrumental conductor to understand how each of his instruments creates sound, so, too, is it important for the choral conductor to understand how the voice speaks and what gestures will evoke and release sound from singers' bodies! The gesture of the vocal conductor must at all times reflect the movement of air through the vocal mechanism. Suddenly angular patterns and subdivided rebounds adversely affect the flow of the air and then directly affects the intensity and color of the tone. At the same time, spontaneous musical line is impeded.

To review, if one traces the development of choral conducting, one could certainly examine its roots in the conducting of chant, or chironomy. In the conducting of chant, a predominantly horizontal curving gesture that resembled a sideways figure eight was employed because it was directly related to the sound that was desired. Legato, with an emphasis on the movement of sound forward, with a minimum of strong rhythmic accent. In conducting chant, the hand, wrist, and arm moved logically and naturally from extreme to extreme. Motion was primarily horizontal. Changes in direction of movement were accomplished via natural movement of the hand and arm.

With the advent of instrumental conducting in the Classical period, the vertical demarcation of the pulse became important to keep larger instrumental ensembles together. The horizontal nature of chironomy gave way to an additional vertical gestural vocabulary. While the vertical additions of instrumental conducting were needed, the role and nature of the horizontal in conducting gesture seemed to occupy a secondary role.

CONDUCTING GESTURES

If one believes that conducting patterns are a reflection of sound, then it follows that conducting gesture should be both a reflection of the sound and provide a certain gestural evoking of sound from the singers. The flexibility of the wrist and hand plays an important role concerning the influence on the sound. To help accomplish and understand this, one need only to observe the hand as it moves horizontally. Imagine that you are mixing bath water. How does you hand move from side to side? How do you change the direction of your hand?

You will see that you hand is capable of a smooth change of direction because of the wrist's ability to move in a circular fashion. If you draw a horizontal figure eight in the air, you will notice that your hand is able to change direction with little or no angular effort. The entire hand seems almost to follow along after the wrist. Conducting patterns for choral ensembles must use this natural, continuous movement of the hand and wrist to reflect the continuous flow of air. The sound in the choir will always reflect, in part, the use of the hand and wrist.

GEOMETRY OF THE CONDUCTING GESTURE. There are several broadly accepted gestural maps of paths that conducting patterns take. It is important, however, to understand their origin. Earlier in this text you learned the "dropped-vee" pattern and ictus locations for the essential meter organizations, two, three, five, and seven. At this point, it would be helpful to review those patterns. As mentioned in the earlier chapter, if you decide to practice these gestures, make certain that you never gesture without making a sound to go with the gesture.

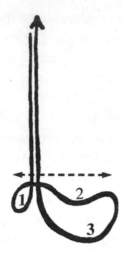

FIG. 9.1. FLEXIBILITY OF HAND MOTION ON HORIZONTAL: THE EXPANSIVE PART OF THE ICTUS LOCATION PATTERN USING A THREE-BEAT AS AN EXAMPLE

USE OF BOTH HANDS, AND THE DEPTH OF THE CONDUCTING GESTURE. This conducting text encourages the use of both hands from the beginning of conducting study. The reason for doing so is rooted in the fact that with two hands, the conductor is better able to evoke a low, deep-seated breath from the singers. Use of only one hand at the beginning stages of conducting encourages shallow breathing from the singers. Moreover, it makes it more difficult for the conductor to seat their breath low. The left hand should mirror the right when conducting. Both hands need not be kept at the same relative depth throughout the conducting gesture. There is a prioritizing of the hands that takes place when conducting. The right hand is in the foreground while the left hand, at times, is in the background. In general, the omnipresence of the left hand is of great assistance to maintaining low breath within the singers.

In the previous chapter, the geometry of the patterns was introduced. This chapter will ask you to revisit those patterns, but now focusing on another important part of the pattern apart from the drop: the horizontal, expansive portion of the pattern.

EXPANSIVE PART OF THE CONDUCTING GESTURE. In chapter 8 you learned the conducting patterns for various meters. It is important to understand the portions of each meter that allow a choir to sing, that is, what part of the gesture evokes legato and line from the singers. In a triple meter, it is the second beat of the bar, which when expanded both gesturally and internally will allow the line to sing. Stated another way, when you are experiencing the *horizontal, expansive portions of the meter,* your gesture needs to become broader. In a duple meter such as 4/4, the expansive portion of the meter occurs between beats 2 and 3. In a five-beat meter (depending on how the five pulses are grouped), the expansive part of the meter comes between pulses 3 and 4. In a simple two-beat, the expansion occurs between beats 1 and 2.

Now we return to the ictus locations depicted earlier in chapter 8 for each meter. The dotted lines denote the expansive part of the pattern, that is, the part of the pattern that must use more horizontal space if the musical line is to be allowed to "sing." In the illustrations that follow (figures 9.10–9.12), examine the natural response of the hands to this horizontal expansion of the pattern.

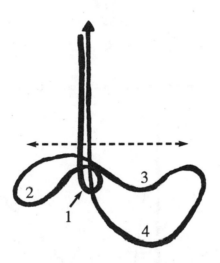

FIG. 9.2. EXPANSIVE HORIZONTAL GESTURE WITHIN
A FOUR-BEAT PATTERN

The accepted conducting patterns that are found in most conducting texts are simply combinations of the pattern shown in figure 9.3. For example, if you perform the dropped one-beat pattern three times, moving the second beat to your right and third beat back toward center again, depending upon the music, the "traditional" three-beat pattern in figure 9.4 might be the result.

If the piece were of a more legato nature, the paths to the ictus locations might resemble the image in figure 9.5.

If the piece were of a more marcato nature, the paths to the ictus locations might resemble the image in figure 9.6.

Similarly, if you drop downward for beat 1, drop to your left for beat 2, to your right for beat 3, and back toward the center for beat 4, the result is a four-beat pattern. If the style of the piece is legato, figure 9.7 may provide a representation of the general pattern.

FIG. 9.3. DROPPED ONE-BEAT ICTUS LOCATION

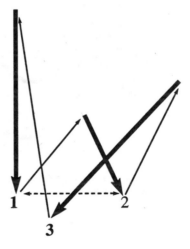

FIG. 9.4. TRADITIONAL THREE-BEAT ICTUS LOCATION

If the style of the piece is marcato, figure 9.8 may provide a representation of the general pattern.

Now, if you perform a first beat again and move slightly to the right and let the second beat fall slightly deeper, a traditional two-beat pattern will be the result. If the style is legato, then the pattern may resemble that in figure 9.9.

These same legato and marcato principles can be applied to the five-beat location patterns and the seven-beat ictus location patterns discussed earlier in the book.

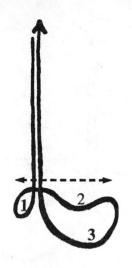

FIG. 9.5. TRADITIONAL THREE-BEAT ICTUS LOCATION:
LEGATO

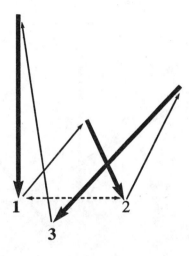

FIG. 9.6. TRADITIONAL THREE-BEAT ICTUS LOCATION:
MARCATO

TRANSITION FROM MARCATO PATTERNS TO LEGATO
PATTERNS. In chapter 8 you were asked to make single sounds on *tee, dah,* and
noo in order to discover the relationship of sound to gesture. Recall those experiences with sound and gesture. Recall the exercise using *noo*. Perform seven *noo*
sounds again, with a breath on beat 8. Now perform four of the *noos* again, this time
moving to your left on the second *noo*, to your right on the third *noo*, and back to
the center for the *noo* on beat 4. Your hand should move in between beats in a similar fashion to the horizontal figure-eight pattern discussed earlier. The palms of
the hands should begin in a "handshake" position and move naturally

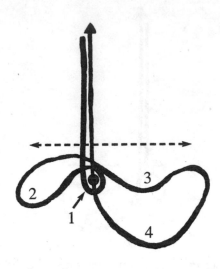

FIG. 9.7. FOUR-BEAT PATTERN ICTUS LOCATION: LEGATO

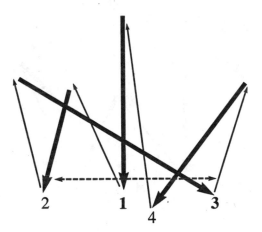

FIG. 9.8. FOUR-BEAT PATTERN ICTUS LOCATION: MARCATO

throughout the pattern with the middle finger being the focus point for the pattern. The hands should never be held in a rigid, stabile position. The most common questionable hand position is the one that remains parallel to the floor. Such a hand position severely inhibits the sound and spontaneity of the choir. Figure 9.10 illustrates the desired result.

Similarly, figure 9.11 illustrates a legato three-beat pattern.

A two-beat pattern is shown in figure 9.12.

FIG. 9.9. TRADITIONAL TWO-BEAT ICTUS LOCATION: LEGATO

STACCATO PATTERNS. Staccato patterns, based upon the *tee* exercise in chapter 8 can be generalized directly from the marcato patterns. The rebound in staccato patterns will be faster and smaller than marcato.

PATTERNS BEYOND THOSE PRESENTED IN THIS TEXT. The scope of this text is to introduce you to the fundamentals of conducting. Patterns that go beyond the ones suggested in the text are simply combinations of those already stated. The reader is referred to the texts by McElheran, Elizabeth Green, and Rudolf in the Bibliography and Suggested List for Further Reading of this book for information concerning particular conducting challenges.

MAINTAINING OPENNESS IN THE ANTICIPATORY POSITION

After absorbing all of the information presented about conducting patterns and ictus locations, it is important to revisit an element of conducting that usually becomes almost an unseen problem in most conductors as they begin to conduct music, as is suggested in part 2 of this text. Aside from maintaining correct alignment, one of the most important things a conductor can do to encourage a free and open sound that tunes well is to maintain spaciousness across the upper chest. Imagining that one's shoulders move toward the rear wall is one way to move toward that goal. However, one of the most effective techniques is to stand in front of the choir with your arms totally opened so that they are flat and are at 45-degree angles and in line with the trunk of your body. This is the same position that you would assume if you laid flat on your back on the floor and extended your arms at 45-degree angles to your body and placed them flat on the floor. After you have assumed this position, have the choir sing for you. You should not conduct; just stand there and listen. After you have done that, maintain the spaciousness that you felt in the "opened" position and begin conducting. You will notice that the sound is more open and free. The spaciousness of the upper body across the upper chest is usually the area that conductors unconsciously close or restrict when they don't trust the choir to sing or when they doubt their own music instincts. This opening of oneself will do much to evoke a beautiful, honest sound from singers.

CONDUCTING FERMATAS

The conducting of fermatas, or pauses, generally causes trouble for most beginning conductors. By definition, a fermata is an extension, or prolongation, of one or more beats. Many times a fermata exists because energy that has been created by the musical line cannot be resolved or handled in a strict rhythm framework. Similar to a ritardando, a fermata resolves, or prolongs, energy built up from the preceding phrase. Consequently, the conductor's responsibility is to understand how much energy has been created and how long the fermata and the consequent break must be to play it out.

Fermatas are not difficult to conduct if the gesture is kept simple and one can remember a few easy rules.

GUIDE FOR CONDUCTING FERMATAS

1. Decide where the held sound comes in the bar, and how long it lasts. On the beat where the fermata appears, hold the hands at that ictus location and "hold" the sound with both hands

2. When you desire to move ahead, simply *repeat* the beat in the pattern on which the fermata appears, breathe simultaneously with the repetition of that beat in the pattern, and proceed with the pattern. Remember that fermatas may be followed by a breath of one beat, or can be longer than a beat, or by no beat at all. In some rare instances, the fermata can come on the breath itself.

3. Note the character of the subsequent music.

4. Finally, decide on the fermata and its release. Duration and volume are factors in the conducting of a fermata. The greater the duration and the volume, the greater the necessity to prepare the location of the release. A forte fermata may require a full beat of repeated beat on which the fermata occurs. A brief, piano fermata may only require a small movement

FIG. 9.10. LEGATO FOUR-BEAT ICTUS LOCATION SEQUENCE

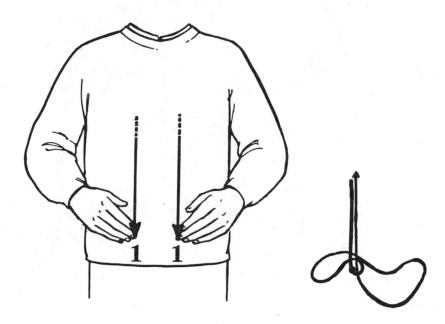

A. PRECEDE WITH BREATH IMPULSE GESTURE SEQUENCE;
DROP TO BEAT 1

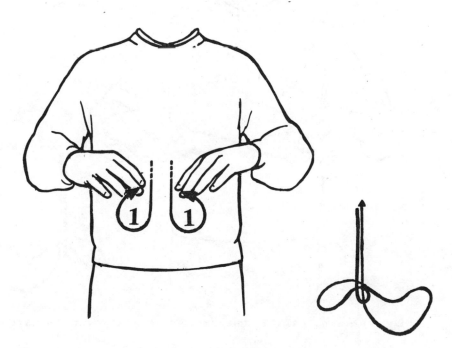

B. COMING AROUND BEAT 1; RIGHT HAND TURNS TO THE LEFT

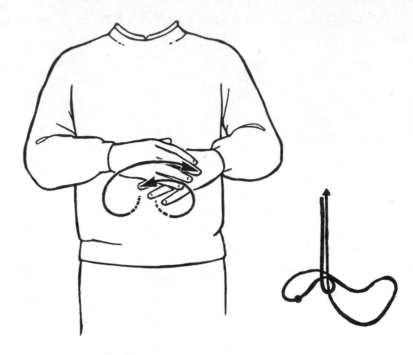

C. MOVING TO BEAT 2

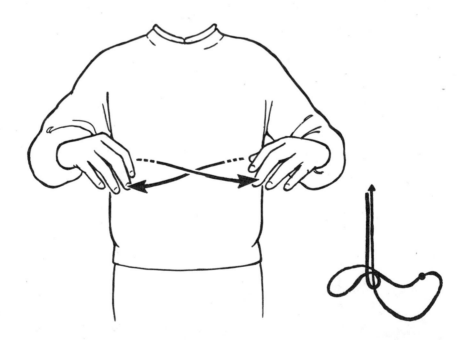

D. DROPPING TO BEAT 3; THE EXPANSIVE PART OF THE GESTURE

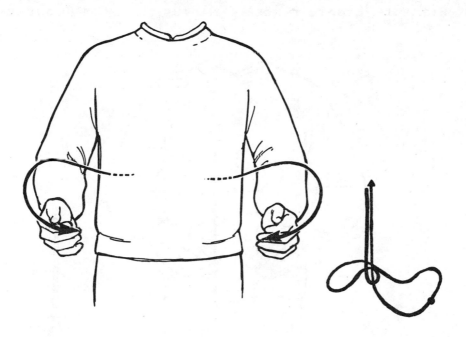

E. STAYING DOWN AND AROUND BEAT 3

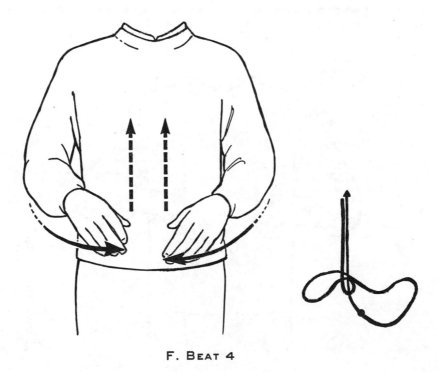

F. BEAT 4

Fig. 9.11. Legato three-beat ictus location sequence

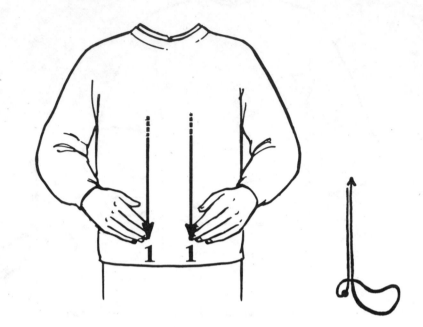

A. Precede with breath impulse gesture sequence; drop to beat 1

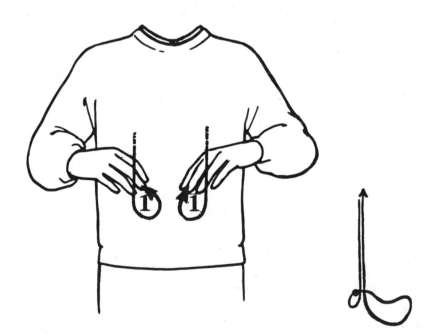

B. Coming around beat 1; right hand turns to the right

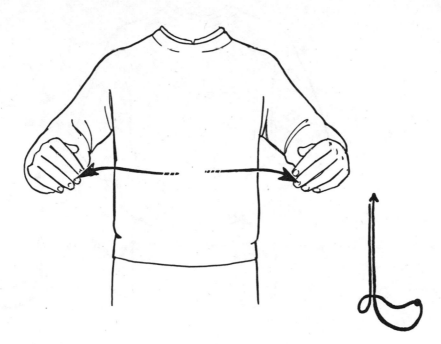

C. MOVING TO BEAT 2; THE EXPANSIVE PART OF THE GESTURE

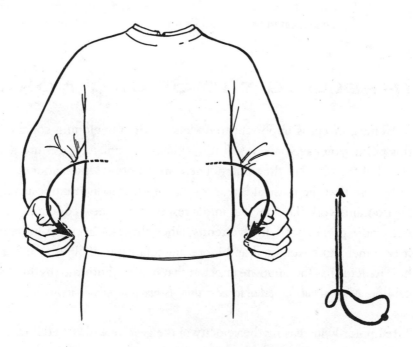

D. MOVING TOWARD BEAT 3, STAYING DOWN AND
AROUND THE OUTSIDE OF BEAT 2

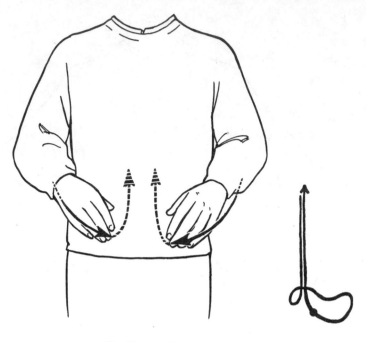

E. BEAT 3

of the arms to effect a release. No matter what the dynamic, however, only one repeated beat should be used to release the fermata.

IMPELLING THE SOUND FORWARD

This concept is important to understand in a beginning conducting text. To this point, you have been asked to maintain a conducting gesture that is slightly ahead of the sound of the singers. There are points at which your ear will lead you to believe that the musical line is losing forward momentum, especially within a legato framework. The obvious initial response by a new conductor is to make the ictus more pronounced. Inadvertently, when the ictus becomes more pronounced, it becomes more weighted and more muscularity is applied to the gesture. This heavier ictus has the opposite effect in that it slows both the rhythm and the musical line. *Musical line is impelled forward through two principal devices:*

1. temporarily increasing the velocity of the gesture without adding weight to that gesture and

2. indicating an ictus (devoid of weight) through the third fingertip of each hand

FIG. 9.12 LEGATO TWO-BEAT ICTUS LOCATION SEQUENCE

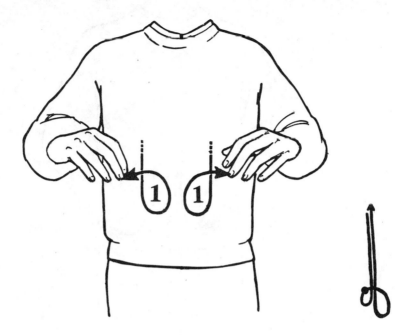

A. COMING AROUND BEAT 1; RIGHT HAND TURNS TO THE RIGHT

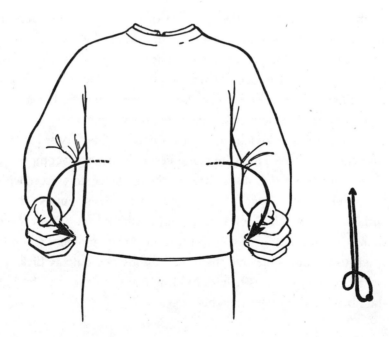

B. MOVING TOWARD BEAT 2

By temporarily increasing the *velocity* of the gesture without adding weight to that gesture, an internal momentum is generated within the musical line that is spontaneously sensed by the singers. The gesture with the quickened velocity

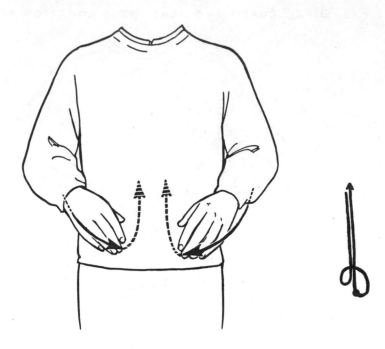

C. Beat two

(without weight) makes the spinning of the air of the singers increase, thereby adding forward momentum to the musical line. The challenge to conductors is to hear when the momentum of the line has been reestablished, and then return to the normal velocity of the conducting gesture. Conductors will know immediately if the velocity of their gesture has been overemphasized because the musical line, instead of gaining momentum, gains tempo and rushes.

The second approach to moving a musical line forward is to indicate an ictus with the fingertips. There are many gestural ways to accomplish this. The principle is that you are indicating through the dry staccato gesture with your fingertips the point at which you feel and hear the strongest pulses. You give the gesture without weight. Think of a quick, light dabbing motion or a motion where the thumb and index finger are held together. At the moment when the rhythm pulse needs to be communicated, the fingers lightly and quickly flick apart, or can lightly dab. Many times it is helpful to bring clarity to the ictus by lightly holding the thumb and index finger together.

FINAL RELEASES

Releasing the sound at the end of a piece of music should reflect the quality of the decay of the sound that the conductor wishes to communicate. This is directly related to the consonant or vowel that ends the word. The basic gesture for a release of sound can be called a cushioned up-down release. When the final sound is reached, the hand floats at the point where the ictus would normally appear. Prior to the ending of the sound, the hand moves gently upward (directly reflecting the quality of sound desired, i.e., dynamic and color) and then drops to an imaginary soft rubber cushion, which represents the sound itself. The sound will be released by the singers when the hand touches the imaginary cushion and gently rebounds at its own speed upward from it. If the final sound of a piece occurs on a vowel, then no further gesture is needed to effect a release of the sound. If, however, the final sound is closed with a consonant, care must be taken by the conductor to relay in the fingertips the exact nature of the articulation of the consonant, that is, the inherent sound quality of each consonant: staccato, legato, or marcato. The table in figure 9.13 illustrates this concept. Special note should be taken of those consonants that can carry more than one articulation. As an exercise, first say the consonants and then "feel" those consonants as one articulation. As another exercise, say the consonants and then "feel" those consonants as one conducts, using the fingertips to approximately mirror the sound (articulation) of that particular consonant.

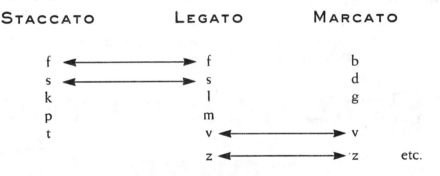

FIG. 9.13. RELATIVE CONSONANT ARTICULATIONS

EXERCISES

1. Become familiar with Madeleine Marshall's *Singer's Manual of English Diction*. Read the respective chapters for *p* and *b*, *t*, *v*, *m* and *n* and *ng*. After reading Marshall's explanation of how the consonant is articulated, speak the consonant correctly and then use a gesture that reflects the consonant accurately. Choose other chapters and develop a gestural vocabulary of consonants.

2. Begin to use the literature suggestions in part 2 of this text. Read the instructions for the use of the rating scales at the beginning of the section. You may choose between exercises 4, 5, 6, and 16.

Chapter X

Receiving the Sound, Listening, and Active Reaction to the Sound

The more I live the life of music the more I am convinced that it is the freely imaginative mind that is at the core of all vital music making and music listening. (P. 7)

A concert is not a sermon. It is a performance—a reincarnation of a series of ideas implicit in the work of art. (P. 17)

The way the music sounds, or the sonorous image, as I call it, is nothing more than an auditory concept that floats in the mind of the executant or composer; a prethinking of the exact nature of the tones to be produced. (P. 21)

You cannot produce a beautiful sonority or combination of sonorities without first hearing the imagined sound in the inner ear. (P. 22)

One might almost maintain that musical interpretation demands of the performer an even wider range than that of the actor, because the musician must play every role in the piece. (P. 48)

Aaron Copland
Music and Imagination

An act of the self, that's what one must make. An act of the self, from me to you. From center to center. We must mean what we say, from our innermost heart to the outermost galaxy. Otherwise we are lost and dizzy in a maze of reflections. We carry light within us. There is no need merely to reflect. Others carry light within them. These lights must wake each other. My face is real. Yours is. Let us find our way to our initiative. (P. 18)

Mary Caroline Richards
Centering

Audiation takes place when we hear *and comprehend* music for which sound is no longer or may never have been physically present. In contrast, aural perception takes place when we simply hear sound that is physically present. *Sound is not comprehended as music until it is audiated after it is heard.*

We audiate while listening to, recalling, performing, interpreting, creating, improvising, reading and writing music. Though it may seem contradictory that we can listen to music at the same time we audiate music, we take for granted that we can think about words at the same time that we are hearing words spoken. The fact is that as we listen to music, we are aurally perceiving the sound the moment it is heard. It is not until a moment or so after the sound is heard that we audiate and give meaning to the sound while aurally perceiving and giving meaning to additional sounds that will follow in the music. (P. 13)

Through audiation, we interiorize singing and movement psychologically before we actually sing and move physically. That is, we learn from the outside in, from the general to the specific. Though we are capable of memorizing without comprehending what we memorized, we will quickly forget it. Consider the words "language," "speech," and "thought." Language is a result of the need to communicate. Speech is how communication takes place. Thought is what is communicated. The words "music," "performance," and "audiation" have parallel meanings. Music is a result of the need to communicate. Performance is how communication takes place. Audiation is what is communicated. Music is a literature. Music is not a language primarily because it has no grammar; it has only syntax, which is the orderly arrangement of sounds. It is interesting to speculate, however, whether language may indeed be a music. (P. 14)

Edwin E. Gordon
Learning Sequences in Music, 1993

What is done without joy is zero. (P. 63)

What is meant to be heard in music must be heard within you before anyone else can hear it. I cannot participate in music where rhythm or line is forgotten. (P. 70)

Do nothing for effect. Do it for truth. (P. 71)

All music must be dramatized. Whether it be a masculine character or feminine character . . . It must have character or it has no life. (P. 74)

We are often mistaken about art. Art is not emotion. Art is the medium in which emotion is expressed. (P. 77)

My main concern now is to develop the conscience of the musician, which is his ear. (P. 88)

Nadia Boulanger
in *Master Teacher*, Don G. Campbell

It is a mistake to believe that in our conducting we must have points to our beats so that the choir can keep time. Singers do not keep time because of what they see. They keep time because of the forward-moving rhythmic pace the conductor creates through empathy. When one sings under a great master he cannot make a mistake because he is too busy to stop and think. The conductor presses him forward with such electrifying power that he hasn't time to think how many beats he gives to a note or even what pitch he is singing. Everything in sound moves forward with such urgency that it is impossible to do anything other than the right thing. (P. 198)

John Finley Williamson
in *John Finley Williamson (1887–1964): His Life and Contribution to Choral Music*, David A. Wehr

Listening is easy. But true ease, like anything worthwhile, may be hard to cultivate. We hear all the time, even in sleep, though we always don't listen to what we hear. In music, as in living, fragments of question and answer might try the door of consciousness, then pass unknown and leave us ignorant of what we've missed. Few people develop their capacity for perceiving what is always around; most ears follow a line of least resistance that allows only pleasant passive hearing. Active listening provokes reaction which is not always pleasant, for pleasure is the target of entertainment—a side issue of great music as of great crucifixions. (P 316)

Unconscious listening is more dependable. Carlyle maintained that if you "see deep enough . . . you see musically; the heart of nature being everywhere musical, if you can only reach it." In signifying only itself, music becomes a language translatable by the universal awareness latent in everything. This most complex of expressions is also the oldest and so appeals to our primitive level, inexplicable through reason. At that level we all hear music the same way though surface reactions vary with social advancement. Tears and concerts, for instance, are recent Western distortions. (P. 321)

> Ned Rorem
> *Setting the Tone*

If asked to describe one of my most important growth concerns I would answer that we become more fully alive by finding and maintaining a vital connection with the creative impulse of life. Some of you may call this impulse "God," some "the spiritual source," some "the creative center." . . .

How does one find connection to this impulse? I think the crux of the matter is to discover ways which allow us to become more open, more receptive, more vulnerable—whether through prayer, through meditation or through whatever means allows us to experience a relationship with the spiritual source. For musicians this also means learning to listen. To listen deeply. To listen to the song within. To silence the clatter of the cognitive brain and learn to be in the moment. Then we will have the possibility of hearing our own intuitive, spontaneous voice—that powerful still small voice which comes from the same impulse that generates all creation.

> Joseph Flummerfelt
> *Charge to the Graduating Class*
> *of Westminster Choir College*
> May, 1993

Taking an interest in one's own soul requires a certain amount of space for reflection and appreciation. . . . Most of us bring to everyday life a somewhat naive psychological attitude in our expectations that our lives and relationships will be simple. Love of Soul asks for some appreciation for its complexity. (P. 14)

The point of art is not simply to express ourselves, but to create an external, concrete form in which the soul of our lives can be evoked and contained.

Children paint everyday and love to show their works on walls and refrigerator doors. But as we become adults, we abandon this important soul task of childhood. We assume, I suppose, that children are just learning motor coordination and alphabets. But maybe they are doing something more fundamental: finding forms that reflect what is going on in their souls. (P. 302)

Care of the soul is not a project of self-improvement nor a way of being released from the troubles and pains of human existence. It is not at all concerned with living properly or with emotional health. These are the concerns of temporal, heroic, Promethean life. Care of the soul touches another dimension, in no way separate from life, but not identical either with the problem solving that occupies so much of our consciousness. We care for the soul solely by honoring its expressions, by giving it time and opportunity to reveal itself, and by living life in a way that fosters depth, interiority, and quality in which it flourishes. Soul has its own purpose and end. To the soul, memory is more important than planning, art more compelling than reason, and love more fulfilling than understanding. We know we are well on the way toward soul when we feel attachment to the world and the people around us and when we live as much from the heart as from the head. We know soul is being cared for when our pleasures feel deeper than usual, when we can let go of the need to be free of complexity and confusion, and when compassion takes the place of distrust and fear. (P. 304)

Thomas Moore
Care of the Soul

In the last analysis, what we *are* communicates far more eloquently than anything we *say* or do. We all know it. There are people we trust absolutely because we know their character. Whether they're eloquent or not, whether they have the human relations techniques or not, we trust them, and we work successfully for them.

In the words of William George Jordan, "Into the hands of every individual is given a marvelous power for good or evil—the silent, unconscious influence of his life. This is simply the constant radiation of what man is, not what he pretends to be." (P. 22–23)

> Stephen R. Covey
> *The Seven Habits of Highly Effective People*

It is common medical knowledge that many elderly patients who have suffered cerebral hemorrhages on the left hemisphere such that they cannot speak can still sing (P. 365)

> Julian Jaynes
> *The Origin of Consciousness
> in the Breakdown of the Bicameral Mind*

• • • • •

This chapter begins with a rather lengthy list of quoted wisdom spanning from the capsulated and excerpted thoughts of an artist and a conductor to those of a psychotherapist-musician-philosopher. Few conducting texts are foolish enough to attempt to approach the subject matter of this chapter. Moreover, there is clear danger in using a lot of words to describe a nonverbal process. Yet, it is the subject matter of this chapter which moves the music making of choirs from the mundane to artistic, no matter what the level or ability of the choir. For that reason alone, we must explore the subject of opening oneself to receive sound so that one can, in turn, listen and react spontaneously to the miracle of song.

Chapter 6 spoke of "opening the inside" and gave suggestions for reconnecting to one's inside. Recall the feeling of giving a gift or meeting a very close friend. Such meaningful events in our lives are able to strip away outside façades and allow those close to us to see us as we really are. In those life events there is a spacious interiority that allows us to receive any and all emotions directly from those who are sharing them with us. We do not turn their feelings of care and such away, but openly receive and enjoy them.

Conducting is not unlike life. Every time we stand in front of a corpus of persons labeled as a choir, we face human beings who have things to share with us through the sounds of song. Our task as conductors is to be receivers of sound that react instinctively to that sound being produced. Just as when we anticipate meet-ing a dear friend at the train station, that inner body anticipation must be present in us at all times as conductors. We must be able to receive and listen to what is being created by singers, evoked by our gesture, which is guided by our own mind's ear of how the piece being performed should sound. Our job as conductors is simply to receive the sound without thinking about it, and then actively react to it so that we can enhance and assist the composer's intent. As we listen and then conduct, our gesture should always stay ever so slightly ahead of the choir's sound. By staying ahead of the sound, we can encourage spontaneity and almost "court" the choir for-ward in time. To stay ahead of the sound with one's gesture allows both the voices of the singers and the voice of the composer to speak. To gesture at the exact moment that the sound is being produced from the singers is to severely limit spon-taneity, and, in reality, to impose the ego of the conductor onto the sound. Thus, neither singer nor composer can then speak.

The idea of staying ahead of the sound is stupendously simple. This guiding principle will allow any choir to sing to the height of their capabilities. Imagine this situation: You are taking a child whom you care for very deeply to the playground. As you get closer and closer to the playground, the child gets more excited and begins tugging at your hand to move faster and faster. You have a choice. You can either begin running with the child so that you can stay ahead and protect the child, especially when crossing streets, or you can resist. If you resist, the child will continue to tug at your hand. If you hold your ground and refuse to join in the child's play, the child, most likely, will become very unhappy. But you, as the adult, will feel in control of the situation.

I have seen the reverse of this situation with my own father and my daughter. My father had the uncanny ability to become a child at the mere tug of my daugh-ter's hand. He never let go. He would run ahead of her, just ever so slightly guiding her along to the playground. Once inside the playground, he would let go of her hand and follow quickly behind her as she ran to her favorite swingset. As she arrived at her swings, he would pick her up and place her on the swing. They would laugh so as he pushed her higher and higher. They would run from swing to seesaw, hand in hand; he always at the lead. If he would pull her hand to make her speed up she would laugh, and then come along. Dad and Elizabeth did this incredible inter-action for hours at a time. Both would return home exhausted and very happy.

The playground example exactly parallels the choir-conductor relationship. The choir is my daughter, Elizabeth, and the conductor is my father. My father can make the choice either to actively react to Elizabeth's spontaneity and playfulness and enjoy the moment, or to resist and impose his idea of what playground fun should be. He chooses to enter into a spontaneous play with her; always staying one step ahead of her, yet allowing her will and play to speak. Receiving the sound of the choir is to accept what they have to give, and then enter into the music-making almost like a musical lure. The breath sets the musical play in motion. The conductor, open to receive their sound, listens to it and uses gesture to lure it forward here, change the color there, never doing too much so as to dampen the choir's spontaneity and musical playfulness (musical idea and line). To enter into this musical play with the choir, one must be able to not only receive their sound and to listen to it, but trust one's deepest musical instincts and impulses. As conductor's, whether we be experienced or novices, there is a tendency for us to "re-create" the musical ideas of either teachers or idolized conductors. Our performances attempt to be xeroxed aural recreations of another person's work, rather than a reflection of music that is a healthy interaction of the choir's singing with the conductor's active reaction to their singing.

Being open, welcoming, and receptive of the choir's sound is paramount to music making with any choir. Then, just being and listening without thinking will allow gesture to be meaningful. But there is considerable confusion in conducting pedagogy concerning the appropriate role of gesture and its relationship to music making. This book adopts the position that gesture is a byproduct of listening. Conducting gesture, like spontaneous dance, should be a reaction to something heard.

One of the difficulties regarding conducting pedagogy is that many approaches teach gesture separated from the sounds that are evoked by the gesture. Conducting is often taught as geometric gesturing in air, devoid of sound. Taught in this manner, gesture takes on a meaningless and detached role to the music making process. Gesture learned and acquired in that fashion exhibits undue rhythmic and color restrictions upon the choir because of its lack of connection to what conductors hear within themselves.

As you prepare all exercises and music examples, you must not think about gesture, nor think about how your arms move, nor for that matter, think about anything other than the sound in the room at the time it is being created. The side of the brain that houses our cognitive or thinking abilities can override the other side of our brain—the intuitive, creative, and spontaneous side, which houses the gift of song. As one "conducts," or rather gestures, what is a spontaneous reaction to both the sounds within and the sounds being released from the singers bodies, one should *not* think about anything. One should not think "That sound is flat," "Wrong pitch in the bass section," and so on. Instead, one should allow the sounds to enter one's being through listening to everything with no opinion or pre-judgment. When the performance (in or outside of the rehearsal) is finished, the intuitive, creative side of the brain instantaneously plays back to the cognitive side of the brain for a musical analysis (i.e., that is flat, that is sharp, the vowel color is wrong, and so on). To try to hear those problems while the music is being performed severely limits the scope of what you are able to hear. Thinking while conducting limits what you hear and, most importantly, restricts your singers from spontaneously singing. By thinking while you conduct, an unspoken language is communicated to the choir through an unspontaneous gesture that basically does not allow them to sing. This message is most often carried in an unreleased rebound gesture, which tries to be more to the conducting gesture than a simple release of energy from the ictus. Throughout all the music you conduct, challenge yourself to listen and not think, and to find the voice of the music within yourself.

Thomas Benjamin, in an article entitled "On Teaching Composition" in the *Journal of Music Theory Pedagogy* (Spring, 1987), attempts to place in proper perspective the relationship of theory versus practice. His observations about teaching composition can illuminate a parallel in the teaching and learning of conducting.

> For the composer, again, the whole aim of technical studies is to develop an answerable, practical craft, beyond mere "theoretical" knowledge. J. S. Bach "started his pupils at once with what was practical and omitted all the *dry species* of counterpoint that we are given in Fux." Writes Sessions, "An Art is . . a craft; and a craft is mastered through prolonged practice—not through theory or 'learning' in the traditional sense." Instruction should be based on psychological and acoustic fact, not on theories about music. That is to say, theory in the best sense *is* practice. Which suggests again an integrated, broad curriculum, with maximum attention given to the *reality* of music: hearing, performing, experiencing. Hindemith urges a "practical music" training for composers, rather than an overly-specialized one, leading to the broadest competency in the field. "Don't teach composition . . . teach musicians." (P. 63)

It follows that we should not teach conducting as an exercise in spatial contortion, but teach musicians who function as conductors who are able to be open receivers of sound.

EXERCISE

Select your favorite recordings and devote some time to reacquaint yourself with listening each day. Listen for the sake of listening. Try not to analyze while you listen. Be open to the sound and do not judge it. Try to remember what it was like to listen to music when you were young. You listened with no preconceived agenda. In fact, many times you were overwhelmed by what you heard. Because you did not possess the "theory" to analyze what you heard, you just sat and received the sound. Reacquaint yourself with listening for listening's sake.

CHAPTER XI

NATURAL IMPULSE
AND ICTUS

INITIATION OF THE MUSICAL LINE

In a consideration of the facets of *phrasing* it is helpful, it seems to me, to think of melody as musical *energy*. The child's definition is not utter nonsense:"melody is a note looking for a place to sit down." Melody, as an abstraction, lies in the amount of tension or relaxation passed by each note to its successor (or received from its predecessor) until the musical sentence is complete and the moment of rest occurs. . . .

Abstractions are seldom without a set of contradictory data, but I have found it helpful to theorize that there are but three "postures" (or conditions) of melodic "energy":

   1. "Departing from . . ."
   2. "Passing through . . ." and
   3. "Arriving at . . ."

Or more simply, but less precisely, "beginning, middling and end-ing." (P 7)

Robert Shaw
in *The Choral Journal*

Each tone has a particular affinity for another note, and so the hand that guides the tone must never become inert. It must beat against the director's most primitive musical instinct to arrest motion in the process of music making . . . His hands should never come to a halt while the music is still sounding. This contradicts the activity of singing as a continuous inhalation and exhalation process, and the choir director who really identifies himself with this rhythmic wave will, if he resorts to "static motions," have the feeling that he is stemming the tide of the musical stream of sound. (P. 126)

The music should completely fill and inspire the conductor while he conducts. He should always anticipate the sound of the music, constantly keep an ideal tonal image before him, and try to realize this concept with the actual sound from his singers. He must continually think along with the music and always be slightly ahead of the choir in the giving of signals and of gestures; a director's movements should never have to follow the choir. (P. 127)

> Wilhelm Ehmann
> *Choral Directing*

The field of the unconscious, wherein temperament, sensibility and intuition are at work, needs to be enlarged by the acquisition of conscious qualities which enable the temperament first to balance the intellect and then to dominate it without inflicting injury on reason and order. (P. 36)

To be master of one's body, in all its relations with the intellect and with the senses, is to break down the oppositions which paralyse the free development of one's powers of imagination and creation. (P. 36)

There are two kinds of movement: spontaneous and deliberate. The former depends on the temperament and creates rhythms; the latter depends on the character and creates measure. (P. 51)

Rhythm, i.e. the expression of order and symmetry, penetrates by way of the body into the soul and into the entire man, revealing to him the harmony of his whole personality. (P. 102)

> Emile Jaques-Dalcroze
> *Eurhythmics Art and Education*

• • • • •

The manifestation of rhythm and natural forward impetus that is rooted in one's spontaneous impulse can begin to define the term ictus. The point at which energy is released through the conducting gesture that is prepared and released by the breath is truly a miracle. The ictus, when clearly presented, provides the energy from which musical line is born. Impulsive spontaneity, and thus instinctive and spontaneous music making, can the when the conductor understands what is embodied in the ictus and it's rebound, and the singers' appropriate reaction to the ictus.

QUALITIES OF THE ICTUS

Many novice conductors misunderstand the relationship of the ictus to the musical sound and line. Some believe that sound should be produced from the ensemble simultaneously with the impulse of the ictus. In that case, the immediate effect on the sound will be that the tempo or pulse of the piece will slow and will become slower as the piece progresses. Moreover, the color of the ensemble sound will become clouded. Diction will become sluggish and tuning will be difficult.

If one thinks a bit about the acoustic properties surrounding the release of a sound from an ensemble, several factors become apparent. First, sound traveling from the ensemble to the ear of the conductor takes an amount of time. Second, if sound is released from singers at the moment when they connect with the conductor and his ictus, the ictus, which initiates the sound will come first and the sound will follow. A rhythmic dilemma arises when conductors "hold" the rebound of the ictus in midair and wait for the sound to reach their ears before their hand moves forward through the conducting pattern to the next ictus. The reality of conducting is that the ictus impulse occurs a small fraction of a second before the sound is released from the choir. The conductor, after the ictus is shown, should not wait for the sound to "speak" from the choir. The conductor's gesture should be impelled forward through a trampoline-like effect of the inhalation breath and natural forward impelling motion of the ictus. Thus, the conducting gesture moves immediately forward without waiting for the choral sound to speak and then travel to the conductor's ears. In actuality, the sound speaks from the choir as the rebound occurs from the ictus; that is, the ictus elicits the sound from the choir, but does not momentarily wait "in time" for that sound to reach the conductor's ear. If the above process is followed—prepared with an open body, followed by the appropriate anticipatory breath by the conductor—the conductor will find that the color of the choral sound will more closely resemble what he hears and that the musical line is free and spontaneous. *Above all, do not wait for the sound after the ictus is elicited!*

QUALITIES OF THE REBOUND

Imagine throwing a ball to the ground. The ball, moving toward the ground, picks up speed as gravity pulls it toward the ground. As it hits the ground, it bounces upward, but at a *slower* rate of motion because of the pull of gravity. The rebound gesture after the ictus is similar to the bouncing ball. The conductor must *wait* for the rebound to occur and should not pull the arm upward to give the illusion of an ictus. It will seem as if the arm moves slower on the rebound upward. It does. The rebound, in its purest sense, is a release. The rebound does not carry any rhythmic subdivision; it is a simple release of energy of the downward energy and momentum elicited through the ictus. It must also be realized that the choir establishes a tempo for a performance based upon the ictus, not the rebound! When the rebound is made to assume a rhythmic quality, a subdivision results which will cripple the musical line.

At this point in your study, it may be beneficial to return once again to the drumsticks and practice pad. Perform the exercises once again using *tee, noo,* and *dah* while striking the stick against the pad. Notice the quality of the rebound when you are using the drumstick. What is the feeling in your arms and shoulders as you perform these drills again? Now put the sticks down and conduct. The drop to the ictus should be the same, as should the rebound.

BEING WITH THE SOUND

Once the musical line has been released through the impulse of the ictus, the conductor need only be "with the sound." Being "with the sound" means that the hand or hands are moving synchronously with the sound being produced. Another analogy is to believe that after the impelling ictus occurs, at times one merely is a mime of the sound being produced by the color. The hands mirror the motion that has been propelled by the ictus. That is, the distance traveled by the hand from the impelling ictus to the next impelling ictus mimes the rate of speed of the line that is actually occurring, and the shape of the hand mirrors the color of the sound. If one is receiving the sound produced by the choir, and one has an aural image of the notes, rhythms, forward movement, and color of the sound, the hand will mirror all of those qualities. The motion that occurs in the gesture between ictus, should reflect the quality of legato or non-legato that is required by the piece. Being with the sound also requires the conductor to develop an imaginary tactile sense in his hands. This tactile sense sets up the image within the conductor's fantasy that the sound is in his hands. The intervening sound between ictus is sometimes touched by his fingertips, sometimes held and supported by the hands. At times the hands mirror the expansive character of the meter.

SPEED AND VELOCITY OF GESTURE AND ITS EFFECT ON LINE

Confusion often abounds when one tries to "move the music forward." In most instances, the opposite happens. The music slows, intonation problems occur, and the choir sings without clarity or color. This is the result of a gesture that attempts to move sound forward with weight. Musical line can be moved forward when the conducting gesture uses velocity or speed without weight. If the conductor is listening, he will discover that a relatively weightless gesture that uses speed will move the line forward. At that point, it is the conductor's challenge to decide when not to conduct and allow the music to sing on its own, so to speak. When one hears that the line is not moving forward, velocity of gesture can again be brought into play to move the sound forward, but always without weight in the gesture.

SKIMMING

Many beginning conductors may initially find it difficult to provide a clear ictus to the choir. This may happen for many reasons. The most frequent cause is that the conductor has lost sight of the correct alignment; hence, the muscles of the body begin to compensate for the lack of correct alignment by "holding" the body in place. This muscular tension then manifests itself as an inability to produce a natural downward drop and the resulting natural rebound. The resulting gesture tends toward a legato and tends to encircle and wrap around, or avoid, the point at which the ictus occurs. In simple language, it is an avoidance of confronting the pulse head-on. This can be labeled as skimming. Skimming will produce a performance that lacks rhythmic clarity and spontaneous musical line, and it will foster intonation problems.

The reaction by the choir to the ictus and the nature of the impulse of the ictus and its primal relationship to the birthing of the musical line must be understood clearly by the conductor. It is the understanding of the dynamic interplay of the ictus with propelling the sound forward that makes the conducting gesture effective and spontaneous. The end product of all the above will be a choir that will sing with a free and spontaneous sound!

METRIC TRANSFORMATION EXERCISES: ASSURING UNDERLYING SUBDIVISION

An ictus can only be elicited if there is an internal subdivision present within the conductor. Even for experienced conductors, it is important to perform the following exercises with metronome in hand to check on yourself. The exercises should be performed at various random tempi.

Throughout the following exercises remember: Do not move to rhythm syllables until you can perform the exercise on *bm* while conducting in consistent tempo. If you have problems with consistent tempo, return to the coordinative sequence suggested in number 1 or perform the exercises seated, keeping the large beat in the heels of your feet.

1. Begin by conducting ♩ = 60. Perform the following exercise with the measure signatures (with the corresponding beat pattern) of 4/4, 3/4, 2/4, 6/8, and 5/4 (3+2 and 2+3).

First, chant two subdivisions of each beat on the syllable *bm*. When that is in consistent tempo, then chant on *du-de* two subdivisions of the large beat while conducting, maintaining a consistent tempo. If you have a problem maintaining a consistent tempo, it might be helpful to review the material in chapter 5. That material is summarized below:

a. Walk the room to step and rhythmically chant the piece to find the micro beat. Walk about the room and step to the work while you chant it on a neutral syllable such as *bum, doo, pah,* etc. The pulse you most naturally step to (*regardless of the measure signature*) is the macro beat, or largest rhythm unit of the work. Remember that the unit of pulse you step to may not be the unit of pulse signified by the measure signature. Always rely on what you hear, not what you see on the printed page. If you have any difficulty doing this, perform the movement coordination sequence discussed at the beginning of chapter 5 *b. Locate the micro beat in your hands while concurrently tapping the macro beat in your feet.* After walking the piece, be seated. Tap the beat that you just stepped in your feet. While chanting the piece, determine whether the beat in your feet can be divided into twos or threes by lightly tapping your index and middle fingers of your right hand lightly onto your upturned left palm

c. Chant through the piece, breathing for each entrance. Continue tapping the macro beat in your feet and the micro beat in your hands. Rhythmically chant the entire piece on a neutral syllable, taking care to breathe for each entrance. Inconsistent tempo problems are most often caused by the nonrhythmic breathing of conductors. Rhythmic breathing, key to a choir's consistent tempo, grows out of an inner consistent tempo of the conductor that is rooted in the concurrent macro and micro beat

d. Chant through the piece without tapping. Remove the tapping of the macro beats in the feet and the micro beats in the hands, and rhythmically chant the piece, while still breathing for each entrance. This will determine whether the consistent tempo of the piece is anchored within your audiation. If you have difficulty doing this, repeat steps 1–3 until the tempo stabilizes.

After two subdivisions of the beat are in consistent tempo, chant three subdivisions of each beat on the syllable *bm*. When that is in consistent tempo, then conduct and chant three subdivisions of the beat using the rhythm syllables *du-dah-di*.

After three subdivisions of the beat are in consistent tempo, chant four subdivisions of each beat on the syllable *bm*. When that is in consistent tempo, then conduct and chant four subdivisions of each pulse using the rhythm syllables *du-ta-de-ta*.

After four subdivisions of the beat are in consistent tempo, chant five subdivisions of each beat on the syllable *bm*. When that is in consistent tempo, try conducting and chanting five subdivisions of the beat using the rhythm syllables *du-bay-du-ba-bi*.

2. After you have performed the above exercise at ♩ = 60, then perform the exercise at other tempi of your choice.

3. Continue the meter transformation exercise into unusual meter. The syllable *be* is pronounced "bay."

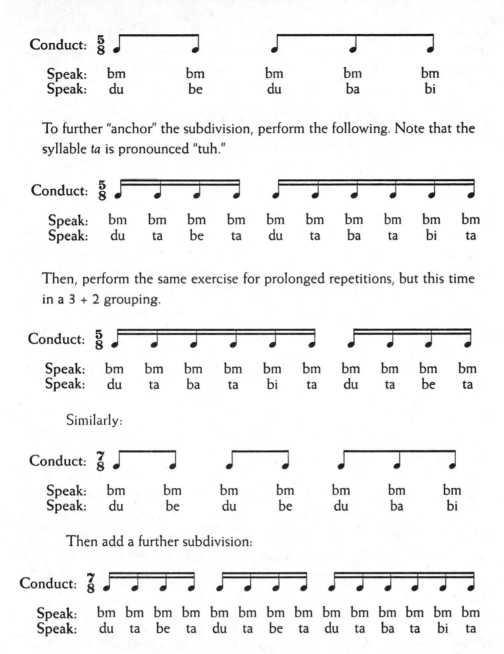

Conduct: 5/8

Speak: bm   bm   bm   bm   bm
Speak: du   be   du   ba   bi

To further "anchor" the subdivision, perform the following. Note that the syllable *ta* is pronounced "tuh."

Conduct: 5/8

Speak: bm bm bm bm bm bm bm bm bm bm
Speak: du ta be ta du ta ba ta bi ta

Then, perform the same exercise for prolonged repetitions, but this time in a 3 + 2 grouping.

Conduct: 5/8

Speak: bm bm bm bm bm bm bm bm bm bm
Speak: du ta ba ta bi ta du ta be ta

Similarly:

Conduct: 7/8

Speak: bm   bm   bm   bm   bm   bm   bm
Speak: du   be   du   be   du   ba   bi

Then add a further subdivision:

Conduct: 7/8

Speak: bm bm bm bm bm bm bm bm bm bm bm bm bm bm
Speak: du ta be ta du ta be ta du ta ba ta bi ta

In the preceding exercises, it must be remembered that rhythm syllables are a means to an end. The syllables tend to label rhythm patterns in a consistent manner so that they can be processed and understood by the musician. The syllables above, developed by Edwin Gordon, are based upon beat function. It is a system based on the relationships of the actual sounds of the rhythm patterns that are heard or audiated, and not on the time values of individual notes. Because of the internal logic of the system, students can learn the system quickly, and as a result of its internal logic, students are guided in audiating meter. For further explanation of this system of rhythm solfège, refer to Edwin E. Gordon, *Learning Sequences in Music*, 1993 edition, pages 275–290, and Appendix I of this book

The Inspirited Hand: Texture-Vowel Color and Consonants

If the conductor has an aural image of the piece—i.e., its rhythm, its tonal content, its phrasing direction, the color of the piece, and the relationship of the consonants to the texture of the piece—all of this will naturally be manifest in the hands of the conductor. This will be manifest only if alignment is good and there is not any muscular holding of the gesture. What is it, then, that permits all of the above characteristics to occur naturally in the hand?

First, remember that the hand cannot be programmed from the "outside." Conductors must hear all of the qualities mentioned above in their own aural world and then be open to receive the sound of the choir. Upon receiving the sound, they then react spontaneously to the sound through gesture to make their own aural image align itself with the sound that the choir is singing. What should happen to the hand as sound is received and as conductors hear the piece being performed within their own aural world?

Subconsciously, as one is with the sound, the colors that one hears in a choral texture are mirrored in the shape of the hand. What produces the textural colors in a choral sound? The vowels. It follows that the hand position for an *ah* vowel will be different from that of an *ee* vowel and so on. Moreover, the colors of all the vowels will change from style period to style period and from composer to composer. Finally, the color of a piece is mitigated by the overall affect, or spirit, that a conductor brings to the music.

Conducting Transitions between Phrases: Breath Cueing

Gesture between phrases should insure the connection of breath between phrases for the singers. At phrase endings, there are two things that can be indicated to the singers: (1) taking the breath for the next phrase and (2) the consonant that occurs at the end of the phrase. Many conductors believe that they must indicate both separately; that is, they must indicate the exact placement of the consonant followed by an indication of breath—and these followed by the "attack" for the start of the next phrase. The choice of what the gesture should indicate should rely on the technique that the singers use to sing between phrases.

The technique for the proper execution of one phrase ending and moving to the start of the next phrase is quite simple. For the singer, as the consonant is being produced, the breath is taken in for the next phrase *at the same moment*. Placing the final consonant and taking the breath are *simultaneous* acts. Sing the first two phrases of "My Country 'Tis of Thee." The first time you sing those phrases, delib-erately place the *g* of *sing* on beat 3 of the bar and then breathe and begin the next phrase. Now, sing the first two phrases again, this time breathe at the same moment that you sing the *g* of *sing*, and begin the next phrase. With the second example, you will notice in your own body that the breath is able to connect the two phrases in a way that it could not in the first example. You will also notice that in the second example the forward motion of the line was more natural and spontaneous when it grew directly from the breath. Further, the second phrase began as a natural reaction to the breath; you did not have to indicate the start of the second phrase—it began out of the breath.

Do the second example again and "conduct" yourself as you sing. You should discover that you do not conduct the *g* consonant of *sing* as a separate entity from the breath for the next phrase. At the point at which you might be inclined to conduct the *g*, just breathe and don't worry about the consonant. The consonant will take care of itself. *In reality, you begin your breath for the next phrase while the choir is finishing their phrase.* This "overlapping" breathing technique assures a connection between phrases with the breath, and additionally assures a spontaneous forward momentum of the phrase.

The "conducting" of consonants between phrases and separated from the breath disrupts the natural forward momentum of the phrase. This happens because by conducting the consonant, you inadvertently disrupt the underlying rhythmic pulse of the phrase, which, in turn, disrupts the breathing of the singers, and this in turn disrupts the tone color and overall musical aesthetic of the piece. If you can master this concept of breath cueing between phrases, your choir will breath better, their sound will be freer, and the music, in turn, will be able to speak.

A RETURN TO BREATHING: ISSUES OF COLOR AND TEXTURE

Much has been said about breathing, and now we return to it again. All of the conducting "technique" discussed thus far is of no use unless the body is allowed to open and the breath can fall in. Most important to the art of conducting is that the conductor listen to his breath and to the breath of the choir. It is that opened and listening state of the conductor that provides all of the necessary performance information to the singers. Listening to the breath of the choir provides the conductor an immediate connection to the choir that will allow the music to begin spontaneously. Within the breath of the conductor is mirrored all the conductor's musical intentions! The ability to breathe and listen is directly related to one's musical effectiveness as a conductor.

In addition, the breath can also relay to the choir the conductor's concept of color or texture. In beginning conducting, as one inhales, one can begin to explore the world of color and texture. To begin in an elementary way, try to associate a color or colors with the piece that you are conducting. Think of a 100-count box of Crayola crayons. Choose the color or colors that best represent the piece. As you inhale, imagine the color in your breath, that is, breathe both the vowel that the choir will sing and the color. Hear the effect of your "breath color" on the choir!

You will discover that the above color imagery has a direct effect on your breath as the conductor and hence on the sound of the choir. But why does it have such a pronounced effect? By thinking about color, you are affecting the internal space of your body that the breath occupies, which is then communicated to the choir. It is simply not enough to breathe. The breath must mirror the color of the sound and the rhythmic character of the piece that is about to be sung. Your "inner space" must reflect the textural color of the piece. As one becomes more proficient with conducting, the color imagery can be abandoned. You will find that when you have a concept of the color of a piece, that "vocal color" will translate immediately to your inner breath space and will be relayed spontaneously to the choir.

EXERCISES

1. Have a partner sing "My Country 'Tis of Thee." As your partner sings, move your hands in a conducting-like gesture to the sound, mirroring the color and the movement of the sound.

2. Use "My Country 'Tis of Thee" again This time while you conduct, imagine that you are a marionette. Imagine that someone else is working the strings that are attached to your arms as you conduct What is the effect of this activity upon the *weight* of your gesture?

3. Speak running eighth notes on the syllable *du* in a consistent tempo. As you chant these running eighth notes, conduct using a pattern of your choice. Practice the following:

  a. Placing the ictus immediately prior to the chanted pulses.
  b. After the above has been accomplished, allow the hand to be with the sound after the ictus. That is, the hand is not moving ahead of the sound between beats, but is right with the sound. Another way to think of this drill is to "mime" the sound as you did in the above exercise between ictus

4. This exercise consists of two parts.

  a. Sing and conduct yourself on a sustained pitch or a series of repeated pitches on one of the vowels. Notice your hand position for that vowel. Now perform the exercise again, but sing a different vowel. The shape of your hand should be slightly different. Perform this exercise on the five pure vowels. Be certain that you breathe the vowel before you sing it, that is, if you are about to sing an *ah* vowel, then breathe in through the *ah* vowel

  b. Perform the above exercise again, but this time, before you sing the vowel, think of the color that you would like the vowel to be, e.g., blue, rose, pink, etc. Repeat this color drill for each of the five pure vowels. You should notice that while singing the same vowel, and varying the color, the shape of your hands changes slightly

5. Consonants provide both rhythm and texture to the choral performance. The technique for reflecting consonants in the fingers is developed over a long period of time through one's experience with sound in the choral rehearsal. But the process by which one becomes familiar with the "colors" of consonants can begin with a simple drill. When confronted with a consonant, especially at the beginning or the end of text, it is helpful to determine the inherent sound qualities in each consonant: staccato, legato, or marcato. The table below illustrates this concept. Special note should be taken of those consonants which carry more than one articulation. As an exercise, first say the consonant, and then "conduct" the consonant, using the fingertips and hand to approximately mirror the sound (articulation) of that particular consonant. One's knowledge of how the consonant is sounded is directly related to the diction mechanics of how the consonant is produced. As a help to the exercise below, you should consult the *Singer's Manual of English Diction* by Madeleine Marshall concerning her description of how the

consonant is actually executed. Her insights will then provide you with the understanding of the production of the consonant that will in turn provide a gesture that will mirror the correct production of the consonant.

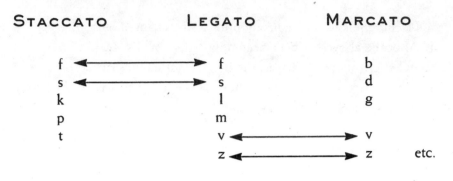

CHAPTER XII

MUSIC APTITUDE

MEASURING AND REALIZING YOUR MUSIC POTENTIAL AS A CONDUCTOR

Music aptitude is a measure of a student's potential to achieve in music. Music achievement is a measure of what a student has learned. Music aptitude may be thought of as relating to the "inner possibility," and music achievement to the "outer reality." The concealed (hitherto unknown) music aptitudes of many students, regardless of whether they have received formal or informal instruction in music are quickly revealed by a valid music aptitude test. Although students who score high on a music achievement test also score high on a music aptitude test, the reverse is not necessarily true. Not all students who score low on a music achievement test score low on a music aptitude test. The fact is that some students who demonstrate little or no music achievement score extremely high on a music test. It has been discovered that, unfortunately, almost 50 percent of the fourth through twelfth grade students whose overall music aptitude is at or above the 80th percentile do not receive special instruction in music, nor do they volunteer to enroll in music performance activities in school. They are not recognized by their teachers as having great potential for understanding and appreciating music, that is, for achieving in music. It is estimated that that percentage is even greater for college and university students. (P. 5)

Edwin E. Gordon
Manual for the Advanced Measures of Music Audiation

Under no circumstances should the results of a music aptitude test exclude a student from instruction in music or from participation in music activities. When a teacher knows that a student has a low level of music aptitude, he can provide the appropriate compensatory instruction that will allow the student to achieve in accordance with his potential to achieve. Regardless of a student's low level of music aptitude, that student is capable of learning music to some extent. (P. 6)

Edwin E. Gordon
Learning Sequences in Music, 1988

It seems that a child will never have a higher level of music aptitude than at the moment of birth. Moments after a child is born, the level of music aptitude begins to decrease. Sounds, including voices, in her immediate environment are not automatically conducive to reinforcing her senses of pitches and durations. With appropriate informal guidance and formal music instruction, every child's level of developmental music aptitude can be brought back toward its birth level, but no higher. The extent to which a child's developmental music aptitude is increased, however, will have a profound effect on her music achievement in and out of school. (P. 3)

Edwin E. Gordon
Learning Sequences in Music, 1993

The only thing you can do is try to understand a person and then discuss with him what he has not done. Really, you cannot develop or change anything in anybody. You can respect what he is and try to make him a true picture of himself. (P. 65)

As a teacher, my whole life is based on understanding others, not on making them understand me. What the student thinks, what he wants to do—that is the important thing. I must try to make him express himself and prepare him to do that for which he is best fitted. (P. 65)

Nadia Boulanger
in *Master Teacher,* Don G. Campbell

• • • • •

Have you ever wondered what your musical ability actually is? Regardless of the amount of training that you have received, have you wondered just how good your "ear" is? Have you been frustrated with sight singing because you know you can "hear" the music but were unable to read it as rapidly as you hear it? Do you feel that reading music at times slows your music learning? Do you believe that you have a good "ear," but are frustrated because you are not sure whether you can trust your instincts? Can you take a measure of your music ability so that you are better able to understand what you are capable of hearing and learning?

DEVELOPMENTAL AND STABILIZED MUSIC APTITUDE

Music aptitude, the potential to learn music, is a product of nature and nurture. Research has been unable to specify which quantities of each make up what is known as music aptitude. Music aptitude as an inherited trait has not been researched. During the past ten years, the work of Edwin E. Gordon has clearly established that, despite the level of music aptitude a child is born with, a child must have positive early childhood experiences in order to maintain the level of aptitude with which he or she was born.[1] Moreover, despite positive informal experiences in music, the levels of a person's music aptitude cannot progress beyond the level with which he or she was born.[2] Because the child's music aptitude is in a state of flux until the age of nine years, it is called *developmental music aptitude*. For choral conductors and church musicians, the following statement should be considered:

> It cannot be overemphasized that early informal and formal instruction in
> music, particularly from birth to age nine, is of greater consequence than

---

[1] See Edwin E. Gordon, *Manual for the Primary Measures of Music Audiation and the Intermediate Measures of Music Audiation* (Chicago: GIA Publications, Inc., 1986), pp.97–118 and Edwin E. Gordon, *The Manifestation of Developmental Music Aptitude in the Audiation of "Same" and "Different" as Sound in Music* (Chicago: GIA Publications, Inc., 1981), pp.25–46.

[2] Informal instruction in music is a relatively new concept in music education. At the beginning of a person's music experience, whether they be newborn children, toddlers, or adults, some type of informal experiences in music must occur to form the foundation of formal music learning. Informal instruction exposes the person to music, but reqiures nothing of that person. He may choose to respond or may choose to listen. The important aspect of informal music instruction is that listening and moving take place. It has been observed that persons in this stage are in music babble; that is, they experiment and explore music. That process cannot be accelerated, and it must take place before formal learning in music begins. A child or adult is beyond music babble when he can maintain a consistent tempo and hum the resting tone of a tune he hears.

formal instruction in music after age nine. The more appropriate early informal experiences and formal instruction in music are, the higher the level at which a student's music aptitude will stabilize. Also, the younger a child is when he begins to receive early informal and formal instruction in music, the more he canprofit from such instruction and the higher level at which his music aptitude will eventually stabilize. A child can profit from informal and formal music instruction very much more at age five than at age six, more at six than at age seven, and very little more at age seven than at age eight.[3]

Research has substantiated that music aptitude does not continue to develop after age nine; rather, the aptitude level the child possesses at age nine stabilizes and remains relatively constant throughout his life. Consequently, after age nine, music aptitude is referred to as *stabilized music aptitude*

AUDIATION

Edwin Gordon has coined the word *audiation*. Audiation takes place when the sound is not physically present. Audiation is multidimensional because one can audiate separate elements of music, that is, melodic, harmonic, rhythmic Moreover, Gordon has theorized seven types of audiation: (1) listening to familiar or unfamiliar music, (2) reading familiar or unfamiliar music, (3) notating familiar or unfamiliar music, (4) recalling familiar music and possibly performing it, (5) recalling familiar music and notating it, (6) creating and improvising unfamiliar music and possibly performing it, and (7) creating and improvising unfamiliar music and notating it.

Audiation must be understood by the choral conductor because it is the basis of music aptitude. Gordon states, "Unless one can audiate what he has aurally perceived, music will have little or no meaning for him. The extent to which one can audiate without formal music achievement what he has perceived in unfamiliar music is a measure of his developmental music aptitude. Though they are significantly different, music aptitude and music achievement are not mutually exclusive."[4]

---

[3] Edwin E. Gordon, *The Nature, Description, Measurement, and Evaluation of Music Aptitudes* (Chicago: GIA Publications, Inc., 1987), p. 9.
[4] Ibid., p. 15.

A TEST OF STABILIZED MUSIC APTITUDE

There are many approaches to the measurement of music aptitude. While there are many other tests currently available, the summaries of the tests listed below represent the finest instruments available for use by choral conductors to assess their own music potential. The following test of stabilized music aptitude is recommended. The test will yield a tonal and rhythm score.

THE ADVANCED MEASURES OF MUSIC AUDIATION (AMMA)

Author:	Edwin E. Gordon
Age:	Grade 7 through college
Test results:	Tonal score, rhythm score, and composite score
Time:	15 minutes
Publisher:	GIA Publications, Inc., Chicago, Illinois

University professors have been requesting short tonal and rhythm aptitude tests that may be used for adapting instruction in music theory and music education courses to the musical strengths and weaknesses of individual students. The *Advanced Measures of Music Audiation* (AMMA) is a test of *stabilized music aptitude* for college-aged students. The test yields a tonal and a rhythm score, as well as a composite score. AMMA is a cassette-recorded test that requires approximately fifteen minutes to administer. Included are thirty questions, each containing a pair of short musical phrases. In addition to the test questions, directions for taking the test, along with practice examples are recorded on the cassette. The AMMA may be given to small and large groups of students and to individual students. There are two subtests included in the AMMA: tonal and rhythm.

Formal music achievement is not a requirement for taking the AMMA. Regardless of whether a student can play a music instrument, read notation, or has taken courses in music theory, he or she may score high on the test. Students simply indicate by filling a space on the answer sheet whether two short musical phrases sound the same, whether they sound different because of a tonal change, or whether they sound different because of a rhythm change. There is only one correct answer for each question. At this time, it is recommended that AMMA now be used with undergraduate and graduate students in colleges and universities.

INTERPRETATION OF AMMA TEST RESULTS

The author of AMMA, Edwin Gordon, states that AMMA scores may be used for one or more of the following purposes:

1. To serve as a part of the criteria for entrance to a college or university music department or school of music. Music aptitude is at least as important as any type of music achievement for ultimate success in music.

2. To identify college and university students, non-music as well as music majors, who possess the music aptitude to achieve high standards in music. It is improbable that a student who demonstrates technical proficiency on a music instrument but who does not possess high music aptitude will become a fine musician.

3. To establish objective and realistic expectations for the music achievement of college and university music and non-music majors. A music aptitude test is more valid for this purpose than is a standardized academic aptitude test or an academic achievement test.

4. To efficiently and diagnostically adapt music teaching in private instruction and within a classroom or an ensemble to the individual musical differences found among college and university students.

5. To assign college and university students to specific music classes, ensembles, and types of private instruction that are designed to meet their individual musical needs.

6. To assist college and university music students in making career decisions.

7. To efficiently and diagnostically adapt music teaching within a classroom or an ensemble and in private instruction to the individual musical differences found among high school students.

Implied in Gordon's writing is the use of the test by persons studying conducting. The test yields a tonal score and a rhythm score. Those scores reveal the hearing potential of the person taking the test. Many times, especially in the case of the amateur musician (the person does not hold a degree in music), one's opinion about one's personal musicianship is based upon the subjective opinion either of oneself or of a favored teacher. The AMMA provides a measure of one's potential to hear, and thus function well in the realm of conducting. If you score "high" on AMMA, you will most likely feel that you may have underestimated the depth of your ability. If you score "average" or "below average," this does not mean that you cannot function as a conductor. It does mean, however, that it may take you longer to learn a score when compared to a person with high music aptitude. The use of AMMA will enhance your abilities as a conductor because it will provide an objective opinion concerning your ability to hear.

CHAPTER XIII

PREPARING THE SCORE

ALLOWING THE MUSIC TO SPEAK

No matter how diverse their views on every other topic, most musicians agree that finding the right tempo is at least half the interpretation. Wagner went further, asserting that the right tempo *was* the interpretation. In his essay *On Conducting* he writes: "I am persistently returning to the question of tempo because, as I said before, this is the point at which it becomes evident whether a conductor understands his business or not." Tempo is also the principal feature singled out by critics in commenting on performers. With all this consensus on the crucial importance of tempo, it may seem curious that musicians hardly ever agree on the proper choice of tempo. Accord in theory has never spread into agreement in practice. (P. 101)

Erich Leinsdorf
The Composer's Advocate

There is a vitality, a life force, an energy, a quickening, that is translated through you into action, and because there is only one of you in all time, this expression is unique. And if you block it, it will never exist through any other medium and will be lost. (P. 75)

> Martha Graham
> in *The Artist's Way, Julia Cameron*

It might sound like only a game with words when one says that there is a difference between "learning about things" and "learning things," just as there is a difference between "speaking about religion" and "speaking religion" or "speaking about music" and "speaking music." However, we know that it is easier to have an opinion about life than it is to live wisely. It is also considerably easier to have an opinion about great music than it is to bring it to life. There is a subtle difference between intelligent, even sensitive interpretation and bringing music into existence: in the case of intelligent interpretation, the emphasis is on the opinion of the interpreter, but when music comes into existence, it speaks for itself. (P. 23)

Some of our greatest and deepest enjoyment as conductors can come not in performance, but the quiet and intense process of learning during which the simple but profound truths of the score revel themselves. We must constantly strive to come closer to the simple truths, so that we may stimulate our singers (and audiences) toward such a search of their own. Our great subject is actually the search for those values which caused Bach's (or Mozart's or Stravinsky's) work. If they are discovered, it is hoped that we might reconquer them in order to possess them, so that they may become the cause of a more basic life of our own and be shared with those whom we conduct. (P. 24)

> Julius Herford
> in *The Choral Journal*

Play is the exultation of the possible. (P. 198)

> Martin Buber
> in *The Artist's Way, Julia Cameron*

A metronome is an undependable criterion; the only designation which can't be misapplied is *presto possible*. Tempos vary with generations like the rapidity of language. Music's velocity has less organic import than its phraseology and rhythmic qualities; what counts in performance is the artistry of the phrase and beat within a tempo. A composer is never sure of tempo before a rehearsal, for preoccupation with such detail during composition slackens creative flow. Writing time corresponds in no way to performance time, and intuitions regarding the latter are, at best, approximate. (P. 326)

Tempo indication is not creation, but an afterthought related to performance. Naturally, an inherently fast piece must be played fast, a slow one slow—but to just what extent is a decision for players. If the composer happens to be the performer, so much the better. Rhythm and phrasing, nevertheless, do pertain to composition and are always misconceived (though sometimes beautifully), for as I say, notation is inexact.

When a composer determines his tempo as a final gesture to the product, he does so as an interpreter. Since his tempo varies with the life of the times, his marking is inaccurate, his emotional conjectures will not have authentic translation into sound. The composer will never hear his music in reality as he heard in spirit. (P. 326)

Ned Rorem
Setting the Tone

Although one can agree that a composer begins with a text, and that it is his inspiration to a certain respect, it is the responsibility of the performer, it seems to me, to satisfy as nearly as he can the composers language and then seek what the inside of the composer sought, how he might have felt about the text rather than arriving at a textual, philosophical relationship with the text that is ones' own personal interpretation and forcing that upon the composer. I can remember once that somebody said that Bach was the greatest witness to the crucifixion of Jesus; not that he happened to be present, but because he was a witness to the meaning of the crucifixion.

Robert Shaw
Preparing a Masterpiece: The Brahms Requiem, video

To become truly immortal, a work of art must escape all human limits: logic and common sense will only interfere. But once these barriers are broken, it will enter the realms of childhood vision and dreams. (P. 84)

Giorgio De Chirico
in *The Artist's Way, Julia Cameron*

•••••
PREPARING AND MARKING THE SCORE

The first step in preparing for the rehearsal is the obvious step of preparing and marking the score. The learning of the notes and the rhythms of all the parts is prerequisite to the other levels of score preparation. The following steps are recommended.

1. *Hum or moan through the piece.* Intensely hum the overall piece (following its principal rhythms) on the consonants *mm* or *nn* at a mezzo forte or forte level. Breathe for as many of the entrances as possible. This technique allows the conductor to actively participate in and make decisions concerning the phrase directions of the work. The humming or moaning establishes a connection between the notes on the page and the sound of a musical line in motion. It is during this activity when breath locations are established.

2. *Play and sing all parts.* Play and/or sing all parts individually. Then, play one part and sing another until all combinations of parts have been experienced. Finally begin by singing one part and then switching immediately to another part. This procedure is especially helpful in contrapuntal music.

3. *Reinforce Alexander-based alignment sensations and thoughts.* When preparing a score, always prepare it from a sitting or standing position that is reflective of the singing process. There is an intimate but unseen connection between body posture and the music learning process. When a piece of music is performed, the body's "muscle memory" will recreate the posture and body alignment that was in evidence as the score was being learned. The conductor should view score preparation as both an aural and kinesthetic exercise. The kinesthetic attitude of the body is established at the time the initial note learning of the score takes place. *Constantly reinforce* all the Alexander-based alignment issues that were presented earlier in chapter 2.

4. *Mark the score.* One of the most obvious aids in rehearsal technique is often overlooked by both experienced and novice conductors. Marking the score in an organized manner will assist both the preparation for rehearsal and serve as a visual reminder for the conductor in rehearsal.

While such score marking may be time consuming, most conductors find that it hastens the score learning process.

The key to score marking is to establish a consistent procedure. Establish standard color codes for the most important aspects of the score. Below is a suggested color-coding system that may be used as a model. Unless otherwise indicated, colors refer to a colored pencil.

red	circle all forte dynamics
green	circle all piano dynamics
dark green	circle all mezzo forte dynamics
light green highlighter	trace over all crescendos and decrescendos
orange	enlarge all meter changes
yellow highlighter	trace and track thematic and imitative material
blue	indicate textual words that receive stress
purple	connect notes between voice parts that are in suspension or create a dissonance
pink highlighter	trace over accents
maroon	place harmonic analysis underneath score; use highlighter to draw attention to unusual harmonic progressions
turquoise	circle thirds in triads and other intervals which may cause intonation problems
light green	underline all tempo changes
pencil	indicate necessary possible vowel modifications above voice part and trace over with blue highlighter; draw arrows where necessary to track entrances

5. *Conduct while humming or moaning through the piece.* Now conduct and intensely hum the overall piece on the consonants *mm* or *nn* at a mezzo forte or forte level. Breathe for as many of the entrances as possible.

6. *Study and experience the breath of the piece carefully.* When learning scores, it is important to have a clear sense of where the choir will breathe within the phrase structure and between phrases. This serves an important function. The consistent tempo of a piece is often altered *by the conductor* because he or she does not breathe with the singers and hence rushes the tempo. One of the most important factors in maintaining a consistent tempo is to make sure that the breath process of the singers is rhythmic. As stated above, in

the initial stages of the score preparation process it is very important for the conductor to not only breathe where the choir breathes, but to exhale air constantly in the motion of the piece to simulate the forward motion of the phrases. One can also moan or hum in a monotone. Regardless of the rhythm of the work, the humming or moaning should be *continuous* and not simply echo the melodic rhythm (exact rhythm) of the piece. This encourages the conductor to always be connected with the "sound" of the piece while learning the score. One should avoid learning a piece of music without connecting oneself and one's singing mechanism to the ongoing rhythmic motion and flow of the work. Moreover, if the conductor does this, it will help to free the conducting gesture.

7. *Conduct the piece while inhaling and exhaling constantly.* Continually inhaling and exhaling while conducting the piece is a valuable score preparation technique. Many times conducting gesture is totally unrelated to the sound and line of a piece; that is, the conducting gesture is not directly connected to both the energy of the body and the energy of the breath. Connecting the gesture to the body and to the breath is essential to good rehearsal technique. Much can be taught to the choir without words if the gesture is connected in such a fashion. By inhaling and exhaling on *tss* or *shh* (or any consonantal combination which provides a resistance), this connection between gesture, body, and breath can be established.

8. *Breathe the color of the style and affect of the piece.* While programmatic approaches to music making can be dangerous, it is very helpful to consider the character of the breath for each piece that you conduct and rehearse. In chapter 7, establishing a sense of textural color was introduced through associating colors with the music. Since the vocal "color" of a piece is set through the inhalation process, the conductor must predetermine the color and mood of the breath that is taken to start phrases so that the color of the ensemble is set in the breath that they take. If you "hear" a particular passage as purple, it is often effective to ask the choir to "inhale" the color purple. Such a technique will elicit a darker sound than if one asks the choir to "breathe" red, and so on.

9. *Study and experience the breath process that connects phrases.* When teaching a piece, take special care to teach how the breath begins simultaneously with the end of a phrase. Amateur singers tend to finish the phonation of the tone and then start the breath process for the start of the next phrase. If one examines the process as a singer, the inhalation of breath happens

at the same moment as the finishing of the tone. When conducting, the conductor should not conduct the end of the phrase, but simply breathe for the next phrase—cue the breath. By doing so, the previous phrase ending will take care of itself, and the tone color, pitch, and forward rhythmic motion of the phrase will be maintained.

PREPARING THE TONAL MATERIALS OF THE MUSIC

After gaining an understanding of the rhythmic life of the piece, you must establish a procedure for learning the tonal aspects of the score. Many persons play through the score at the keyboard. This certainly will give them an idea concerning the harmonic movement, but actually does very little to establish the direction of phrase of the lines of the piece. It is best if one begins by first singing the soprano part. On subsequent repetitions, sing and conduct the soprano part. After it becomes very familiar to you, then move ahead and do the same with the alto, tenor, and other parts. The time that you spend singing and conducting individual parts is, perhaps, the most valuable aspect of score preparation. If you know each of the parts, the musical mind is then able to combine them. Familiarity with the part also means that, as you are conducting the work, your ear will be easily able to switch between parts while continuing to track the parts that you are not focusing on. This procedure should be followed for every score that you conduct. If instrumental or keyboard parts are present, you should learn those parts in a similar fashion.

ANTICIPATING VOCAL PROBLEMS WITHIN THE SCORE

Aside from preparing the tonal, rhythmic, and harmonic aspects of the score so that you can "hear" the score you are to conduct, it is valuable for the conductor to study the score with respect to the vocal technique problems that one may encounter as an amateur choral singer. In many cases, a tonal or rhythm error may be evident that is caused by the singer's inability to correctly execute the pitch they are hearing. Obviously, the space allotted to a summary such as this does not allow for a detailed explanation or solution of this problem. However, below you will find a list of problems to look for. In some cases, short solutions or "tools" will be offered. For further pedagogical answers, the reader is referred to the text by

Frauke Haasemann and James Jordan, *Group Vocal Technique*, listed in the bibliography of this text.

If one would compile a list of possible vocal problems that need to be examined in any work, the list would be as follows:

MAINTAINING POSTURE FOR CORRECT SINGING

DIAPHRAGM ACTIVITY (FOR DICTION AND FOR ARTICULATION OF THE RHYTHM)

BREATHING (EXHALATION, INHALATION AND SUPPORT)

APPROPRIATE RESONANCE (FOR THE STYLE OF THE MUSIC)

FIVE PURE VOWELS (WITHOUT DIPHTHONGS, TO MAINTAIN PITCH AND TONE COLOR)

FINDING HEAD VOICE (YAWN-SIGH TO MAINTAIN PROPER TONE COLOR)

EXPANDING THE VOCAL TRACT (TO ASSURE A FREE, OPEN SINGING SOUND)

RANGE EXTENSION AND REGISTER CONSISTENCY (AS REQUIRED BY THE PIECE)

FLEXIBILITY (RUNS)

RESONANCE AND PLACEMENT (TO EXECUTE A SPECIFIC STYLE)

RHYTHMIC STYLE

MARTELLATO

STACCATO

LEGATO

DYNAMICS

ACCENTS (SFORZATOS)

CRESCENDO AND DECRESCENDO

EXECUTION OF LEAPS

VOWEL MODIFICATION (FOR BLEND AND INTONATION)

When preparing a score for rehearsal, one should sing each vocal part and search each part for technical problems in the above areas. By familiarizing oneself with these problems and the proper solutions before rehearsal, the conductor will be able to keep the rehearsal pace moving and be able to provide the choir with "tools" to fix these problems. Many times, new conductors may hear some of the problems, but they often lack the pedagogical expertise to correct the problem. Hence, the rehearsal pac

MAINTAINING POSTURE FOR CORRECT SINGING: THE FOUNDATION FOR THE INHALATION PROCESS. Examine the score meticulously for those points where the breath must be taken. Rehearse the inhalation process as one counts through the work. Make sure that the breath is being taken low enough and is not shallow. Make sure that the choir is able to set the sound with the breath. This can only be done if the body is able to accept air through correct posture and alignment.

DIAPHRAGM ACTIVITY (FOR DICTION AND FOR ARTICULATION OF THE RHYTHM). The process of using the breath for singing should be taught to the choir as a two-step process. Diaphragm activity is not support. Diaphragm activity is used only for cleaner, sharper diction and accents. If air is only taken into the body to the perceived level of the diaphragm, shallow breath will result. Moreover, if the diaphragm is used to propel the air through the vocal mechanism rather than through the lower "support" mechanism, a harsh, pushed sound will certainly result.

BREATHING: EXHALATION, INHALATION, AND SUPPORT. The manner in which the breath is allowed to fall into the body and the sensation of support for the particular piece of music you will be rehearsing are important to establish for the choir. The choir members need to "feel" what the support sensation is like for that piece of music. They need to connect the feeling of support for that piece to their bodies.

APPROPRIATE RESONANCE FOR THE STYLE OF THE MUSIC. Conductors must hear within themselves an appropriate color or sound for the particular piece that they are going to rehearse before they enter the rehearsal room. That sound is borne out of their own experience and tone preference. An initial decision, however, must be made concerning whether the piece to be rehearsed will require a bright tone color or a dark one.

FIVE PURE VOWELS (WITHOUT DIPHTHONGS) TO MAINTAIN PITCH AND TONE COLOR. As stated earlier, rehearse the piece using the five pure vowels. Do not use diphthongs when rehearsing a piece. Because the choir is not skilled in diphthong execution, poorly executed diphthongs will manifest themselves as a veiled or unusual tone color or a variance in pitch. After the choir has learned the piece on neutral syllables, then move the choir to the text of the piece. Locate all diphthongs in the text and be prepared to teach the proper performance of the diphthong.

FINDING HEAD VOICE (YAWN-SIGH) TO MAINTAIN PROPER TONE COLOR. The conductor must be vigilant that the appropriate amount of head tone is maintained in each respective voice part, regardless of the tessituras of the work. Often, parts that lay low in the tessitura for a voice part, sung without the proper amount of head tone, will immediately result in pitch difficulties, inability to perform a wide range of dynamics, and obvious inconsistencies in tone color.

EXPANDING THE VOCAL TRACT TO ASSURE A FREE, OPEN SINGING SOUND. If a variety of vocal ranges are required to perform the work, maintaining a free vocal tract will present some problems to the conductor.

RANGE EXTENSION AND REGISTER CONSISTENCY AS REQUIRED BY THE PIECE. If extremes of tessitura are required by the work, an approach to range extension and, more importantly, register consistency needs should be addressed. In fact, a choir's ability to maintain register consistency (the same relative color throughout the entire range) is a major determinant of choral tone.

FLEXIBILITY (RUNS). For certain styles of music, especially those pieces in the Baroque and Classical periods, the ability to execute runs is important to the rhythmic clarity of the piece. The choir should be taught the technique of singing *martellato*. When martellato is taught, the conductor will find that the choir is able to sing extended melismas with ease.

RHYTHMIC STYLES. In studying the score, the conductor will make a determination based upon his concept of the piece of the inherent rhythmic style included in the piece. As stated earlier, much work can be accomplished toward that end through the correct choice of neutral syllable and consonant combinations when the work is introduced and taught. Rehearse the inherent rhythm style of the piece, focusing on staccato, legato, dynamics, and accents (sforzatos).

CRESCENDO, DECRESCENDO, AND MESSA DI VOCE. This may seem like an oversimplification, but amateur choirs need to be instructed as to the proper execution of crescendos and decrescendos as they are required by the score. Most amateur choral singers will provide more air (support) to sing a crescendo without dropping the jaw. This results in a harsh, unrealistic crescendo. The use of messa di voce (crescendo and decrescendo on one pitch) heightens the expressive color and the range of emotional expression of the choir. Choirs should be made very familiar with messa di voce and how it is produced. This technique is especially necessary in contrapuntal music.

EXECUTION OF LEAPS. Leaps within all voice parts should be located. The choir should be given the "tools" concerning the execution of leaps. Basically stated, the choir should be taught to drop the jaw and "fishmouth" for every ascending leap. This technique also is the foundation for vowel modification.

VOWEL MODIFICATION (FOR BLEND AND INTONATION). Help must be given to the choir when their voice parts approach extremes in range. This is especially important in both female and treble parts. Failure to deal with vowel modification issues will result in poor tone color in addition to pitch difficulties. In many instances, problems that appear to be inaccurate pitches are simply vowel modification issues.

PREPARING THE TEXT

In addition to making yourself aware of the vocal technique aspects of the score, take considerable time to understand the diction issues of the work you are about to conduct. To understand the diction is to understand the inherent color of the work. For English diction, study Madeleine Marshall, *The Singer's Manual of English Diction*, and for other languages, John Moriarty, *Diction*, both listed in the bibliography.

EXERCISE

Apart from the processes described above, there is a choral score reading program available that gives conductors feedback concerning their ability to detect errors within a choral performance. The program also includes a self-study workbook to help improve one's ability to detect errors. The program is *The Choral Score Reading Program* by Richard F. Grunow and Milford H. Fargo, from GIA Publications, Inc.

Chapter XIV

Giving Meaning to the Music through the Text instead of Taking Meaning

Toward Universal Human Truths in Music

"Technique, wonderful sound . . . all of this is sometimes astonishing—but it is not enough."

"As Western students of Oriental culture have discovered, the First Principle does not lend itself to precise translation," said my Chinese friend, an art historian. "It is something definite, yet it is indescribable. It is how you feel when you enter a room and sense that everything in it is somehow harmonious; you know that you are at peace there. It is how your life seems to change when you fall in love. It is the way in which your spirit comes into subtle accord with the movement of life around you; at the same time it is an experience within yourself—at the very centre. It is active and passive, embracing and releasing; it is a profound sense of being." (P. 1)

Casals: "Real understanding does not come from what we learn in books; it comes from what we learn from love—love of nature, of music, of man. For only what is learned in that way is truly understood." (P. 210)

> David Blum
> *Casals and the Art of Interpretation*

The invention of melody, the disclosure in it of all the deepest secrets of human willing and feeling, is the work of genius, whose effect is more apparent here than anywhere else, is far removed from all reflection and conscious intention, and might be called an inspiration. Here, as everywhere in art, the concept is unproductive. The composer reveals the innermost nature of the world, and expresses the profoundest wisdom in a language that his reasoning faculty does not understand. (P. 260)

Therefore music is by no means like the other arts, namely a copy of the Ideas, but a copy of the will itself, the objectivity of which are the Ideas. For this reason, the effect of the music is so very much more powerful and penetrating than is that of the other arts, for these others speak only of the shadow, but music of the essence. (P. 257)

> Arthur Schopenhauer
> *The World as Will and Representation*

Words divide, tones unite. The unity of existence that the word constantly breaks up, dividing thing from thing, subject from object, is constantly restored in the tone. Music prevents the world from being entirely transformed into language, from becoming nothing but object, and prevents man from becoming nothing but subject. . . . It is certainly no accident that the highest unfolding of the power of tones in modern instrumental music and the highest unfolding of the power of objectifying words in modern science coincided historically with the sharpest divisions ever drawn between subjectivity and objectivity (P. 75).

> Victor Zuckerkandl
> *Man and the Musician, Sound and Symbol*

My life is a story of the self-realisation of the unconscious. (P. 17)

> C. G. Jung
> *Memories, Dreams and Reflections*

The basic ingredient of music is not so much sound as movement. . . . I would even go a step farther, and say that music is significant for us as human beings principally because it embodies movement of a specifically human type that goes to the roots of our being and takes shape in the inner gestures which embody our deepest and most intimate responses. (P. 18–19)

Roger Sessions
The Musical Experience of Composer, Performer and Listener

• • • • •

Perhaps one of the most important tasks for any conductor is to have a viewpoint concerning the composer's intent when the text was set to music. Many conductors simply translate the text and share that literal translation with the choir, using the music as a type of text painting device that paints a musical portrait of the work at hand. Other conductors translate the text and then apply their personal religiosity to that text, irrespective of the composer's point of view.

All the above approaches are certainly better than ignoring the relationship of text to music. However, it is our responsibility as conductors to listen to the music and the text as a total artistic unit, and attempt to give meaning to the text—to search for, if you will, the most profound inner meaning. The approaches noted in the above paragraph simply take meaning from the text and music on a very superficial level. Perhaps it is the way we live our lives, but there is a tendency to take the shortest, quickest route to find an answer in everything we do. Fortunately, great music—and great art in general—does not allow us to do so. There is a profound difference between taking meaning from a text and giving meaning to a text. A conductor's responsibility is to search for a *universal meaning* in each piece that he conducts, a meaning that contains a truth or truths that are applicable to life and living. Whether it be a simple church anthem or a major choral work, it is our responsibility to give meaning to the text so that that meaning derived from the relationship of the text and the music connects in a direct way with the lives of the persons singing the work and those who will hear the work performed.

For example, many choirs sing various arrangements of the American folk Song "Shenandoah." I have heard some conductors talk about the beauty of the Shenandoah river and how the music should move along like a river, and so on. That programmatic approach to interpretation where the music simply illustrates the text will produce a result. However, the truth in the text of "Shenandoah" speaks of a real life truth, separation. Choir members who have experienced separation as part of their lives will be able to bring their life experience to the music. The resulting performance will have an honesty in the sound that reaches the listeners in a direct and profound way.

Often when dealing with biblical or other religious texts, interpretations are frequently arrived at through a literal translation of the text that is filtered through one's personal religiosity. The conductor must look beyond the limitations of her or his own personal religious outlook and try to find within the music a more universal truth concerning the text. If one examines only the text, then one will have limited possibilities for interpretation. But when one studies how the music and the text interact to deepen the meaning, a more universally applicable interpretation that has validity for everyday life will be found.

I often wonder why conductors believe that music performs only a programmatic function rather than speaking to real life truths through its notes. To some degree, as I mentioned above, we are all reflective of the society in which we live. The speed at which we carry on our daily existence and the superficial nature of our lifestyles carry into our music making. If daily life does not demand that we go deeper into ourselves, why should the music we make? Our lives leave little time for inward reflection, time to listen to our own inner voice, which many times holds truth for our own life. But, because we have not been taught in a societal way to trust ourselves, we arrive at surface meanings that do not inherently hold life truths. The educational process for most of us demanded a surface mastery of facts without sufficient time or direction to infer and probe deeper into basic ideas and, most importantly, instincts.

The gift of music is that it has the ability to go beyond the mere literal meaning of words. The quotes of both Schopenhauer and Zukerkandl contained at the beginning of this section illuminate that point eloquently. While it is important for the members of a choir to bring their life experience to any text, it is even more important for the conductors to know where that music sits inside themselves, that is, how the truths of their own life experience locate a place deep within themselves from which music then can sing. It is that innermost place from which all music impulse and honest fantasy come that is communicated through gesture and breath.

CHAPTER XV

TRUST AND CONDUCTING

INTERPRETER OR TRANSMITTER? A FEW FINAL WORDS

Music has not failed us; it is we at times who have failed music. We have depended upon gadgets and gimmicks, methods and procedures—many of which are outdated—to make our music successful. And all the while our principal purpose should be that of allowing the music to speak for itself. (P. 84)

When a mutual and sympathetic understanding of the human spirit is built, people finally become persons. (P. 149).

Howard Swan
Conscience of a Profession

Trust isn't the kind of thing you exactly learn—you either trust or you don't. And when you feel you can't trust, you can't let go. So why is it sometimes so difficult to trust? I've found that there are often obstacles between us and our capacity to trust, and in order to overcome them, we first need to know what they are and how they work. . . .

These three examples indicate three major obstacles to trust: worries about self-image, the feelings that things are out of your control, and doubts and fears about your own ability. (P. 78–79)

> Barry Green
> *The Inner Game of Music*

Only when he no longer knows what he is doing does the painter do good things. (P. 174)

> Edgar Degas
> in *The Artist's Way*, Julia Cameron

Music is your own experience, your thoughts, your wisdom. If you don't live it, it won't come out your horn. (P. 159)

> Charlie Parker
> in *The Artist's Way* Julia Cameron

If we add up "sense of rightness," "tranquillity," "balance," "catharsis," "expressivity," we begin to approach the meaning of "fun." Add to these "participation," "creativity," "order," "sublimation," and "energy release," and you almost have it. Fun is all the things we find it impossible to say when we hear the Opus 131 or witness Letter to the World. (Beethoven and Martha Graham must have had this kind of fun making those works.) Fun is the final goal in the collected aesthetic searchings of David Prall, Dewey, Richards and Santayana. Fun is the "x" of the equation that tries to solve the riddle of why art exists at all. (P. 104)

Every artist copes with reality by means of his fantasy. Fantasy, better known as imagination, is his greatest treasure, his basic equipment for life. And since his work *is* his life, his fantasy is constantly in play. He dreams life. Psychologists tell us that a child's imagination reaches its peak at the age of six or seven, then is gradually inhibited, diminished to conform with the attitudes of his elders—that is, reality. Alas. Perhaps what distinguishes artists from regular folks is that for whatever reasons, their imaginative drive is less inhibited; they have retained in adulthood more of that five-year-old's fantasy than others have. This is not to say that an artist is the childlike madman the old romantic traditions have made him out to be; he is usually capable of brushing his teeth, keeping track of his love life, or counting his change in a taxicab. When I speak of his *fantasy* I am not suggesting a constant state of abstraction, but rather the continuous imaginative powers that inform his creative acts as well as his reactions to the world around him. And out of that creativity, and those imaginative reactions come not idle dreams, but truths— all those abiding truth-formations and constellations that nourish us, from Dante to Joyce, from Bach to the Beatles, from Praxiteles to Picasso. (P. 358–359)

Leonard Bernstein
Findings

Yes, we do need to extend our psychological space. This is one of therapy's main concerns. The soul has shrunk because its imagination has withered, and so we have little psychological space for fantasying, for holding things and mulling, for letting be. Events pass right through us, traceless. Or they press us into tight corners, no room to maneuver, no inner distance. We can hold more in mind than in soul, so that the contents of our minds are largely without psychological significance, input without digestion. "We had the experience but missed the meaning" (T. S. Elliot). (P. 93)

James Hillman
Re-Visioning Psychology

Beginners acquire new theories and techniques until their minds are cluttered with options. Advanced students forget their many options. They allow the theories and techniques that they have learned to recede into the background.

Learn to unclutter your mind. Learn to simplify your work.

As you rely less and less on knowing just what to do, your work will become more direct and more powerful. You will discover that the quality of your consciousness is more potent than any technique or theory of interpretation. (P. 95)

John Heider
The Tao of Leadership

What's the use of disguises and artificialities in a work of art? What counts is what is spontaneous, impulsive. That is the truthful truth. What we impose upon ourselves does not emanate from ourselves. (P. 85)

Pablo Picasso
in *Picasso: In His Words*, Hiro Clark

The solution which I am urging is to eradicate the fatal disconnection of subjects which kills the vitality of our modern curriculum. There is only one subject-matter for education, and that is life in all its manifestations. (P. 18)

Moral education is impossible without the habitual vision of greatness. . . . An atmosphere of excitement, arising from imaginative consideration [of greatness] transforms knowledge. A fact is no longer a bare fact: it is invested with all its possibilities. It is no longer a burden on the memory: it is energized as the poet of our dreams, as the architect of our purposes. (P. 139–140)

Alfred North Whitehead
The Aims of Education and Other Essays

Vaughan Williams once compared a page of music to a railway timetable. The page, he says, tells us no more about the living experience of the music than the timetable tells us about the sights to be enjoyed during the journey. (P. 1)

Peter Le Hurray
Authenticity in Performance

Living is a form of not being sure, not knowing what next or how. The moment you know how, you begin to die a little. The artist never entirely knows. We guess. We may be wrong, but we take leap after leap in the dark. (P. 121)

Agnes de Mille
in *The Artist's Way*, Julia Cameron

Most people like music because it gives them certain emotions, such as joy, grief, sadness, an image of nature, a subject for daydreams, or—still better—oblivion from "everyday life." They want a drug "dope." It matters little whether this way of thinking of music is expressed directly or is wrapped up in a veil of artificial circumlocutions. Music would not be worth much if it were reduced to such an end. When people have learned to love music for itself, when they listen with other ears, their enjoyment will be of a far higher and more potent order, and they will be able to judge it on a higher plane and realize its intrinsic value. Obviously such an attitude presupposes a certain degree of musical development and intellectual culture, but that is not very difficult of attainment. Unfortunately, the teaching of music, with a few exceptions, is bad from the beginning. One only has to think about the sentimental twaddle so often talked about Chopin, Beethoven, and even about Bach—and that in schools for the training of professional musicians! Those tedious commentaries on the side issues of music not only do not facilitate its understanding, but, on the contrary, are a serious obstacle which prevents the understanding of its essence and substance. (p. 163)

Igor Stravinsky
An Autobiography

Imagination is more important than knowledge. (P. 131)

Albert Einstein
in *The Artist's Way*, Julia Cameron

There flows from music irrespective of its ever-changing emotional expression an unchanging message of comfort. . . . Music as an element has an optimistic quality and I believe that therein lies the source of my innate optimism. . . . I have been vouchsafed the grace to be a servant of music. It has been a beacon on my way and has kept me in the direction towards which I have been striving—darkly when I was a child, consciously later. There lies my hope and my confidence. (P. 344)

Bruno Walter
Theme and Variations

The essential point here is that there are several stages of creative thought: first, a stage of preparation in which the problem is consciously worked over; then a period of incubation without any conscious concentration upon the problem; and then the illumination which is later justified by logic. The parallel between these important and complex problems and the simple problems of judging weights or the circle-triangle series is obvious. The period of preparation is essentially the setting up of a complex struction together with conscious attention to the materials on which the struction is to work. But then the actual process of reasoning, the dark leap into huge discovery, just as in the simple trivial judgement of weights, has no representation in consciousness. Indeed, it is sometimes almost as if the problem had to be forgotten to be solved. (P. 44)

But more complex reasoning without consciousness is continually going on. Our minds work much faster than consciousness can keep up with.

We commonly make general assertions based on our past experiences in an automatic way, and only as an afterthought are sometimes able to retrieve any of the past experiences on which an assertion is based. How often we reach sound conclusions and are unable to justify them! Because reasoning is not conscious. And consider the kind of reasoning that we do about others' feelings and character, or in reasoning out the motives of others from their actions. These are clearly the result of automatic inferences by our nervous systems which consciousness is not only unnecessary, but, as we have seen in the performance of motor skills, would probably hinder the process. (P. 42)

> Julian Jaynes
> *The Origin of Consciousness*
> *in the Breakdown of the Bicameral Mind*

And what I had observed with a patient in England, a musicologist with profound amnesia from a temporal lobe encephalitis, unable to remember events or facts for more than a few seconds, but able to remember, and indeed to learn, elaborate musical pieces, to conduct them, to perform them, and even to improvise at the organ. This patient is the subject of a remarkable BBC film made by Jonathan Miller, *Prisoner of Consciousness* (November, 1988). (P. 65)

> Oliver Sacks
> *An Anthropologist on Mars*

"When I studied physics in Taiwan," said Huang, "we called it Wu Li (pronounced Woo Lee). It means Patterns of Organic Energy." (P. 31)

My western education left me unable to accept a nondefinition for the definition of "Master," so I began to read Huang's book, *Embrace Tiger, Return to Mountain*. There, in the foreword by Alan Watts in a paragraph describing Al Huang, I found what I sought. Said Alan Watts of Al Huang:

> He begins from the center and not from the fringe. He imparts an understanding of the basic principles of the art before going on to the meticulous details, and he refuses to break down the t'ai chi movements into a one-two-three drill so as to make the student into a robot. The traditional way . . . is to teach by rote, and to give the impression that long periods of boredom are the most essential part of training. In that way a student may go on for years without ever getting the feel of what he is doing.

Here was just the definition of Master that I sought. A Master teaches essence. When the essence is perceived, he teaches what is necessary to expand the perception. (P. 35)

I asked Huang how he structures his classes.

"Every lesson is the first lesson," he told me. "Every time we dance, we do it for the first time."

"But surely you cannot be starting new each lesson," I said. "Lesson number two must be built on what you taught in lesson number one, and lesson three likewise must be built on lessons one and two, and so on."

"When I say that every lesson is the first lesson," he replied, "it does not mean that we forget what we already know. It means that what we are doing is always new, because we are always doing it for the first time."

This is another characteristic of a Master. Whatever he does, he does with the enthusiasm of doing it for the first time. This is the source of unlimited energy. Every lesson that he teaches (or learns) is a first lesson. Every dance that he dances, he dances for the first time. It is always new, personal and alive. (P. 35–36)

Gary Zukav
The Dancing Wu Li Masters

By soul I mean, first of all, a perspective rather than a substance, a viewpoint toward things rather than a thing itself. The perspective is reflective; it mediates events and makes differences between ourselves and everything that happens. Between us and events, between the doer and the deed, there is a reflective moment—and soul-making means differentiating this middle ground.

It is as if consciousness rests upon a self-sustaining and imagining substrate—an inner place or deeper person or ongoing presence—that is simply there even when our subjectivity, ego, and consciousness go into eclipse. Soul appears as a factor independent of the events in which we are immersed. Though I cannot identify soul with anything else, I can never grasp it by itself apart from other things, perhaps it is like a reflection in a flowing mirror, or like the moon which mediates only borrowed light. But just this peculiar and paradoxical intervening variable gives one the sense of having or being a soul. However intangible and indefinable it is, soul carries highest importance in hierarchies of human values, frequently being identified with the principle of life and even dignity. (P. 20–21)

James Hillman
in *A Blue Fire*, Thomas Moore

People usually complain that music is so ambiguous, that it leaves them in such doubt as to what they are supposed to think, whereas words can be understood by everyone. But to me it seems exactly the opposite. (P. 170)

Felix Mendelssohn
in *The Musician's World*, Hans Gal

•••••

This book has taken an a traditional approach to the teaching of the fundamentals of conducting. Whether you are a trained musician with a college degree or degrees, or the conductor of a church choir, there is a common factor that links us all as conductors and musicians. For those of us who were trained within a college or conservatory atmosphere, there is a tendency for us to look to professors and those with whom we study for musical answers to our musical questions. Certainly, these persons can broaden our musical experience, but many of us try, through conducting, to replicate performances that they directed or molded. We look outside of ourselves for musical ideas and musical answers. If we do this often enough, without realizing it, we develop a musical insecurity and dependence upon others for musical ideas.

Many church musicians I have known, especially those who do not possess music degrees, believe that because they do not have "professional" training, they can never be "legitimate" conductors. They continually doubt their own natural instincts and justify that doubt because of the lack of a formalized and extended education in music. They, too, take conducting courses with the hope of learning how to "conduct," but continually apologize because of their inexperience. Experience in conducting study is usually correlated with their own perception of their musicianship. They are constantly worried about where their hands go.

What is common to both the professionally trained conductor and the novice conductor is that, early on in their study, gesture takes precedent over listening. Moreover, conducting is taught to them devoid of sound. So, they learn gesture devoid of sound and that the execution of the "correct conducting gesture" is most important. Many times, such conductors do not listen. Because they are not listening to the music being shared with them, they are also inadvertently closing themselves off from their own musical voice. They are not listening to their ensemble nor are they listening to their instincts.

Like it or not, all of us must realize and accept the fact that while we may be able to recreate another conductor's performance, our first responsibility is to allow the singers who sing for us to sing. We need to listen to their singing and learn from it. We need to listen to our own inner voice, which is our innermost personal musical idea. At all times, we must both listen to the music within us and learn to trust that inner music voice. While great teachers can broaden our musical experiences, in the end we can rely only on what speaks inside of us if the music is to be both spontaneous and believable. Any dishonesty about the origin of music will manifest itself in the tone of the choir. It will be manifest in their rhythm and in their diction. Their spirits will not be able to speak through the composer.

The conductor must trust the choir to sing. He must trust his innermost musical voice. He must find ways to go deeper inside himself for the musical answers and avoid looking outside himself. He needs to allow the music to speak so that it can speak to him and to the choir. Each one of us must learn to trust and listen to our own musical instincts. It is from that trust and listening that great music making is born.

But ultimately, if one listens, a unique transformation can take place in the way one learns conducting. Instead of learning gesture via a conducting class or a favored professor, the sound can become your teacher. If you are willing to trust the choir to sing, have begun to listen without bias, and can accept the responsibility that sounds from the choir are a direct result of the influence of your gesture, then the sound, the musical voice of each composer, can be your teacher. Great conductors have learned that the sound of their ensemble is their best teacher.

PART II

LITERATURE FOR STUDY AND SELF-EVALUATION

USE OF RATING SCALES

The measurement and evaluation of performance often is subjective. While the evaluation of performance will ultimately be subjective, some objective measures can be used to improve aspects of conducting, which can directly impact upon performance. Presented in this chapter are rating scales with each piece that is suggested for study so that you can measure and evaluate specific skills.

With each of the scales suggested for each of the pieces, you should measure yourself based upon the criteria listed in each scale. Videotape yourself conducting the exercise listed at the top of the measurement sheet. A grade of 4 is the high score, while the grade of 0 is a low score. A score of 2 on the rating scale should denote what average achievement should be in that category. While the ideal would be to achieve a 4 in all categories, the purpose of these scales is simply to identify, or *measure*, areas that are in need of improvement. Often times in the study of conducting, specific technical issues are not sufficiently isolated during the process; hence, progress is achieved, but at a much slower pace. These rating scales can be used for self-evaluation by the student, or they can be used by the instructor to give appropriate and objective feedback to the student. For a detailed explanation concerning the use and construction of rating scales, the reader is referred to *Learning Sequences in Music* (1993) by Edwin Gordon, pages 342–348.

REMINDERS ABOUT
SCORE PREPARATION

One of the challenges of studying the art of conducting is that, unlike study on the voice or an instrument, you cannot practice on the instrument that you are studying. The absence of an ensemble with which to practice conducting issues is a distinct problem! While there is no substitute for conducting an ensemble, there are certain techniques that can be used to maintain a connection between gesture and sound. For each example that you study, it is important to keep the following practice principles in mind.

1. *Always practice conducting from the same body alignment position that you will be using when you conduct. There is an intimate, direct, and powerful connection between body posture and the music learning and conducting process.* You must realize that because music speaks through our entire being, every time a piece of music is performed or prepared for conducting, the body's "muscle memory" will recreate the exact body posture, body attitude, and spirit that existed as the music was being learned. From the beginning of the study of conducting, the student of conducting should view score preparation as both an aural and kinesthetic exercise. The kinesthetic attitude of the body is established simultaneously when the initial learning of the score takes place; that is, if one learns a score in a slouched seated position, it is very likely that the major aspects of that posture will return subconsciously when the music is sounded. Many times it is difficult to establish a correct body alignment when posture and music learning have been unknowingly associated in this fashion.

2. *Make certain that you breathe as if you were conducting. Open the body and let breath drop into the body. Inhale for the "preparation" to start the piece and exhale while you are conducting.*

3. *Never practice conducting gesture that is not intimately connected to sound.*

4. *At the very least, practice conducting with a partner to experience the music making with another person.* It is important that after the initial preparation of mate-

rials has been accomplished through singing and conducting, one conducts at least one other person to experience the human connection that occurs as one participates in the music making process as conductor-singer. By using a partner, you can also gain valuable feedback concerning whether what you are doing is effective in achieving the desired musical result.

5. *When you conduct other persons, let the sound be your teacher.* As you conduct your partner or a group of persons, remember that the sounds that you hear are directly reflective of your body and gesture. It is important to establish a high level of honesty with regard to this aspect of conducting practice. If the sound coming back to you is not what you want, you must be willing to accept that the sound is a mirror image of your conducting. When the sound is not "good," try to change it more toward your ideal by understanding the interrelationship of gesture to sound. Ultimately, the goal of any conducting teacher is to move the students to the point where they can teach themselves through listening to the sounds that are shared with them and through them by the choir.

6. *Listen to the breath of those you conduct.* The most basic of connections to the choir is established at the moment inhalation takes place in both the conductor and the choir. The moment at which sound is released from the singers can only be forecast through listening to the breath of the ensemble. Not only must the conductor listen to the breath in the choir, but choir members must listen to each other breathe so as to establish a sense of ensemble. That sense of ensemble begins in the communal breath.

7. *Sing and conduct when preparing musical materials for conducting class.* The feeling of what it is to sing a phrase and the feeling of sound being released from the body are the "feelings" and "body attitudes" that need to be relayed to and reinforced in singers. Conducting gesture is reflective of what we feel as a singer as the phrase is being recreated; that is, gesture comes from the inside out. If one "plans" the geometry of one's conducting, it will never allow for spontaneous music making. Sing the music. Experience what it feels like to sing that phrase. Then, conduct while singing. Next, conduct without singing and maintain the same body feeling that you had when you were singing. You will find that learning conducting "technique" can be an effortless process when pursued in this way.

EXERCISE ONE:
EXPERIENCING LEGATO SOUNDS

Take both arms and move them horizontally, exhaling as you move them. Imagine mixing bubble bath into the water before a bath. Now do the same gesture vertically while you continue to sigh an *oo* sound. Lift your hands upward as you breathe (imagine a marionetteer working your hands with strings) and release your *oo* sound when you are full of air at the appropriate time at the top of the upward gesture. You knew when the sound should begin because you felt it within your body. You can feel the release of the sound within your body. Now, instead of the large external vertical movement outside of your body, minimize the large vertical gesture and place most of the movement *inside* your body. Do only as much gesturing as will help facilitate and evoke the sound. Concentrate on the movement of air inside your body and relax the muscularity of the gesture so that it reflects the sound your choir is to produce. Now sing *noo*. Make sure the gesture stays ahead of the sound. As you take the breath, be certain that you take the breath in the tempo you want and do not slow down. In legato passages, it is often the tendency to take slower and slower breaths, thereby impacting the tempo dramatically. As you move your hands on *noo*, begin to move them more horizontally than vertically and mirror the sound. Imagine you are a cellist bowing this legato sound.

LEGATO RATING SCALE

Videotape yourself conducting this exercise with singers. View the videotape and use the rating scale below to measure your progress. You may need to view the tape several times to accurately measure yourself in some of the areas. Evaluate the specific areas for which you need improvement. Tape yourself again, trying to improve your performance in those areas that were in need of improvement.

NAME_____

4 = high 0 = low	Trial 1	Trial 2
Alignment	4 3 2 1 0	4 3 2 1 0
Neck is released	4 3 2 1 0	4 3 2 1 0
Wrists are released	4 3 2 1 0	4 3 2 1 0
Openness of gesture	4 3 2 1 0	4 3 2 1 0
Arm position	4 3 2 1 0	4 3 2 1 0

Correct anticipatory position for air to enter body	4 3 2 1 0	4 3 2 1 0
Opens body for breath	4 3 2 1 0	4 3 2 1 0
Releases breath into ensemble sound	4 3 2 1 0	4 3 2 1 0
Breath impulse gesture present	4 3 2 1 0	4 3 2 1 0
Breath (inhalation) in character of the music	4 3 2 1 0	4 3 2 1 0
Facial breath countenance	4 3 2 1 0	4 3 2 1 0
Release of sound	4 3 2 1 0	4 3 2 1 0
Arm and shoulder freedom	4 3 2 1 0	4 3 2 1 0

Overall Evaluation   (Average)   _____   _____

EXERCISE TWO:
Experiencing Staccato Sounds

Perform the same exercise as in exercise 1, but this time substitute the forte word *tee* for the forte word *noo*. Breathe and speak seven forte *tees*. When you breathe, the breath should go deep into your pelvis, well below your navel. *Listen to sound that you produce*. Describe the intensity and quality of that forte staccato sound. As you breathe with the energy of a staccato and conduct the staccato, notice that as you take the breath your arms move upward and slightly outward, with the predominant motion moving straight upward from your elbow hinge with no shoulder involvement. Your arms then drop straight down in a free fall without any muscular holding. At the point at which you speak *tee*, your hands, led by your third fingers, move quickly and decisively into the center of the beat, similar to a quick dabbing gesture. Use the marcato beat pattern for staccato, but with less weight in the gesture. The hands do not slide forward or swing away from the beat; they fall straight down and rebound straight up.

If you find yourself skimming the beat, hold your left forearm out in front of you. Speak the word *dab* and drop your right forearm on your left forearm. In staccato, you will notice that your right forearm thrusts into your left forearm. Feel the release of your arms straight upward after the staccato is articulated.

Also check your arm position. For a forte staccato sound, your arms should reflect the quality and depth of the sound that your body desires as reflected in the breath. If the arms are held too high, then a forte staccato character of sound cannot be achieved by the choir. If you imagine that you are carrying two large paper sacks of groceries, your arms will assume a lower, and rounder, arm position. When conducting a forte staccato, your arms should similarly reflect a lower, rounder sound seated low in the body.

Size of beat for forte sounds. In the exercises, you need to monitor the relationship of the size of beat to the quantity of sound. A large beat pattern does not necessarily produce a large, forte sound. It is the intensity of the breath and its corresponding gesture that imparts the character of the dynamic to the singer. If the inside of the body is forte, then the gesture will reflect forte. Dynamics are not merely a question of volume; they are changes of intensity borne out of the breath.

Note: It is important that staccato articulations—and marcato articulations in the next exercise—stay in motion at all times for the sound to continue forward! The further you move gesturally away from the impulse gesture or ictus, the slower the velocity of the gesture, and the more vague the gesture becomes.

STACCATO RATING SCALE

Videotape yourself conducting this exercise with singers. View the videotape and use the rating scale below to measure your progress. You may need to view the tape several times to accurately measure yourself in some of the areas. Evaluate the specific areas for which you need improvement. Tape yourself again, trying to improve your performance in those areas that were in need of improvement.

NAME _____

4 = high 0 = low	Trial 1	Trial 2
Alignment	4 3 2 1 0	4 3 2 1 0
Neck is released	4 3 2 1 0	4 3 2 1 0
Wrists are released	4 3 2 1 0	4 3 2 1 0
Openness of gesture	4 3 2 1 0	4 3 2 1 0
Arm position	4 3 2 1 0	4 3 2 1 0
Correct anticipatory position for air to enter body	4 3 2 1 0	4 3 2 1 0
Opens body for breath	4 3 2 1 0	4 3 2 1 0
Releases breath into ensemble sound	4 3 2 1 0	4 3 2 1 0
Breath impulse gesture present	4 3 2 1 0	4 3 2 1 0
Breath (inhalation) in character of the music	4 3 2 1 0	4 3 2 1 0
Facial breath countenance	4 3 2 1 0	4 3 2 1 0
Release of sound	4 3 2 1 0	4 3 2 1 0
Arm and shoulder freedom	4 3 2 1 0	4 3 2 1 0

Overall Evaluation   (Average)   _____   _____

EXERCISE THREE:
EXPERIENCING MARCATO SOUNDS

Perform the same exercise as in exercise 1, but this time substitute the forte word *dah* for the forte word *noo*. Breathe and speak seven forte *dah*s. When you breathe, the breath should go deep into your pelvis, well below your navel. *Listen to sound that you produce.* Describe the intensity and quality of that forte marcato sound. The marcato sound is characterized by a rhythmic thrust behind the sound followed by a decay of the sound. Perform the marcato *dah* exercise again, this time making note of the thrust and decay of the sound that defines a marcato articulation. As you now breathe with the energy of a marcato and conduct the marcato, notice that with the taking of the breath your arms move upward, with the predominant motion moving straight upward from your elbow hinge. Your arms then drop straight down in a free fall without any muscular holding. At the point at which you speak *dah*, your hands, led by your third fingers, sink clearly and decisively into the center of the beat. The hands do not slide forward or swing away from the beat; they fall straight down and rebound straight up. Also notice that the marcato syllable *dah* cannot sound like the staccato syllable *tee*. With a marcato, you thrust into the "gut," or center, of sound for the marcato articulation, which is then followed immediately by a decay of the sound.

If you find yourself skimming the beat, hold your left forearm out in front of you. Speak the word *dah* and drop your right forearm on your left forearm. In marcato, you will notice that your right forearm thrusts into your left forearm. Feel the release of your arms straight upward after the marcato is articulated.

Also check your arm position. For a forte marcato sound, your arms should reflect the quality and depth of the sound that your body desires as reflected in the breath. If the arms are held too high, then a forte marcato character of sound cannot be achieved by the choir. If you imagine that you are carrying two large paper sacks of groceries, your arms will assume a lower, and rounder, arm position. When conducting a forte marcato, your arms should similarly reflect a lower, rounder sound seated low in the body.

Size of beat for forte sounds. In the exercises, you need to monitor the relationship of the size of beat to the quantity of sound. A large beat pattern does not necessarily produce a large sound. It is the intensity of the breath and its corresponding gesture that imparts the character of the dynamic to the singer. Dynamics are not merely a question of volume; they are changes of intensity borne out of the breath.

Note: It is important that staccato and marcato articulations stay in motion at all times for the sound to continue forward! The further you move gesturally away from the impulse gesture or ictus, the slower the velocity of the gesture.

MARCATO RATING SCALE

Videotape yourself conducting this exercise with singers. View the videotape and use the rating scale below to measure your progress. You may need to view the tape several times to accurately measure yourself in some of the areas. Evaluate the specific areas for which you need improvement. Tape yourself again, trying to improve your performance in those areas that were in need of improvement.

NAME _____

4 = high 0 = low	Trial 1	Trial 2
Alignment	4 3 2 1 0	4 3 2 1 0
Neck is released	4 3 2 1 0	4 3 2 1 0
Wrists are released	4 3 2 1 0	4 3 2 1 0
Openness of gesture	4 3 2 1 0	4 3 2 1 0
Arm position	4 3 2 1 0	4 3 2 1 0
Correct anticipatory position for air to enter body	4 3 2 1 0	4 3 2 1 0
Opens body for breath	4 3 2 1 0	4 3 2 1 0
Releases breath into ensemble sound	4 3 2 1 0	4 3 2 1 0
Breath impulse gesture present	4 3 2 1 0	4 3 2 1 0
Breath (inhalation) in character of the music	4 3 2 1 0	4 3 2 1 0
Facial breath countenance	4 3 2 1 0	4 3 2 1 0
Release of sound	4 3 2 1 0	4 3 2 1 0
Arm and shoulder freedom	4 3 2 1 0	4 3 2 1 0

Overall Evaluation   (Average)   _____   _____

Staccato/Legato/Marcato Rating Scale

Now combine the previous three exercises into one continuous exercise: three beats of *tee* followed by a breath, three beats of *noo* followed by a breath, and three beats of *dah*. Use the rating scale below to measure your progress.

NAME_____

4 = high 0 = low	Trial 1	Trial 2
Alignment	4 3 2 1 0	4 3 2 1 0
Neck is released	4 3 2 1 0	4 3 2 1 0
Wrists are released	4 3 2 1 0	4 3 2 1 0
Openness of gesture	4 3 2 1 0	4 3 2 1 0
Arm position	4 3 2 1 0	4 3 2 1 0
Correct anticipatory position for air to enter body	4 3 2 1 0	4 3 2 1 0
Opens body for breath	4 3 2 1 0	4 3 2 1 0
Releases breath into ensemble sound	4 3 2 1 0	4 3 2 1 0
Breath impulse gesture present	4 3 2 1 0	4 3 2 1 0
Breath (inhalation) in character of the music	4 3 2 1 0	4 3 2 1 0
Facial breath countenance	4 3 2 1 0	4 3 2 1 0
Release of sound	4 3 2 1 0	4 3 2 1 0
Arm and shoulder freedom	4 3 2 1 0	4 3 2 1 0
Ictus is clearly in the third fingertip of each hand	4 3 2 1 0	4 3 2 1 0
Gesture is ahead of the sound	4 3 2 1 0	4 3 2 1 0

Overall Evaluation   (Average)   _____   _____

EXERCISE FOUR:
THESAURUS MUSICUS:
MY COUNTRY, 'TIS OF THEE

STUDY GUIDE

"My Country, 'Tis of Thee" contains the following issues for conducting study:

- anticipatory position
- impulse gesture and corresponding breath
- facial countenance when breath is taken
- openness of body prior to breathing
- release of breath into the choral sound
- release of sound
- exhalation of air while conducting
- reception of and reaction to sound
- listening
- use of a three-beat pattern in which beat 2 is expansive
- use of a legato three-beat pattern
- use of a conducting gesture that is not held and with no subdivision
- gesture ahead of the sound to allow for rhythmic spontaneity
- breath cue technique between phrases
- breathing the textural color of the piece and contrasting phrases
- decisions concerning the length of consonants
- "conducting" of consonants
- conducting a final release that is in the character of that consonant

MY COUNTRY, 'TIS OF THEE

1. My coun - try, 'tis of thee, Sweet land of
2. My na - tive coun - try, thee, Land of the
3. Let mu - sic swell the breeze, And ring from
4. Our fa - thers' God, to thee, Au - thor of

lib - er - ty, Of thee I sing; Land where my
no - ble, free; Thy name I love; I love thy
all the trees Sweet free - dom's song; Let mor - tal
lib - er - ty, To thee we sing; Long may our

fa - thers died, Land of the pil - grim's pride,
rocks and rills, Thy woods and tem - pled hills;
tongues a - wake; Let all that breathe par - take;
land be bright With free - dom's ho - ly light;

From ev - 'ry moun - tain - side Let free - dom ring!
My heart with rap - ture thrills, Like that a - bove.
Let rocks their si - lence break, The sound pro - long.
Pro - tect us by thy might, Great God, our King.

Text: Samuel F. Smith, 1808-1895
Tune: AMERICA, 66 4 666 4; *Thesaurus Musicus*, 1744

RATING SCALE
THESAURUS MUSICUS:
MY COUNTRY, 'TIS OF THEE

Videotape yourself conducting this exercise with singers. View the videotape and use the rating scale below to measure your progress. You may need to view the tape several times to accurately measure yourself in some of the areas. Evaluate the specific areas for which you need improvement. Tape yourself again, trying to improve your performance in those areas that were in need of improvement.

NAME_____

4 = high 0 = low	Trial 1	Trial 2
Alignment	4 3 2 1 0	4 3 2 1 0
Spaciousness across chest	4 3 2 1 0	4 3 2 1 0
Neck is released	4 3 2 1 0	4 3 2 1 0
Wrists are released	4 3 2 1 0	4 3 2 1 0
Openness of gesture	4 3 2 1 0	4 3 2 1 0
Arm position	4 3 2 1 0	4 3 2 1 0
Correct anticipatory position for air to enter body	4 3 2 1 0	4 3 2 1 0
Opens body for breath	4 3 2 1 0	4 3 2 1 0
Releases breath into ensemble sound	4 3 2 1 0	4 3 2 1 0
Breath impulse gesture present	4 3 2 1 0	4 3 2 1 0
Breath (inhalation) in character of the music	4 3 2 1 0	4 3 2 1 0
Facial breath countenance	4 3 2 1 0	4 3 2 1 0
Release of sound	4 3 2 1 0	4 3 2 1 0
Arm and shoulder freedom	4 3 2 1 0	4 3 2 1 0
Ictus is clearly in the third fingertip of each hand	4 3 2 1 0	4 3 2 1 0
Gesture is ahead of the sound	4 3 2 1 0	4 3 2 1 0
Correct patter is maintained throughout	4 3 2 1 0	4 3 2 1 0

Overall Evaluation   (Average)   _____   _____

EXERCISE FIVE:
STANFORD: WHEN, IN OUR MUSIC, GOD IS GLORIFIED

STUDY GUIDE

"When, in Our Music, God Is Glorified" contains the following issues for conducting study:

- anticipatory position
- beginning with the accompaniment and then executing breath cue on beat one
- impulse gesture and corresponding breath
- facial countenance when breath is taken
- release of sound
- exhalation of air while conducting
- openness of the body prior to breathing
- release of breath into the choral sound
- reception of and reaction to sound
- use of a conducting gesture that is supportive of vocal technique needed for choir to sing octave leap
- use of impelling gesture in fingertips (dab) on the dotted rhythm values to impel musical line forward
- listening
- gesture ahead of the sound to allow for rhythmic spontaneity
- use of a four-beat pattern in which beat 3 is expansive
- use of a legato four-beat pattern
- use of a conducting gesture that is not held and with no subdivision
- breath cue technique between phrases
- breathing the textural color of the piece and contrasting phrases
- decisions concerning the length of consonants
- "conducting" of consonants
- conducting a final release that is in the character of the vowel without a consonant to end the sound
- final whole note should be treated as a fermata, then released

WHEN, IN OUR MUSIC, GOD IS GLORIFIED

1. When, in our mu - sic, God is glo - ri - fied,
2. How of - ten, mak - ing mu - sic, we have found
3. So has the Church, in lit - ur - gy and song,
4. And did not Je - sus sing a psalm that night
5. Let ev - 'ry in - stru-ment be tuned for praise!

And ad - o - ra - tion leaves no room for pride,
A new di - men - sion in the world of sound,
In faith and love, through cen - tu - ries of wrong,
When ut - most e - vil strove a - gainst the Light?
Let all re - joice who have a voice to raise!

It is as though the whole cre - a - tion cried:
As wor - ship moved us to a more pro - found
Borne wit - ness to the truth in ev - 'ry tongue:
Then let us sing, for whom he won the fight:
And may God give us faith to sing al - ways:

Tune: ENGELBERG, 10 10 10 with alleluia; Charles V. Stanford, 1852 1924

RATING SCALE
STANFORD: WHEN, IN OUR MUSIC, GOD IS GLORIFIED

Videotape yourself conducting this hymn with singers and accompaniment. View the videotape and use the rating scale below to measure your progress. You may need to view the tape several times to accurately measure yourself in some of the areas. Evaluate the specific areas for which you need improvement. Tape yourself again, trying to improve your performance in those areas that were in need of improvement.

NAME_____

4 = high 0 = low	Trial 1	Trial 2
Alignment	4 3 2 1 0	4 3 2 1 0
Spaciousness across chest	4 3 2 1 0	4 3 2 1 0
Neck is released	4 3 2 1 0	4 3 2 1 0
Wrists are released	4 3 2 1 0	4 3 2 1 0
Openness of gesture	4 3 2 1 0	4 3 2 1 0
Arm position	4 3 2 1 0	4 3 2 1 0
Correct anticipatory position for air to enter body	4 3 2 1 0	4 3 2 1 0
Opens body for breath	4 3 2 1 0	4 3 2 1 0
Releases breath into ensemble sound	4 3 2 1 0	4 3 2 1 0
Breath impulse gesture present	4 3 2 1 0	4 3 2 1 0
Breath (inhalation) in character of the music	4 3 2 1 0	4 3 2 1 0
Facial breath countenance	4 3 2 1 0	4 3 2 1 0
Release of sound	4 3 2 1 0	4 3 2 1 0
Arm and shoulder freedom	4 3 2 1 0	4 3 2 1 0
Ictus is clearly in the third fingertip of each hand	4 3 2 1 0	4 3 2 1 0
Gesture is ahead of the sound	4 3 2 1 0	4 3 2 1 0
Correct patter is maintained throughout	4 3 2 1 0	4 3 2 1 0
Expansiveness in gesture that allows line to sing	4 3 2 1 0	4 3 2 1 0
Breaths between phrases that combine the final consonant with inhalation	4 3 2 1 0	4 3 2 1 0
Evidence of texture in hands	4 3 2 1 0	4 3 2 1 0
Final release	4 3 2 1 0	4 3 2 1 0
Locking of gesture not evident	4 3 2 1 0	4 3 2 1 0
Overall Evaluation (Average)	_____	_____

EXERCISE SIX:
BOURGEOUIS: NEW SONGS OF CELEBRATION RENDER

STUDY GUIDE

"New Songs of Celebration Render" contains the following issues for conducting study:

- anticipatory position
- beginning with the accompaniment and choir together
- impulse gesture and corresponding breath
- facial countenance when breath is taken
- release of sound
- release of breath into the choral sound
- openness of the body prior to breathing
- reception of and reaction to sound
- listening
- breathing the textural color of the piece and contrasting phrases
- gesture ahead of the sound to allow for rhythmic spontaneity
- use of a four-beat pattern in which beat 3 is expansive
- use of a legato four-beat pattern
- use of a conducting gesture that is not held and with no subdivision
- breath cue technique between phrases
- decisions concerning the length of consonants
- "conducting" of consonants
- conducting a final release that is in the character of the vowel without a consonant to end the sound

NEW SONGS OF CELEBRATION RENDER

1. New songs of cel - e - bra - tion ren - der To him who has great
2. Joy - ful - ly, heart - i - ly re - sound - ing, Let ev - 'ry in - stru -
3. Riv - ers and seas and tor - rents roar - ing, Hon - or the Lord with

won - ders done; Love sits en - throned in age - less
ment and voice Peal out the praise of grace a -
wild ac - claim; Moun - tains and stones, look up a -

splen - dor; Come and a - dore the might - y One.
bound - ing, Call - ing the whole world to re - joice.
dor - ing, And find a voice to praise his name.

He has made known his great sal - va - tion
Trum - pets and or - gans, set in mo - tion
Right - eous, com - mand - ing, ev - er glo - rious,

Which all his friends with joy con - fess.
Such sounds as make the heav - ens ring;
Prais - es be his that nev - er cease:

He has re - vealed to ev - 'ry na - tion
All things that live in earth and o - cean
Just is our God, whose truth vic - to - rious

His ev - er - last - ing right - eous - ness.
Make mu - sic for your might - y King.
Es - tab - lish - es the world in peace.

Text: Psalm 98; Erik Routley, 1917-1982
Tune: RENDEZ À DIEU, 9 8 9 8 D; *Strasbourg Psalter*, 1545, rev. in *Genevan Psalter*, 1551; harm. by John W. Wilson, b.1905
© 1974, Hope Publishing Co., Carol Stream, IL 60188. All rights reserved. Used by permission.

RATING SCALE
BOURGEOIS: NEW SONGS
OF CELEBRATION RENDER

Videotape yourself conducting this hymn with singers and accompaniment. View the videotape and use the rating scale below to measure your progress. You may need to view the tape several times to accurately measure yourself in some of the areas. Evaluate the specific areas for which you need improvement. Tape yourself again, trying to improve your performance in those areas that were in need of improvement.

NAME _____

4 = high 0 = low	Trial 1	Trial 2
Alignment	4 3 2 1 0	4 3 2 1 0
Spaciousness across chest	4 3 2 1 0	4 3 2 1 0
Neck is released	4 3 2 1 0	4 3 2 1 0
Wrists are released	4 3 2 1 0	4 3 2 1 0
Openness of gesture	4 3 2 1 0	4 3 2 1 0
Arm position	4 3 2 1 0	4 3 2 1 0
Correct anticipatory position for air to enter body	4 3 2 1 0	4 3 2 1 0
Opens body for breath	4 3 2 1 0	4 3 2 1 0
Releases breath into ensemble sound	4 3 2 1 0	4 3 2 1 0
Breath impulse gesture present	4 3 2 1 0	4 3 2 1 0
Breath (inhalation) in character of the music	4 3 2 1 0	4 3 2 1 0
Facial breath countenance	4 3 2 1 0	4 3 2 1 0
Release of sound	4 3 2 1 0	4 3 2 1 0
Arm and shoulder freedom	4 3 2 1 0	4 3 2 1 0
Ictus is clearly in the third fingertip of each hand	4 3 2 1 0	4 3 2 1 0
Gesture is ahead of the sound	4 3 2 1 0	4 3 2 1 0
Correct patter is maintained throughout	4 3 2 1 0	4 3 2 1 0
Expansiveness in gesture that allows line to sing	4 3 2 1 0	4 3 2 1 0
Breaths between phrases that combine the final consonant with inhalation	4 3 2 1 0	4 3 2 1 0
Evidence of texture in hands	4 3 2 1 0	4 3 2 1 0
Final release	4 3 2 1 0	4 3 2 1 0
Locking of gesture not evident	4 3 2 1 0	4 3 2 1 0
Overall Evaluation (Average)	_____	_____

EXERCISE SEVEN: VULPIUS: LO, HOW A ROSE E'ER BLOOMING

First, conduct the canon as a unison exercise. Breathe at the appropriate points. Use the experience with the single voice to understand the shape and direction of the line. After the single line is mastered, then move on to performing the work in a four-part canon.

A note on the performance of the fermatas: This canon is meant to be performed in three or four parts. Each entrance of a new start for the canon should occur at the first fermata, with the conductor breathing for each entrance. The canon should be taught by the conductor singing through the tune. Treat the fermatas only as breaths; that is, breathe after each one when performing the tune.

STUDY GUIDE

The Vulpius canon "Lo, How a Rose E'er Blooming" contains the following issues for conducting study:

- anticipatory position
- breath cues for each entrance of the four parts
- breathing the color of the sound desired and hearing the effects of that breath on the sound
- openness of the body prior to breathing
- release of breath into the choral sound
- tracking entrances
- impulse gesture and corresponding breath for each of the four entrances
- facial countenance when breath is taken
- release of sound
- exhalation of air while conducting
- reception of and reaction to sound
- listening
- gesture ahead of the sound to allow for rhythmic spontaneity
- use of a four-beat pattern in which beat 3 is expansive
- use of a legato four-beat pattern
- consistency of ictus in third fingertip and its effect on pitch
- use of a conducting gesture that is not held and with no subdivision
- breath cue technique between phrases
- developing the tactile feeling that the sound actually exists in your hands

- decisions concerning the length of consonants
- "conducting" of consonants
- conducting a final release that is in the character of the consonant

LO, HOW A ROSE E'ER BLOOMING

4-part canon

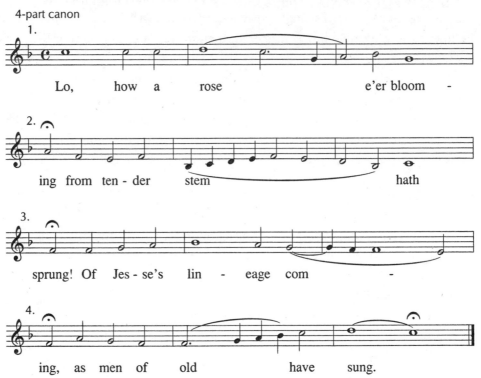

Text: *Det är en ros utsprungen; Es ist ein' Ros' entsprungen; Speier Gebetbuch,* 1599; trans. by Theodore Baker, 1851-1934
Tune: Melchior Vulpius, 1560-1615

RATING SCALE
VULPIUS: LO, HOW A
ROSE E'ER BLOOMING

Videotape yourself conducting this hymn with singers and accompaniment. View the videotape and use the rating scale below to measure your progress. You may need to view the tape several times to accurately measure yourself in some of the areas. Evaluate the specific areas for which you need improvement. Tape yourself again, trying to improve your performance in those areas that were in need of improvement. (Focus first on those areas in boldface.)

NAME_____

4 = high 0 = low	Trial 1	Trial 2
Alignment	4 3 2 1 0	4 3 2 1 0
Anticipatory position present	4 3 2 1 0	4 3 2 1 0
Connect breath between phrases	4 3 2 1 0	4 3 2 1 0
Neck is released	4 3 2 1 0	4 3 2 1 0
Wrists are released	4 3 2 1 0	4 3 2 1 0
Initial, non-held release of sound	4 3 2 1 0	4 3 2 1 0
Gesture low and centered enough to reflect low breath	4 3 2 1 0	4 3 2 1 0
Natural, low breath	4 3 2 1 0	4 3 2 1 0
Openness of body prior to breathing	4 3 2 1 0	4 3 2 1 0
Releases breath into the choral sound	4 3 2 1 0	4 3 2 1 0
Facial breath countenance	4 3 2 1 0	4 3 2 1 0
Expansiveness in gesture that allows line to sing	4 3 2 1 0	4 3 2 1 0
Line of ictus present	4 3 2 1 0	4 3 2 1 0
Ictus present in fingertips	4 3 2 1 0	4 3 2 1 0
Breathes vowel on entrance	4 3 2 1 0	4 3 2 1 0
Breath is activated before gesture	4 3 2 1 0	4 3 2 1 0
Shoulder rigidity absent	4 3 2 1 0	4 3 2 1 0
Non-holding of gesture	4 3 2 1 0	4 3 2 1 0
Non-disconnection from sound	4 3 2 1 0	4 3 2 1 0
Color of sound present prepared by the breath	4 3 2 1 0	4 3 2 1 0
Listening to breath	4 3 2 1 0	4 3 2 1 0
Listening to sound	4 3 2 1 0	4 3 2 1 0
Gesture stays low when tessitura high	4 3 2 1 0	4 3 2 1 0
Gesture stays ahead of sound	4 3 2 1 0	4 3 2 1 0
Rebound with no subdivision	4 3 2 1 0	4 3 2 1 0
Ability to rhythmically initiate and propel sound forward only where necessary	4 3 2 1 0	4 3 2 1 0

Overall Evaluation   (Average)   _____   _____

EXERCISE EIGHT:
DUFAY: GLORIA AD MODUM TUBAE

STUDY GUIDE

The canonic work by Guillaume Dufay, "Gloria ad modum tubae," contains the following issues for conducting study:

- anticipatory position
- breath cues for entrances of each vocal part
- breathing the color of the sound desired and hearing the effects of that breath on the sound
- opening body rhythmically for breath
- release of breath into the choral sound
- use of dropped vee pattern for marcato character of the piece
- tracking parts in two-voice texture
- facial countenance when breath is taken
- release of sound
- exhalation of air while conducting
- reception and reaction to sound
- listening
- gesture ahead of the sound to allow for rhythmic spontaneity
- use of a four-beat pattern in which beat 3 is expansive
- consistency of ictus in third fingertip and effect on pitch
- use of a conducting gesture that is not held and with no subdivision
- breath cue technique between phrases
- developing the tactile feeling that the sound actually exists in your hands
- decisions concerning the length of consonants
- "conducting" of consonants
- affecting color changes between marcato and legato sections of the work
- conducting a final release in the character of the final voiced consonant
- maintaining a consistent tempo
- use of a rebound that is not subdivided

GLORIA AD MODUM TUBAE

Guillaume Dufay composed four know Glorias that are independent pieces and not part of any complete mass settings. These include one with the designation de Quaremiaux (for Lent!); the well-known *Gloria ad modum tubae* (in the manner of a trumpet); and two that alternate plainchant and polyphony. One is based on the Gloria of Gregorian Mass IX (*De Beata Virgine*) and one on the Gloria of Mass XI (*Orbis factor*).

The accompaniment for *Gloria ad modum tubae* was written to be played on two natural (valveless) trumpets. These were straight—about a yard in length—with a slightly conical bore. The ideal modern instruments for this piece would be C trumpets, since the parts can be played entirely on open notes without the use of valves. Most trumpet players, however, use Bb instruments, and most who do have C trumpets are accustomed to transposing Bb parts. Two trombones, playing an octave lower, are also possible, and the accompaniment can be played on two manuals of the organ, preferably using contrasting reed stops.

The choir part, which is a canon, can be sung by equal voices, by women on part one and men on the canon, by sopranos and tenors on one part and altos and basses on the other, or by two choirs (e.g., children and adult).

For a good effect, the two trumpeters and two choirs can be separated. At the very least, separation is achieved by placing one trumpeter on either side of the singers. —*William Tortolano, edition editor. Octavo (G-2150) copyright © 1978 by GIA Publications, Inc. and used with permission.*

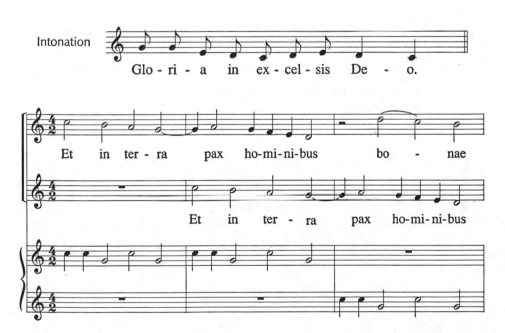

Music: Guillaume Dufay, 1400-1474

RATING SCALE
DUFAY: GLORIA AD MODUM TUBAE

Videotape yourself conducting this work with singers and accompaniment. View the videotape and use the rating scale below to measure your progress. You may need to view the tape several times to accurately measure yourself in some of the areas. Evaluate the specific areas for which you need improvement. Tape yourself again, trying to improve your performance in those areas that were in need of improvement. (Focus first on those areas in boldface.)

NAME _____

4 = high 0 = low	Trial 1	Trial 2
Alignment	4 3 2 1 0	4 3 2 1 0
Anticipatory position present	4 3 2 1 0	4 3 2 1 0

Connect breath between phrases	4 3 2 1 0	4 3 2 1 0
Neck is released	4 3 2 1 0	4 3 2 1 0
Wrists are released	4 3 2 1 0	4 3 2 1 0
Initial, non-held release of sound	4 3 2 1 0	4 3 2 1 0
Gesture low and centered enough to reflect low breath	4 3 2 1 0	4 3 2 1 0
Natural, low breath	4 3 2 1 0	4 3 2 1 0
Openness of body prior to breathing	4 3 2 1 0	4 3 2 1 0
Releases breath into the choral sound	4 3 2 1 0	4 3 2 1 0
Facial breath countenance	4 3 2 1 0	4 3 2 1 0
Expansiveness in gesture that allows line to sing	4 3 2 1 0	4 3 2 1 0
Line of ictus present	4 3 2 1 0	4 3 2 1 0
Ictus present in fingertips	4 3 2 1 0	4 3 2 1 0
Breathes vowel on entrance	4 3 2 1 0	4 3 2 1 0
Breath is activated before gesture	4 3 2 1 0	4 3 2 1 0
Shoulder rigidity absent	4 3 2 1 0	4 3 2 1 0
Non-holding of gesture	4 3 2 1 0	4 3 2 1 0
Non-disconnection from sound	4 3 2 1 0	4 3 2 1 0
Color of sound present prepared by the breath	4 3 2 1 0	4 3 2 1 0
Listening to breath	4 3 2 1 0	4 3 2 1 0
Listening to sound	4 3 2 1 0	4 3 2 1 0
Gesture stays ahead of sound	4 3 2 1 0	4 3 2 1 0
Rebound with no subdivision	4 3 2 1 0	4 3 2 1 0
Ability to rhythmically initiate and propel sound forward only where necessary	4 3 2 1 0	4 3 2 1 0

Overall Evaluation   (Average)   _____   _____

EXERCISE NINE:
DUFAY: KYRIE ORBIS FACTOR

STUDY GUIDE

Guillaume Dufay's unison "Kyrie orbis factor" contains the following issues for conducting study:

- anticipatory position
- breath cues for entrances of each vocal part
- breathing the color of the sound desired and hearing the effects of that breath on the sound

- release of breath into the choral sound
- use of dropped-vee pattern for marcato character of the piece
- facial countenance when breath is taken
- release of sound
- exhalation of air while conducting
- reception of and reaction to sound
- listening
- gesture ahead of the sound to allow for rhythmic spontaneity
- use of a four-beat pattern in which beat 3 is expansive
- consistency of ictus in third fingertip and its effect on pitch
- use of a conducting gesture that is not held and with no subdivision
- breath cue technique between phrases
- developing the tactile feeling that the sound actually exists in your hands
- making decisions concerning the length of consonants
- "conducting" of consonants
- affecting color changes between marcato and legato sections of the work
- conducting a final release in the character of the final voiced consonant
- maintaining a consistent tempo
- use of a rebound that is not subdivided

KYRIE ORBIS FACTOR

Guillaume Dufay wrote several Kyries that are independent works, not part of any complete Mass setting. *The Kyrie Orbis Factor* is based upon the Gregorian chant of the same name.

The chants can be sung by a soloist (cantor), choir, or congregation. The subsequent three-part setting might be somewhat difficult for a congregation, but would be effective by soloist or choir with accompaniment. The accompaniment was originally for strings. It has been adapted for organ in this edition, but alternate string parts for violin and cello, or two violas are [available]. In order to avoid crossing parts, entirely possible in the original, the organ part includes octave changes, but original intervals are in most instances kept intact.

The organ accompaniment could be played on two manuals, with light registration and clearly delineated. —*William Tortolano, edition editor. Octavo (G-2147) copyright © 1978 by GIA Publications, Inc. and used with permission.*

Music: Guillaume Dufay, 1400-1474

RATING SCALE
DUFAY: KYRIE ORBIS FACTOR

Videotape yourself conducting this work with singers and accompaniment. View the videotape and use the rating scale below to measure your progress. You may need to view the tape several times to accurately measure yourself in some of the areas. Evaluate the specific areas for which you need improvement. Tape yourself again, trying to improve your performance in those areas that were in need of improvement. (Focus first on those areas in boldface.)

NAME _____

4 = high 0 = low	Trial 1	Trial 2
Alignment	4 3 2 1 0	4 3 2 1 0
Anticipatory position present	4 3 2 1 0	4 3 2 1 0
Connect breath between phrases	4 3 2 1 0	4 3 2 1 0
Neck is released	4 3 2 1 0	4 3 2 1 0

224

Wrists are released	4 3 2 1 0	4 3 2 1 0
Initial, non-held release of sound	4 3 2 1 0	4 3 2 1 0
Gesture low and centered enough to reflect low breath	4 3 2 1 0	4 3 2 1 0
Natural, low breath	4 3 2 1 0	4 3 2 1 0
Openness of body prior to breathing	4 3 2 1 0	4 3 2 1 0
Releases breath into the choral sound	4 3 2 1 0	4 3 2 1 0
Facial breath countenance	4 3 2 1 0	4 3 2 1 0
Expansiveness in gesture that allows line to sing	4 3 2 1 0	4 3 2 1 0
Line of ictus present	4 3 2 1 0	4 3 2 1 0
Ictus present in fingertips	4 3 2 1 0	4 3 2 1 0
Breathes vowel on entrance	4 3 2 1 0	4 3 2 1 0
Breath is activated before gesture	4 3 2 1 0	4 3 2 1 0
Shoulder rigidity absent	4 3 2 1 0	4 3 2 1 0
Non-holding of gesture	4 3 2 1 0	4 3 2 1 0
Non-disconnection from sound	4 3 2 1 0	4 3 2 1 0
Color of sound present prepared by the breath	4 3 2 1 0	4 3 2 1 0
Listening to breath	4 3 2 1 0	4 3 2 1 0
Listening to sound	4 3 2 1 0	4 3 2 1 0
Gesture stays ahead of sound	4 3 2 1 0	4 3 2 1 0
Rebound with no subdivision	4 3 2 1 0	4 3 2 1 0
Ability to rhythmically initiate and propel sound forward only where necessary	4 3 2 1 0	4 3 2 1 0

Overall Evaluation   (Average)   _____   _____

EXERCISE TEN:
HILL: LADY, HELPE; JESU, MERCE!

STUDY GUIDE

The unison work by Jackson Hill, "Lady, Helpe; Jesu, Merce!" from *Medieval Lyrics*, contains the following issues for conducting study:

- anticipatory position
- breath cues for entrance of vocal part
- openness of the body prior to breathing
- release of breath into the choral sound
- transitions between marcato and legato textures
- breathing the color of the sound desired and hearing the effects of that breath on the sound

- use of dropped-vee pattern for marcato opening
- conducting in unusual meter
- breath cues that are in both half-note and quarter-note values
- breath cue occurring on first beat of measure
- impulse gesture and corresponding breath for each of the four entrances
- facial countenance when breath is taken
- release of sound
- exhalation of air while conducting
- reception of and reaction to sound
- listening
- gesture ahead of the sound to allow for rhythmic spontaneity
- use of a four-beat pattern in which beat 3 is expansive
- use of a legato four-beat, three-beat, and two-beat pattern
- consistency of ictus in third fingertip and to see its effect on pitch
- use of a conducting gesture that is not held and with no subdivision
- breath cue technique between phrases
- developing the tactile feeling that the sound actually exists in your hands
- decisions concerning the length of consonants
- "conducting" of consonants
- affecting color changes between marcato and legato sections of the work
- conducting a final release in the character of the vowel

HILL: LADY, HELPE; JESU, MERCE!

*Reduction of brass quintet.

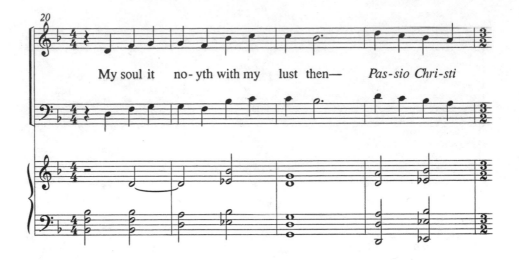

My soul it no-yth with my lust then— *Pas-sio Chri-sti*

con - for-ta me.

Men unis.

For blind ness is a hev-y thing and to be def ther -

fiv - e wound-es of   Je - su   Christ   My   med - i - cine now

mot they be;   the   fiend-es pow-er   down to   cast.

Text: John Audelay, early 15th century, adapted
Music: based on *Urbs beata Ierusalem* Jackson Hill, © 1996

RATING SCALE
HILL: LADY, HELPE; JESU, MERCE!

Videotape yourself conducting this work with singers and accompaniment. View the videotape and use the rating scale below to measure your progress. You may need to view the tape several times to accurately measure yourself in some of the areas. Evaluate the specific areas for which you need improvement. Tape yourself again, trying to improve your performance in those areas that were in need of improvement. (Focus first on those areas in boldface.)

NAME

4 = high 0 = low	Trial 1	Trial 2
Alignment	4 3 2 1 0	4 3 2 1 0
Anticipatory position present	4 3 2 1 0	4 3 2 1 0
Connect breath between phrases	4 3 2 1 0	4 3 2 1 0
Neck is released	4 3 2 1 0	4 3 2 1 0
Wrists are released	4 3 2 1 0	4 3 2 1 0
Initial, non-held release of sound	4 3 2 1 0	4 3 2 1 0
Gesture low and centered enough to reflect low breath	4 3 2 1 0	4 3 2 1 0
Natural, low breath	4 3 2 1 0	4 3 2 1 0
Openness of body prior to breathing	4 3 2 1 0	4 3 2 1 0
Releases breath into the choral sound	4 3 2 1 0	4 3 2 1 0
Facial breath countenance	4 3 2 1 0	4 3 2 1 0
Expansiveness in gesture that allows line to sing	4 3 2 1 0	4 3 2 1 0
Line of ictus present	4 3 2 1 0	4 3 2 1 0
Ictus present in fingertips	4 3 2 1 0	4 3 2 1 0
Breathes vowel on entrance	4 3 2 1 0	4 3 2 1 0
Breath is activated before gesture	4 3 2 1 0	4 3 2 1 0

Shoulder rigidity absent	4 3 2 1 0	4 3 2 1 0
Non-holding of gesture	4 3 2 1 0	4 3 2 1 0
Non-disconnection from sound	4 3 2 1 0	4 3 2 1 0
Color of sound present prepared by the breath	4 3 2 1 0	4 3 2 1 0
Listening to breath	4 3 2 1 0	4 3 2 1 0
Listening to sound	4 3 2 1 0	4 3 2 1 0
Gesture stays low when tessitura high	4 3 2 1 0	4 3 2 1 0
Gesture stays ahead of sound	4 3 2 1 0	4 3 2 1 0
Rebound with no subdivision	4 3 2 1 0	4 3 2 1 0
Ability to rhythmically initiate and propel sound forward only where necessary	4 3 2 1 0	4 3 2 1 0
Ability to make transition between marcato and legato	4 3 2 1 0	4 3 2 1 0
Ability to affect a color change between marcato and legato sections	4 3 2 1 0	4 3 2 1 0

Overall Evaluation   (Average)   _____   _____

EXERCISE ELEVEN:
AMERICAN: SHENANDOAH

STUDY GUIDE

The excerpt from "Shenandoah" can be studied for the following:

- beginning on an eighth-note pickup
- affecting the line by indicating an ictus on the dot of the dotted rhythms
- breaths between phrases
- non-muscularity of gesture
- clarity of diction

SHENANDOAH

see you,   'Way,   we're bound a - way,   A-

cross the   wide   Mis - sou - ri.

Rating Scale
American: Shenandoah

Videotape yourself conducting this work with singers and accompaniment. View the videotape and use the rating scale below to measure your progress. You may need to view the tape several times to accurately measure yourself in some of the areas. Evaluate the specific areas for which you need improvement. Tape yourself again, trying to improve your performance in those areas that were in need of improvement. (Focus first on those areas in boldface.)

NAME _____

4 = high 0 = low	Trial 1	Trial 2
Alignment	4 3 2 1 0	4 3 2 1 0
Anticipatory position present	4 3 2 1 0	4 3 2 1 0
Connect breath between phrases	4 3 2 1 0	4 3 2 1 0
Neck is released	4 3 2 1 0	4 3 2 1 0
Wrists are released	4 3 2 1 0	4 3 2 1 0
Initial, non-held release of sound	4 3 2 1 0	4 3 2 1 0
Gesture low and centered enough to reflect low breath	4 3 2 1 0	4 3 2 1 0
Natural, low breath	4 3 2 1 0	4 3 2 1 0
Openness of body prior to breathing	4 3 2 1 0	4 3 2 1 0
Releases breath into the choral sound	4 3 2 1 0	4 3 2 1 0
Facial breath countenance	4 3 2 1 0	4 3 2 1 0
Expansiveness in gesture that allows line to sing	4 3 2 1 0	4 3 2 1 0
Line of ictus present	4 3 2 1 0	4 3 2 1 0
Ictus present in fingertips	4 3 2 1 0	4 3 2 1 0
Breathes vowel on entrance	4 3 2 1 0	4 3 2 1 0

Breath is activated before gesture	4 3 2 1 0	4 3 2 1 0
Shoulder rigidity absent	4 3 2 1 0	4 3 2 1 0
Non-holding of gesture	4 3 2 1 0	4 3 2 1 0
Non-disconnection from sound	4 3 2 1 0	4 3 2 1 0
Color of sound present prepared by the breath	4 3 2 1 0	4 3 2 1 0
Listening to breath	4 3 2 1 0	4 3 2 1 0
Listening to sound	4 3 2 1 0	4 3 2 1 0
Gesture stays low when tessitura high	4 3 2 1 0	4 3 2 1 0
Gesture stays ahead of sound	4 3 2 1 0	4 3 2 1 0
Rebound with no subdivision	4 3 2 1 0	4 3 2 1 0
Ability to rhythmically initiate and propel sound forward only where necessary	4 3 2 1 0	4 3 2 1 0
Ability to make transition between marcato and legato	4 3 2 1 0	4 3 2 1 0
Ability to move line forward on dotted rhythms	4 3 2 1 0	4 3 2 1 0

Overall Evaluation   (Average)   _____   _____

EXERCISE TWELVE:
Plainsong: Ave Maria

The accompanied plainsong "Ave Maria" presents several challenges to the conductor. In preparing the piece for performance, first make decisions concerning which pitches group into twos and which ones group into threes. Use a single, repeated dropped-vee pattern for each pulse grouping of two or three. After each breath mark (vertical slash at top of the stave) start each phrase as if there were an eighth-note rest, at which point the breath occurs. This implied eighth-note breath-rest occurs in all locations with the exception of the final "Amen." This piece may be performed a cappella or with the accompaniment.

Tempo for the chant should lie somewhere between 120–130 for the eighth-note pulse. In this edition, notational care is already allowed for prolongations. No ritardando should be used with the exception of the final "Amen."

Study Guide

The plainsong "Ave Maria" contains the following issues for conducting study:
- anticipatory position
- breath cues at the start of each phrase that rhythmically impel the phrase forward

240

- breathing the color of the sound desired and hearing the effects of that breath on the sound
- tracking both the vocal part and the accompaniment
- breath impulse gesture for each phrase group
- release of sound
- exhalation of air while conducting
- release of breath into the choral sound
- reception of and reaction to sound
- listening
- gesture ahead of the sound to allow for rhythmic spontaneity
- use of a one-beat pattern that uses speed and velocity of gesture without weight to impel phrase forward
- consistency of ictus in third fingertip and to see its effect on pitch
- use of a conducting gesture that is not held and with no subdivision
- breath cue technique between phrases
- developing the tactile feeling that the sound actually exists in your hands
- decisions concerning the length of consonants
- "conducting" of consonants
- conducting a final release in the character of the consonant

AVE MARIA

Text: Lk. 1:28, 42; Council of Ephesis
Tune: AVE MARIA, Irregular; Mode I; acc. by Richard Proulx, b.1937. © 1988, GIA Publications, Inc.

RATING SCALE
PLAINSONG: AVE MARIA

Videotape yourself conducting this work with singers and accompaniment. View the videotape and use the rating scale below to measure your progress. You may need to view the tape several times to accurately measure yourself in some of the areas. Evaluate the specific areas for which you need improvement. Tape yourself again, trying to improve your performance in those areas that were in need of improvement. (Focus first on those areas in boldface.)

NAME _____

4 = high 0 = low	Trial 1	Trial 2
Alignment	4 3 2 1 0	4 3 2 1 0
Anticipatory position present	4 3 2 1 0	4 3 2 1 0
Connect breath between phrases	4 3 2 1 0	4 3 2 1 0
Neck is released	4 3 2 1 0	4 3 2 1 0
Wrists are released	4 3 2 1 0	4 3 2 1 0
Initial, non-held release of sound	4 3 2 1 0	4 3 2 1 0
Gesture low and centered enough to reflect low breath	4 3 2 1 0	4 3 2 1 0
Natural, low breath	4 3 2 1 0	4 3 2 1 0
Openness of body prior to breathing	4 3 2 1 0	4 3 2 1 0
Releases breath into the choral sound	4 3 2 1 0	4 3 2 1 0
Facial breath countenance	4 3 2 1 0	4 3 2 1 0
Expansiveness in gesture that allows line to sing	4 3 2 1 0	4 3 2 1 0
Line of ictus present	4 3 2 1 0	4 3 2 1 0
Ictus present in fingertips	4 3 2 1 0	4 3 2 1 0
Breathes vowel on entrance	4 3 2 1 0	4 3 2 1 0
Breath is activated before gesture	4 3 2 1 0	4 3 2 1 0
Shoulder rigidity absent	4 3 2 1 0	4 3 2 1 0
Non-holding of gesture	4 3 2 1 0	4 3 2 1 0
Non-disconnection from sound	4 3 2 1 0	4 3 2 1 0
Color of sound present prepared by the breath	4 3 2 1 0	4 3 2 1 0
Listening to breath	4 3 2 1 0	4 3 2 1 0
Listening to sound	4 3 2 1 0	4 3 2 1 0
Gesture stays ahead of sound	4 3 2 1 0	4 3 2 1 0
Rebound with no subdivision	4 3 2 1 0	4 3 2 1 0
Ability to rhythmically initiate and propel sound forward with breath	4 3 2 1 0	4 3 2 1 0

Overall Evaluation (Average) _____ _____

EXERCISE THIRTEEN:
PLAINSONG: SANCTUS

The accompanied plainsong "Sanctus" presents similar challenges to the conductor as did "Ave Maria." In preparing the piece for performance, first make decisions concerning which pitches group into twos and which ones group into threes. Use a single, repeated dropped-vee pattern for each pulse grouping of two or three. This piece may be performed a cappella or with the accompaniment.

Tempo for the chant should lie somewhere between 120 and 130 for the eighth-note pulse. In this edition, notational care is already allowed for prolongations. No ritardando should be used.

STUDY GUIDE

The plainsong "Sanctus" contains the following issues for conducting study:
- anticipatory position
- breath cues at the start of each phrase that rhythmically impel the phrase forward
- breathing the color of the sound desired and hearing the effects of that breath on the sound
- tracking both the vocal part and the accompaniment
- breath impulse gesture for each phrase group
- release of sound
- exhalation of air while conducting
- release of breath into the choral sound
- reception of and reaction to sound
- listening
- gesture ahead of the sound to allow for rhythmic spontaneity
- use of a one-beat pattern that uses speed and velocity of gesture without weight to impel phrase forward
- consistency of ictus in third fingertip and its effect on pitch
- use of a conducting gesture that is not held and with no subdivision
- breath cue technique between phrases
- developing the tactile feeling that the sound actually exists in your hands
- decisions concerning the length of consonants
- "conducting" of consonants
- conducting a final release in the character of the consonant

SANCTUS

Ho - sán - na in ex - cél - sis.

Tune: Vatican edition XVIII

RATING SCALE
PLAINSONG: SANCTUS

Videotape yourself conducting this work with singers and accompaniment. View the videotape and use the rating scale below to measure your progress. You may need to view the tape several times to accurately measure yourself in some of the areas. Evaluate the specific areas for which you need improvement. Tape yourself again, trying to improve your performance in those areas that were in need of improvement. (Focus first on those areas in boldface.)

NAME _____

4 = high 0 = low	Trial 1	Trial 2
Alignment	4 3 2 1 0	4 3 2 1 0
Anticipatory position present	4 3 2 1 0	4 3 2 1 0
Connect breath between phrases	4 3 2 1 0	4 3 2 1 0
Neck is released	4 3 2 1 0	4 3 2 1 0
Wrists are released	4 3 2 1 0	4 3 2 1 0
Initial, non-held release of sound	4 3 2 1 0	4 3 2 1 0
Gesture low and centered enough to reflect low breath	4 3 2 1 0	4 3 2 1 0
Natural, low breath	4 3 2 1 0	4 3 2 1 0
Openness of body prior to breathing	4 3 2 1 0	4 3 2 1 0
Releases breath into the choral sound	4 3 2 1 0	4 3 2 1 0
Facial breath countenance	4 3 2 1 0	4 3 2 1 0
Expansiveness in gesture that allows line to sing	4 3 2 1 0	4 3 2 1 0
Line of ictus present	4 3 2 1 0	4 3 2 1 0

Ictus present in fingertips	4 3 2 1 0	4 3 2 1 0
Breathes vowel on entrance	4 3 2 1 0	4 3 2 1 0
Breath is activated before gesture	4 3 2 1 0	4 3 2 1 0
Shoulder rigidity absent	4 3 2 1 0	4 3 2 1 0
Non-holding of gesture	4 3 2 1 0	4 3 2 1 0
Non-disconnection from sound	4 3 2 1 0	4 3 2 1 0
Color of sound present prepared by the breath	4 3 2 1 0	4 3 2 1 0
Listening to breath	4 3 2 1 0	4 3 2 1 0
Listening to sound	4 3 2 1 0	4 3 2 1 0
Gesture stays ahead of sound	4 3 2 1 0	4 3 2 1 0
Rebound with no subdivision	4 3 2 1 0	4 3 2 1 0
Ability to rhythmically initiate and propel sound forward with breath	4 3 2 1 0	4 3 2 1 0

Overall Evaluation   (Average)   _____   _____

EXERCISE FOURTEEN: MENDELSSOHN: HE THAT SHALL ENDURE TO THE END (FROM ELIJAH)

STUDY GUIDE

For this chorus from Mendelssohn's *Elijah* focus on the following issues:
- breath cueing for each entrance
- hearing a four-part texture and the accompaniment
- initiation of the musical line
- dynamics
- shaping of phrases
- changes of color within the piece
- selection of proper tempo for performance
- non-muscularity of gesture

HE THAT SHALL ENDURE TO THE END

Text: *Elijah*, Felix Mendelssohn, 1809-1847
Tune: Felix Mendelssohn, 1809-1847

RATING SCALE
MENDELSSOHN: HE THAT SHALL
ENDURE TO THE END (FROM ELIJAH)

Videotape yourself conducting this work with singers and accompaniment. View the videotape and use the rating scale below to measure your progress. You may need to view the tape several times to accurately measure yourself in some of the areas. Evaluate the specific areas for which you need improvement. Tape yourself again, trying to improve your performance in those areas that were in need of improvement. (Focus first on those areas in boldface.)

NAME _____

4 = high 0 = low	Trial 1	Trial 2
Alignment	4 3 2 1 0	4 3 2 1 0
Anticipatory position present	4 3 2 1 0	4 3 2 1 0
Connect breath between phrases	4 3 2 1 0	4 3 2 1 0
Neck is released	4 3 2 1 0	4 3 2 1 0
Wrists are released	4 3 2 1 0	4 3 2 1 0
Initial, non-held release of sound	4 3 2 1 0	4 3 2 1 0
Gesture low and centered enough to reflect low breath	4 3 2 1 0	4 3 2 1 0
Natural, low breath	4 3 2 1 0	4 3 2 1 0
Openness of body prior to breathing	4 3 2 1 0	4 3 2 1 0
Releases breath into the choral sound	4 3 2 1 0	4 3 2 1 0
Facial breath countenance	4 3 2 1 0	4 3 2 1 0
Expansiveness in gesture that allows line to sing	4 3 2 1 0	4 3 2 1 0
Line of ictus present	4 3 2 1 0	4 3 2 1 0
Ictus present in fingertips	4 3 2 1 0	4 3 2 1 0
Breathes vowel on entrance	4 3 2 1 0	4 3 2 1 0
Breath is activated before gesture	4 3 2 1 0	4 3 2 1 0
Shoulder rigidity absent	4 3 2 1 0	4 3 2 1 0
Non-holding of gesture	4 3 2 1 0	4 3 2 1 0
Non-disconnection from sound	4 3 2 1 0	4 3 2 1 0
Color of sound present prepared by the breath	4 3 2 1 0	4 3 2 1 0
Listening to breath	4 3 2 1 0	4 3 2 1 0
Listening to sound	4 3 2 1 0	4 3 2 1 0
Gesture stays ahead of sound	4 3 2 1 0	4 3 2 1 0
Rebound with no subdivision	4 3 2 1 0	4 3 2 1 0

Ability to rhythmically initiate and propel sound
forward with breath   4 3 2 1 0   4 3 2 1 0

Overall Evaluation (Average)   _____   _____

EXERCISE FIFTEEN:
Bach chorale:
O Sacred Head Now Wounded

This Bach chorale approaches the issue of the conducting of fermatas and the procedure by which one prepares a four-voice texture. As a review from chapter 9, the guidelines for conducting a fermata are summarized below.

Guide for conducting fermatas

1. On the beat where the fermata appears, hold the hands at that ictus location and "hold" the sound with both hands.

2. When you desire to move ahead, simply repeat the beat in the pattern on which the fermata appears, *breathe simultaneously* with the repetition of that beat in the pattern in the tempo you wish the next phrase, and proceed with the pattern.

In studying the score, learning each of the parts separately is recommended. Sing the music using neutral syllables or use solfège, or both, for each voice part in the score. After each of the parts has been learned, begin at the start of the work, pick a voice part, and sing it either on neutral syllables or solfège syllables. At the fermata, switch immediately to another voice part, and continue with your singing. At each fermata, follow the same procedure and switch the voice part you are singing until the end of the chorale. While playing the entire chorale is helpful to hear and understand its harmonic motion, it is much more valuable to have learned each of the parts. If each of the voice parts have been meticulously prepared, the "musical ear," or audiation, of the conductor will combine them simultaneously while the music is being sounded. In addition to singing each of the parts, analyze the chorale harmonically and make note of suspensions and other nonharmonic devices.

O SACRED HEAD, NOW WOUNDED

Text: Paul Gerhardt, 1607-1676; tr. by Robert Seymour Bridges, 1844-1930
Tune: HERZLICH TUT MICH VERLANGEN, 76 76 D; Hans Leo Hassler, 1564-1612; harm. by J. S. Bach, 1685-1750

Rating Scale
Bach chorale: O Sacred Head
Now Wounded

Videotape yourself conducting this work with singers and accompaniment. View the videotape and use the rating scale below to measure your progress. You may need to view the tape several times to accurately measure yourself in some of the areas. Evaluate the specific areas for which you need improvement. Tape yourself again, trying to improve your performance in those areas that were in need of improvement. (Focus first on those areas in boldface.)

NAME_____

4 = high 0 = low	Trial 1	Trial 2
Alignment	4 3 2 1 0	4 3 2 1 0
Anticipatory position present	4 3 2 1 0	4 3 2 1 0
Connect breath between phrases	4 3 2 1 0	4 3 2 1 0
Neck is released	4 3 2 1 0	4 3 2 1 0
Wrists are released	4 3 2 1 0	4 3 2 1 0
Initial, non-held release of sound	4 3 2 1 0	4 3 2 1 0
Gesture low and centered enough to reflect low breath	4 3 2 1 0	4 3 2 1 0
Natural, low breath	4 3 2 1 0	4 3 2 1 0
Openness of body prior to breathing	4 3 2 1 0	4 3 2 1 0
Releases breath into the choral sound	4 3 2 1 0	4 3 2 1 0
Ability to conduct fermatas and breathe for the start of the next phrase	4 3 2 1 0	4 3 2 1 0
Facial breath countenance	4 3 2 1 0	4 3 2 1 0
Expansiveness in gesture that allows line to sing	4 3 2 1 0	4 3 2 1 0
Line of ictus present	4 3 2 1 0	4 3 2 1 0
Ictus present in fingertips	4 3 2 1 0	4 3 2 1 0
Breathes vowel on entrance	4 3 2 1 0	4 3 2 1 0
Breath is activated before gesture	4 3 2 1 0	4 3 2 1 0
Shoulder rigidity absent	4 3 2 1 0	4 3 2 1 0
Non-holding of gesture	4 3 2 1 0	4 3 2 1 0
Non-disconnection from sound	4 3 2 1 0	4 3 2 1 0
Color of sound present prepared by the breath	4 3 2 1 0	4 3 2 1 0
Listening to breath	4 3 2 1 0	4 3 2 1 0
Listening to sound	4 3 2 1 0	4 3 2 1 0

Gesture stays ahead of sound	4 3 2 1 0	4 3 2 1 0
Rebound with no subdivision	4 3 2 1 0	4 3 2 1 0
Ability to rhythmically initiate and propel sound forward with breath	4 3 2 1 0	4 3 2 1 0
Overall Evaluation (Average)	_____	_____

EXERCISE SIXTEEN:
COLLECTION OF HYMN TUNES

The following collection of hymn tunes are provided as a supplement to what was presented in the earlier exercises. For beginning conductors, the conducting of these hymn tunes will provide facility in the development of conducting patterns and beginning ones contact with choral sound. All the hymn tunes present challenges for starting and more challenges to move the musical line forward. The same rating scale can be used for each of the hymn tunes.

STUDY GUIDE

The hymn tunes contain the following issues for conducting study:

- anticipatory position
- beginning with the accompaniment and choir together
- impulse gesture and corresponding breath
- facial countenance when breath is taken
- release of sound
- release of breath into the choral sound
- openness the body prior to breathing
- reception of and reaction to sound
- listening
- breathing the textural color of the piece and contrasting phrases
- gesture ahead of the sound to allow for rhythmic spontaneity
- use of a four-beat pattern in which beat 3 is expansive
- use of a legato four-beat pattern
- use of a conducting gesture that is not held and with no subdivision
- breath cue technique between phrases
- decisions concerning the length of consonants
- "conducting" of consonants
- conducting a final release in the character of the vowel without a consonant to end the sound

GOD, WHO STRETCHED THE SPANGLED HEAVENS

Melody in the tenor

1. God, who stretched the span - gled heav - ens
2. Proud - ly rise our mod - ern cit - ies,
3. We have ven - tured worlds un - dreamed of
4. As each far ho - ri - zon beck - ons,

In - fi - nite in time and place, Flung the suns in
State - ly build - ings, row on row; Yet their win - dows,
Since the child - hood of our race; Known the ec - sta -
May it chal - lenge us a - new, Chil - dren of cre -

burn - ing ra - diance Through the si - lent fields of space:
blank, un - feel - ing, Stare on can - yoned streets be - low,
sy of wing - ing Through un - trav - eled realms of space;
a - tive pur - pose Serv - ing o - thers, hon - 'ring you.

We, your chil - dren in your like - ness, Share in - ven - tive
Where the lone - ly drift un - no - ticed In the cit - y's
Probed the se - crets of the at - om, Yield - ing un - i -
May our dreams prove rich with prom - ise, Each en - deav - or

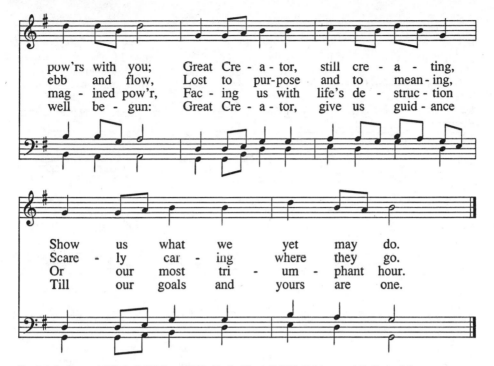

pow'rs with you; Great Cre - a - tor, still cre - a - ting,
ebb and flow, Lost to pur-pose and to mean - ing,
mag - ined pow'r, Fac - ing us with life's de - struc - tion
well be - gun: Great Cre - a - tor, give us guid - ance

Show us what we yet may do.
Scare - ly car - ing where they go.
Or our most tri - um - phant hour.
Till our goals and yours are one.

Text: Catherine Cameron, b.1927, alt., © 1976, Hope Publishing Co., Carol Stream, IL 60188. All rights reserved. Used by permission.
Tune: HOLY MANNA, 87 87 D; from *Southern Harmony*, 1835

WHAT WONDROUS LOVE IS THIS

Melody in the tenor

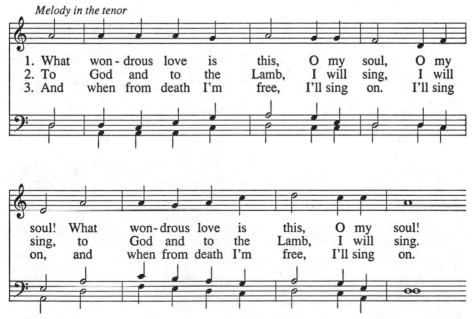

1. What won-drous love is this, O my soul, O my
2. To God and to the Lamb, I will sing, I will
3. And when from death I'm free, I'll sing on. I'll sing

soul! What won-drous love is this, O my soul!
sing, to God and to the Lamb, I will sing.
on, and when from death I'm free, I'll sing on.

What won-drous love is this that caused the Lord of
To God and to the Lamb who is the great I
And when from death I'm free I'll sing and joy - ful

bliss to lay a - side his crown for my soul, for my
AM, while mil - lions join the theme, I will sing, I will
be, and through e - ter - ni - ty I'll sing on, I'll sing

soul, to lay a - side his crown for my soul.
sing, while mil - lions join the theme I will sing.
on, and through e - ter - ni - ty I'll sing on.

Text: American folk hymn
Tune: WONDROUS LOVE, 12 9 12 12 9; *Southern Harmony*, 1835

DRAW US IN THE SPIRIT'S TETHER

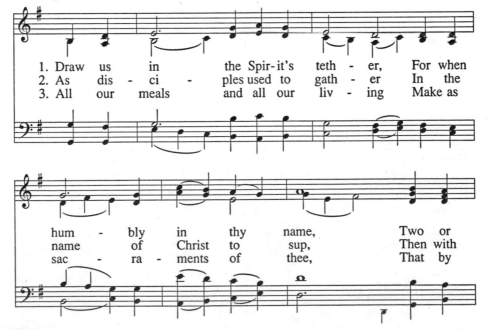

1. Draw us in the Spir-it's teth - er, For when
2. As dis - ci - ples used to gath - er In the
3. All our meals and all our liv - ing Make as

hum - bly in thy name, Two or
name of Christ to sup, Then with
sac - ra - ments of thee, That by

three   are met to - geth - er,   Thou art   in   the
thanks   to God the   Fa - ther   Break the bread   and
car -   ing, help-ing,   giv - ing,   We may true   dis -

midst   of   them.   Al - le - lu -   ia! Al - le -
bless   the   cup;   Al - le - lu -   ia! Al - le -
ci -   ples   be.   Al - le - lu -   ia! Al - le -

lu -   ia! Touch we   now   thy   gar -   ment's hem.
lu -   ia! So   now   bind   our   friend - ship   up.
lu -   ia! We   will   serve   thee   faith - ful - ly.

Text: Mt. 18:20, Percy Dearmer, 1867-1936, from *Enlarged Songs of Praise* by permission of Oxford University Press
Tune: UNION SEMINARY 87 87 44 7, Harold Friedell, 1905-1958, © 1957, 1985, H. W. Gray Co., Inc., harm. by Jet Turner, 1928-1984, © 1967,
    Chalice Press, P.O. Box 179, St. Louis, MO 68116; used by permission

ALL CREATURES OF OUR GOD AND KING

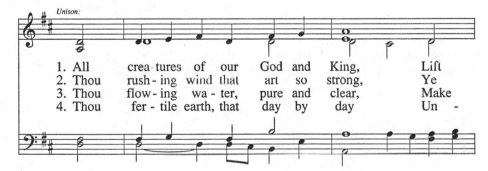

Unison:

1. All   crea-tures of   our   God   and   King,   Lift
2. Thou   rush-ing wind that   art   so   strong,   Ye
3. Thou   flow-ing wa - ter,   pure and   clear,   Make
4. Thou   fer - tile earth, that   day   by   day   Un -

lu - ia! Al-le - lu - ia! Al-le - lu - ia!

COME DOWN, O LOVE DIVINE

1. Come down, O Love di - vine, Seek now this soul of
2. O let it free - ly burn, Till earth - ly pas - sions
3. And so the yearn - ing strong, With which the soul will

mine, And vis - it it with your own ar - dor glow - ing;
turn To dust and ash - es in its heat con - sum - ing;
long, Shall far out-pass the power of hu - man tell - ing;

O Com - fort - er, draw near, With - in my heart ap -
And let your glo - rious light Shine ev - er on my
For none can guess its grace, Till love cre - ates the

pear, And kin-dle it, your ho-ly flame be-stow - ing.
sight, And clothe me round, the while my path il - lum - ing.
place Where-in the Ho - ly Spir-it makes its dwell - ing.

Text: *Discendi, Amor Santo;* Bianco da Siena, d.c.1434; tr. by Richard F. Littledale, 1833-1890
Tune: DOWN AMPNEY, 66 11 D; Ralph Vaughan Williams, 1872-1958, © from the *English Hymnal* by permission of Oxford University Press

PRAISE, MY SOUL, THE KING OF HEAVEN

1. Praise, my soul, the King of heav - en; To his
2. Praise him for his grace and fa - vor To his
3. Fa - ther - like he tends and spares us; Well our
4. Frail as sum-mer's flow'r we flour - ish, Blows the
5. An - gels, help us to a - dore him; You be -

feet your trib-ute bring; Ran - somed, healed, re - stored, for -
peo - ple in dis - tress; Praise him still the same as
fee - ble frame he knows; In his hands he gent - ly
wind and it is gone; But while mor - tals rise and
hold him face to face; Sun and moon, bow down be -

giv - en, Ev - er - more his prais - es sing: Al - le - lu - ia!
ev - er, Slow to chide, and swift to bless: Al - le - lu - ia!
bears us, Res - cues us from all our foes. Al - le - lu - ia!
per - ish, God en - dures un - chang-ing on; Al - le - lu - ia!
fore him, Dwell-ers all in time and space: Al - le - lu - ia!

Al - le - lu - ia! Praise the ev - er - last - ing King.
Al - le - lu - ia! Glo - rious in his faith - ful - ness.
Al - le - lu - ia! Wide - ly yet his mer - cy flows.
Al - le - lu - ia! Praise the high e - ter - nal one!
Al - le - lu - ia! Praise with us the God of grace.

Text: Psalm (102)103; Henry F. Lyte, 1793-1847, alt.
Tune: LAUDA ANIMA, 8 7 8 7 8 7; John Goss, 1800-1880

RATING SCALE: HYMN TUNES
HYMN:_____

Videotape yourself conducting the hymn with singers and, where appropriate, accompaniment. View the videotape and use the rating scale below to measure your progress. You may need to view the tape several times to accurately measure yourself in some of the areas. Evaluate the specific areas for which you need improvement. Tape yourself again, trying to improve your performance in those areas that were in need of improvement.

NAME _____

4 = high 0 = low	Trial 1	Trial 2
Alignment	4 3 2 1 0	4 3 2 1 0
Spaciousness across chest	4 3 2 1 0	4 3 2 1 0
Neck is released	4 3 2 1 0	4 3 2 1 0
Wrists are released	4 3 2 1 0	4 3 2 1 0
Openness of gesture	4 3 2 1 0	4 3 2 1 0
Arm position	4 3 2 1 0	4 3 2 1 0
Correct anticipatory position for air to enter body	4 3 2 1 0	4 3 2 1 0
Opens body for breath	4 3 2 1 0	4 3 2 1 0
Releases breath into ensemble sound	4 3 2 1 0	4 3 2 1 0
Breath impulse gesture present	4 3 2 1 0	4 3 2 1 0
Breath (inhalation) in character of the music	4 3 2 1 0	4 3 2 1 0
Facial breath countenance	4 3 2 1 0	4 3 2 1 0
Release of sound	4 3 2 1 0	4 3 2 1 0
Arm and shoulder freedom	4 3 2 1 0	4 3 2 1 0
Ictus is clearly in the third fingertip of each hand	4 3 2 1 0	4 3 2 1 0
Gesture is ahead of the sound	4 3 2 1 0	4 3 2 1 0
Correct patter is maintained throughout	4 3 2 1 0	4 3 2 1 0
Expansiveness in gesture that allows line to sing	4 3 2 1 0	4 3 2 1 0
Breaths between phrases that combine the final consonant with inhalation	4 3 2 1 0	4 3 2 1 0
Evidence of texture in hands	4 3 2 1 0	4 3 2 1 0
Final release	4 3 2 1 0	4 3 2 1 0
Locking of gesture not evident	4 3 2 1 0	4 3 2 1 0

Overall Evaluation (Average)   _____   _____

[This page may be duplicated for use with this text to evaluate your conducting of other hymns.]

PART III

A PRIMER FOR REHEARSAL TECHNIQUE

I have a vision in my head of what I want to hear and I try to communicate this to the people in front of me using everything I can muster from my Imagination. I may sometimes look foolish in the attempt, but I don't care, because I have something to share and, after all, isn't that the ultimate joy of conducting—to share your knowledge, experiences, joys, and desires, and to receive them back as beautiful gifts when singers realize them in the music? (P. 12)

Paul Salamunovich
in *The Choral Journal*, Dennis Shrock

Have you ever considered the artificiality and phoniness of the usual musical rehearsal and performance? The conductor stands constantly in front of the chorus or the audience; he or she is always in the spotlight. The very nature of a rehearsal causes us to think and to speak in negative terms to our choirs. It is: "No, no—you missed that pitch." "Your blend is terrible." "Sopranos, you are flat." "Precision in attack is quite ragged." "You don't sing with proper quality." "No, *don't*—that's bad," etc. Sometimes it seems that we are so busy trying to promote our-selves that we can hardly afford the time to even learn the names of those who sing in our chorus, let alone make the attempt to understand the thinking and the life styles of our choristers. We become obsessed with a goal of making the programs which we conduct better in their sound and content than those performed by our principal competitor who lives either across town or across the state. . . .

In some ways it seems to me at times that this is all rather pseudo and artificial and downright dishonest. Where is music? Where is beauty? Where is living? (P. 129–130)

When a mutual and sympathetic understanding of the human spirit is built, people finally become persons. (P. 149)

Howard Swan
Conscience of a Profession

To me, the rehearsal is not merely a group therapy session. My *modus operandi* changed drastically during the nineteen years that I was at Temple. I really value another person's time. It is the one thing in the world that can never be made up by something else. If that time is gone, it is gone forever. With a volunteer group, such as the Cleveland Orchestra Chorus, I value every moment that the singers are there, and I want every minute to be filled with something of great import to them through the music. I save all of my energies for the rehearsal. In that two-and-a-half hours I come alive. I erase everything else from my mind, and I expect the singers to do so also. (P. 145–146)

Robert Page
A Quest for Answers

I was interviewed once in Missouri at a little radio station and the inter-viewer asked, "Now, if you were put on a desert island with one piece of music, which would it be?" I said, "Whichever piece I'm working on."

Paul Salamunovich
in *The Choral Journal*, Dennis Shrock

• • • • •

The major problem with many rehearsal techniques is that the conductors who use them were not taught to listen. Second, in addition to not being taught to lis-ten, conducting pedagogy has avoided the study of the influence, both positive and negative, upon the sound and human response of the singers. Third, conductors have not been taught to understand how their choirs learn. Many conductors expect their choirs to learn music exactly as they do, regardless of the music level of their choirs. When rehearsed *efficiently*, children's choirs will learn music much faster than when rehearsed as if they were adults with adult skill levels! The church choir will learn quickly when music is introduced to them at a level at which *their* music understanding can help them both to understand and retain it. *Finally, perhaps the best way to improve a rehearsal is for the conductor to talk less and listen more!* This section of the text will outline the basics of beginning rehearsal technique based upon points one and two above, which have been discussed throughout this text, and will address the third point throughout all the discussion. Throughout all of the discussion, however, it is important to remember that rehearsal technique should be viewed not as an approach to "fixing things" but rather techniques that can be used so that the sound of the pieces can be evoked from the singers. Rehearsal technique, then, should provide the vehicles by which the choir can realize the true sound of the piece and the composer's intent.

ROTE TEACHING AND MUSIC LITERACY FOR CHOIRS

I hear the question asked frequently, "Is rote teaching bad?" My response is always, "It depends on whether it is good rote or bad rote teaching." Whether or not we want to admit it, we acquired our music achievement through rote learning. In fact, we acquired much of what we know through rote learning. Our spoken language was acquired through rote learning. Written language was very easily taught once we had come to school speaking English. Think of how difficult it would have been to learn to read or write if we had not come to school speaking the language. Think of how difficult it would have been if we would have begun our study of English with reading it rather than hearing it and using it on a daily basis. Yet, many conductors force choirs to draw meaning from music notation that does not exist in their ears. They do not hear the sounds that they are being asked to read; consequently, the notation is meaningless. Many choir members are asked to read notation, even though they do not have the aural readiness to read and do not even possess the basics for music understanding: a sense of consistent tempo and resting tone. A philosophy on how a piece is introduced to the choir and how it is "put into their ears" will establish both a meaningful and efficient rehearsal technique.

THE ROLE OF THE CONDUCTOR: CONDUCTING VERSUS TEACHING/REHEARSING

The most challenging aspect of rehearsal procedure for the conductor is listening. One must become comfortable with the myriad details of score analysis so that there is, in reality, no "analytical thinking" going on by the conductor as the music is being made by the singers. Those details include an understanding of how the piece moves forward, its vocal and technical demands, and what vocal and musical elements must be taught and reinforced in order for the piece to "speak."

Conductors need to be able to breathe for and with the choir and to be able to open themselves to listen to the sounds being made by the ensemble: to receive sounds being made by the singers and to, in effect, "store" them for "analysis" after the ensemble has completed singing. A common fault of conductors is to *concurrently* listen and analyze while the music is being created by the ensemble. If this occurs, the amount of music that is accurately heard and retained, as well as the conductor's ability to give the choir needed "tools," will be greatly diminished. A common concern expressed by conductors after their initial rehearsals is that "there is so much to listen to; I don't know what to focus on." The problem is one of simply trying to "think" too much while the music is being sung, instead of concentrating complete energies and focus upon listening. A conducting student once characterized the experience of listening in a rehearsal as having "ears as big as my body." That analogy is not far from the truth. As has been discussed many times in this text, if the conductor listens, the conducting gesture will always be appropriate. Without listening, the conductor's gesture gets in the way of the singers, no matter what their level, and causes the music not to have a voice of itself.

While it is important for the conductor to focus on the *what*, *why*, and *how* of rehearsing, it is even more important while conducting (rehearsing) to develop the skill of total listening *without* concurrent analysis. Conductors who temporarily "shut off" the cognitive side of their brain discover, to their amazement, that can "hear" better as they conduct. They also find that their conducting gesture is exactly appropriate to elicit sound from the choir. They also are amazed that after the music ceases, the wonders of the cognitive (thinking) side of the brain continue to function well and that the musical "mind" is able to quickly "replay" to the cognitive side of the brain the music that has just been sung. It is at that moment that effective rehearsal procedure is born. If the potential problems have been identified before the rehearsal through score study, the cognitive mind has little difficulty matching a previously identified problem with the sound in the conductor's "ear." When the two processes are developed separately, the hopeless listening-pedagogical muddle that usually plagues young conductors will not exist. In fact, an incredible spontaneity develops in rehearsal that is very much like play between the choir and the conductor. A conductor who intensely listens at all times during the music making process and then selects and applies an *appropriate and meaningful* pedagogical solution to the musical problem at hand is well on the way to achieving a rehearsal technique mastered by many of the great choral conductors. Simply stated, good rehearsal procedures merely provide the "how" of fixing problems after they have been heard.

PREPARING A PIECE FOR REHEARSAL: BASIC SCORE STUDY

If you need to, refer back to chapter 13 to refresh yourself concerning the principles of preparing a score for rehearsal. Be certain you have done all the necessary preparations to aurally hear the score before moving into rehearsal and teaching the piece.

A PLAN FOR INTRODUCING A PIECE

When introducing a new piece to a choir, certain fundamental overview issues must be presented to the choir before smaller musical issues are approached. The following overview issues should be kept in mind as one begins *familiarizing* a choir with a new piece. These overview issues should form the basic "plan" for the initial rehearsing of a work are listed below. Discussions of each of the headings will take place after the list. This text will not approach all of the specific elements of vocal production involved in rehearsal technique.

- *Use conducting gesture that provides the correct signals to the choir.*
- *Maintain a consistent tempo and resting tone—to establish the choir's readiness for hearing.*
- *Allow the choir to absorb the harmonic language by rote: consider rehearsing the work at a slower tempo.*
- *Impart the shape and forward movement of the work: establish the movement of air early in the rehearsal process*

- *Teach and familiarize the choir with a work through an approach to count singing that teaches one layer of musical element at a time.*
- *Use neutral syllables to teach the musical elements of a piece.*
- *Be aware of the proper production of the vowels that will influence intonation.*
- *When using count singing or neutral syllable singing, make certain that the choir is counting with an emphasis upon correct attack and correct rhythm. Do not be concerned about sustainment; teach the notes and the rhythms first.*

CORRECT SIGNALS IN GESTURES

Much has been said in this text concerning conducting gesture that is a direct outgrowth of listening. If one is listening, then the conducting gesture will be appropriate. Remember that if the sounds being sung by the choir are inappropriate, always examine your gesture for the signals it may or may not be giving that, in turn, affect the sound.

CONSISTENT TEMPO AND RESTING TONE—READINESS FOR HEARING

Has the choir demonstrated to you that they can maintain a consistent tempo? While rushing problems are usually caused by the lack of full, appropriate breaths by the choir, rhythmic havoc will result if the choir cannot discern a consistent tempo from an inconsistent one! Likewise, has the choir demonstrated an ability to sing the resting tone of the modality (major, minor, dorian, lydian, etc.) that they are about to sing? If not, attempts at proper intonation will not be successful.

TEACHING CONSISTENT TEMPO. Each singer may bring his or her "personal" tempo to the reading and learning of a piece; that is, each singer will hear the tempo of the piece slower or faster than the tempo that the conductor has chosen. The establishment of "communal" tempo must be undertaken for each new work rehearsed. Additionally, this process will teach and reinforce the concept of consistent tempo within each singer.

Consistent tempo may be established using several different techniques. These techniques are similar to those introduced earlier in this text. However, it is helpful to examine those techniques again from the viewpoint of teaching consistent tempo through ensemble rehearsal. Regardless of the technique chosen, several cognitive elements concerning the pedagogy of consistent tempo must be kept in mind before any techniques can be used and be expected to be retained by the ensemble.

1. *Large body movement should be used as the basic starting point for establishing consistent tempo.* As the "beats" of the piece are chanted or played, the choir should be able to move their bodies in free response to the basic rhythmic pulse of the piece. Body movement can take the form of swaying from side to side; clapping hands across the body mid line as if tossing dough from hand to hand; moving the hands and arms in an outward circular motion. It is important to remember that basic rhythmic impulse is learned through what amounts to a disturbance of the body kinesthesia. Swaying from side to side upsets the equilibrium of balance due to the movement of fluid within the inner ear. It is that disequilibrium which first establishes pulse in its broadest sense. Regardless of the activity chosen, the choir should chant on a neutral syllable on each major pulse of the piece until the ensemble does not rush or slow the tempo.

If the ensemble cannot hold a consistent tempo, they must be taught by rote and experience, through conductor example, the feeling of a consistent tempo in the following manner. The conductor should first demonstrate rushing or slowing. The choir should listen, perhaps with eyes closed. The conductor should then demonstrate a consistent tempo to the choir. The choir should keep the large beat in their feet while the conductor chants (using a neutral syllable) in a consistent tempo. The choir should then echo, on a neutral syllable (such as *bm*) the melodic rhythm of the piece.

2. *After large body movement has been established, the large beat (macro beat) should be performed with the feet.* The first subdivision (micro beat) should be performed with a light clapping motion in the hands. The rhythm of the piece (melodic rhythm) is spoken simultaneously in conjunction with the action of the feet (macro beat) and hands (micro beat). A consistent teaching strategy is important when teaching both consistent tempo and the melodic rhythm of the piece to the choir. If the procedure for teaching the rhythmic structure is altered with each piece, it will take longer for the choir to musically understand and retain the essences of the rhythm of the work. Rhythm learning is most efficient when the same "input" mechanism is used, that is, the combination of feet, hands, and mouth, each always performing the same respective element of the rhythm, macro beat, micro beat and the melodic rhythm. One may view the action of the feet and hands as the "input and filing mechanism" for the rhythmic patterns of the piece.

3. *Always perform the melodic rhythm of the piece with neutral syllables first before employing other techniques such as counting, etc.* It is important to remember that before any rhythmic syllable system is used by the choir, the melodic rhythm of the piece be chanted in a monotone syllable such as *bm, du-bee-du-bee* (useful in passages using eighth note or sixteenth note runs), *tee, tah, pum, pah, nyee, nu, du*, etc. By limiting the

choir to such neutral syllables until the pitches and rhythm have been stabilized, the choir will focus on listening without the cognitive-theoretical confusion that ensues when a rhythm syllable system is added. Amateur singers, especially those who do not read music, will complain. In fact, at first, rehearsals may move slower. The conductor will find, however, that the "ears" and overall listening ability of the choir will show a marked improvement. In general, follow the following sequential consistent tempo procedure when rehearsing a piece or when one finds that the choir cannot maintain a consistent tempo. Remember that if you skip a few of the steps, and difficulty results, you should return to step one.

a. Have the choir locate the "large beat" of the music with large body movement, i.e., rocking, swaying, swinging, etc.

b. After the choir has been able to move with their bodies to the "large beats," have the choir put the macro beat in their feet and the micro beat in their hands. Make sure that the choir is in a consistent "communal tempo."

c. After the choir is able to locate the macro beat with their feet and the micro beat with their hands, have them chant the melodic rhythm of their part on a neutral syllable simultaneously with keeping the macro and micro beat in their feet and hands.

d. After the choir is able to perform the melodic rhythm in the above fashion in a consistent tempo, the conductor may ask them to use any syllable or number counting system that is preferred.

Remember that before any number or counting system is used with the choir, the choir must have demonstrated to the conductor an ability to perform the rhythm of the piece on a neutral syllable in a consistent tempo. *A number system used prematurely may inhibit the choirs ability to hear and learn the rhythm of the piece!*

TEACHING RESTING TONE. To teach the resting tone of a work, the conductor needs to clearly establish the tonality of the exercise for the choir, i.e., major, minor, dorian, phrygian, etc. The conductor should make a special effort to sound the resting tone triad, the dominant function triad and the cadential or leading tone triad of that mode. For example, in major, the conductor should either hum or sing in solfège syllables: so-la-so-fa-mi-re-ti-do. After hearing that "preparatory sequence," the conductor should pause to allow the choir to audiate (hear) that tonality. The choir should then be asked to hum the resting tone, do, either with a neutral syllable such as *bm* or with the solfège syllable if the students have received comprehensive instruction concerning solfège syllables. A secure, in-tune response from the choir will indicate to some extent that the choir can "hear" the resting tone of that tonality. Ideally, it would be most beneficial to hear elementary, junior high school, high school, and university choir members perform the exercise in solo. Only when individual choir members can perform in solo is the conductor assured that they are truly "hearing" in that tonality. (Caution must be exercised concerning solo singing with older choir members in church choirs, etc.) Other tonalities are as follows:

Tonality	Solfège Syllables	Resting Tone Response from Choir
Minor	mi fa mi re do ti si la	**LA**
Mixolydian	re mi re do ti la fa so	**SO**
Dorian	la ti la so fa me do re	**RE**

Many times, choirs are unable to negotiate half steps in vocalises because the conductor does not clearly establish the resting tone for the exercise; hence, each choir member is free to assume subjectively in which tonality he or she might be singing. The conductor needs to be sure that the choir members are in agreement as to what tonality they are singing. Ultimately, the choir needs to be taught to hear the pitches without the sound being physically present. That process is known as audiation.

ABSORPTION OF THE HARMONIC LANGUAGE

It is recommended that, when a piece is being introduced to the choir for the first time, the choir be allowed to hear it played from the keyboard while they listen. Too often conductors underestimate the ability of the ears of choir members to absorb considerable musical information about the piece from listening. Many times conductors insist on intervening in the process that will allow the piece of music to speak directly to the singers by becoming over involved in the teaching of the work at the initial reading. Many of us need to put more trust in the power of hearing. If the choir is focused and directed toward listening, they can glean the following from the initial playing of the work: (1) the rhythmic direction and shaping of the work; (2) the tonal and harmonic nature of the work; (3) changes of key or mode; and (4) the style of the work.

Many conductors make the mistake of beginning to rehearse a work at "performance" tempo. While this certainly can be done, rehearsing using a modified, or slower, tempo can be beneficial (1) to allow for the exact intonation to occur—moving at a fast tempo does not allow the choir time to hear the pitch, let alone make adjustments to it; (2) to guide the choir toward hearing the subtleness of the harmonic movement, further assisting tuning; (3) to allow for exact placement and musical execution of artistic and deep-seated breaths; and (4) to establish articulation issues—i.e., length of syllable, color of pitches, style of the piece, and the direction of the musical line—more efficiently than rehearsing at a fast tempo.

SHAPE AND FORWARD MOVEMENT OF THE WORK

After the work has been played by the keyboardist, it should be played again, but this time the choir should be asked to "hiss" each phrase, using a resistant and low supported double-s consonant and a vowel sound, as if they were saying the word *set*. The conductor should hear, regardless of the music style of the work, a continuity of air flow (support). If one hears the melodic rhythm of the piece, this indicates that the choir is incorrectly supporting the tone. Continuous air should be sounded with an increase of air flow to parallel the rise of phrases. Any break in that flow will indicate that the support of the singers has lessened; hence, the tone will not be supported, which will lead to many other problems. It is important to establish in the first reading the support feeling necessary to sing the work, which grows out of how the piece moves. After the choir has "hissed" through the work, they can then begin to sing it on a neutral syllable. It is also recommended that the choir "moan" through a work on *mm* or *nn*. The moaning provides a tool for the conductor to hear and teach the concept of the line for that piece in addition to connecting the support "system" to the singing voice.

EXACT ATTACK AND EXACT PITCH

One of the most important factors when reading a new work is often overlooked by many conductors. Intonation problems are often born during the initial reading of a work. This discussion presupposes that the conductor is *not* reading with text during an initial reading. When reading a work for the first time, whether it be with neutral syllables or count singing, the choir is too often allowed to sing legato. By allowing the choir to read the work legato, the conductor unknowingly allows each choir member the liberty of sliding, or glissing, to each pitch, no matter whether the line moves by step or leap. By allowing this legato, the conductor is allowing each singer not to be totally committed to either the pitch or the rhythm (or both) of each note of the composition. When reading a work, the conductor should use syllables or numbers and insist that the choir sing with exact rhythm and exact pitch; that is, the focus of their attention must be the attack of each note, its exact pitch and its exact rhythm. There should be no attempt to sustain the line after the attack. The choir should be encouraged not to sing sostenuto after each note is sounded. If the conductor asks the choir to do this, the result is different than asking the choir to sing staccato. The effect of this procedure is that it places responsibility on each singer to commit to singing exact pitch and exact rhythm according to his own musical instincts. The insistence of the conductor of singing without excessive legato minimizes glissando, which creates part of the phenomenon of out-of-tune singing. Also, this procedure allows for a "clearing," or space, after each pitch is sounded in its rhythmic context so that the next pitch can be clearly heard or audiated before it is sung. Syllables, no matter whether they be neutral or numeric, sung with particularity, can quickly anchor the exact pitch and exact rhythm of the work. After the choir can sing the work in this fashion, then they will more likely be able to sing the work with an in-tune legato, providing they are able to sing the same vowel sounds.

AN APPROACH TO COUNT SINGING

Many different counting systems are employed by conductors as means of establishing and reestablishing rhythmic pulse within a work. It is also a valuable technique to teach the forward motion and internal rhythm pulse of a work to a choir. It is additionally useful to clearly establish those points within the music for rhythmic breath and phrasing. However, many conductors make the mistake of trying to teach too much too quickly with count singing. Count singing works most effectively when it is use to expose musical "layers" of the piece one at time. Follow the procedure below.

Initial readings: count sing at a low dynamic level (sotto voce), minimizing vibrato and vocal color. By restricting the choir's dynamic level, you automatically withdraw from the note learning process two aspects of vocal technique that can cause serious intonation problems or intonation vagueness. The restricted dynamic level focuses the concentration of the choir on accurate pitch and accurate rhythm. It is at this level that rhythmic breathing is taught in tandem with the rhythm and tonal elements. Make sure that the choir is performing in a consistent tempo. If not, return to the procedure for teaching consistent tempo.

One of the most important aspects of count singing is the style of the count singing used. *When count singing, insist that the choir count with an exact particularity.* That is, when counting, there should be an exactitude about the counting that emphasizes only the pitch and the rhythm of what is being counted, and not the sostenuto quality of the line. By insisting on the choirs attention to the attack of each note, not its decay, the choir members will be forced to commit to singing exact pitch and exact rhythm. It is the attack of each note which determines the pitch and the rhythm. The sostenuto quality of the line tends to mask pitch and rhythm problems for the singers. The exactness of the counting will go a long way towards improving rehearsal efficiency.

The most commonly used technique is to count through the music with the numeric syllables "One and two and tee and four and." (Note that the word *tee* is substituted for the word *three*. The consonantal combination of *th* tends to slow the tempo of the piece.) The problem, however, with numeric syllables is that they presuppose a knowledge of music theory and music reading literacy by the choir. For an amateur choir whose music reading skills are not polished, it is better to count sing using neutral syllables such as *du-du-du* or *du-bah-du-bah*, repeated. The syllables should be spoken on every micro beat (subdivision) regardless of the note value. (For example, for a half note in 4/4 time, speak *du-du-du-du*.) Avoid using syllables with diphthongs, such as *du-day-du-day*, because they will cause poor intonation at this stage of the reading with an amateur choir. An important aspect of count singing that is a necessary component in order for it to work lies in the accurate and precise articulation of the syllables. Since count singing is a technique to clarify both rhythm and pitch, *emphasis must be placed on the precise rhythmic attack of each pitch, not the sostenuto quality of each note.* By insisting on the particularity of the articulation, proper pitch and rhythm will be realized. Be careful not to ask the choir to sing staccato. By asking them to sing staccato, the singers tend to focus on an abrupt release of the tone, thus drawing attention away from exact pitch and attack for the start of each tone.

Aside from the usual use of the count singing by all members of the choir, some variations in the technique add to rehearsal variety and maintain interest.

1. Use numeric or neutral syllables, but leave all rests silent.
2. Divide the choir in half by asking those whose last name begins with A–M to be in the first group, and those with the letters N–Z to be in the second group. Have half the choir chant the melodic rhythm of the piece, while the other half of the choir counts numbers or syllables aloud.
3. Have half the choir perform macro and micro beats in their feet and hands (tapping macros in feet, clapping micros in the hand) while the other half of the choir count sings the music. Have the choir reverse their task on your direction.

4. To further anchor the consistent tempo, have the choir count sing but accent the offbeat after each pulse.

When the correct pitch and correct rhythm have been established, add the appropriate dynamic levels, but still minimize vibrato and maintain the count singing syllable. This is an important next step in the process. The next "layer" of musical element is the dynamics, devoid of as much color as possible. To add vibrato and dynamics at the same time may create intonation problems because the singers have not had enough "aural" time with the pitch and the rhythm. This should not be done for extensive periods of time because it becomes taxing on the voice. Remember to always maintain the particularity of the rhythm; the emphasis should be on exact rhythm and exact pitch, not the sostenuto quality of the line.

When the correct pitch and rhythm are performed in conjunction with the dynamics, the singers can add vibrato to the sound. Many times when rehearsing or count singing, the piece is sung at full color and dynamics. The essential elements of the score, accurate pitch and accurate rhythm, then become veiled or hidden. *Be careful, however, that when each tone is begun, vibrato does not begin at the onset of the note. When this is done, accurate pitch suffers.* Vibrato can be added after the tone has been sounded. It is important to use count singing to separate and illuminate the score in this layering process—pitch and rhythm first, dynamic next, and finally, vocal color.

PERSONAL COMMITMENT FOR GOOD INTONATION

Good pitch in a choir is the product of several technical factors. Obviously, the vowels sung by the choir must be the same within each section and within the choir. However, it cannot be overemphasized that particular singing using neutral syllables and numbers is one of the most important rehearsal procedures to be mastered. When one sings his or her part without "crooning" to each pitch, vocal and pitch clarity can be the result. If, however, intonation is still a problem, it might be best to approach the problem via the energy and commitment of the singers.

Many times, problems of pitch are problems of attitude. One of the more valuable rehearsal procedures is to ask the choir to point directly ahead of themselves as they sing each pitch. It is often fascinating to watch the response from the choir when this is asked of them. Some of them point with incredible directness. Others find it difficult to point at all, albeit with any energy. It is these latter singers who affect the pitch by their lack of personal, human commitment to singing. In trying to remedy this problem, it would be inhumane to point out individuals. What does make sense, however, is to encourage them to point with directness. When they can point with directness, you will hear that the pitch of the work being rehearsed becomes very clear.

NEUTRAL SYLLABLES

One of the rehearsal decisions that conductors are faced with when rehearsing a piece concerns the choice of what syllables should be used in the initial rehearsal/reading/learning of the piece in conjunction with the count singing procedure discussed above. Many conductors choose a favorite rehearsal syllable and begin rehearsing the piece without considering why a syllable is chosen or what purpose it serves. The choice of a syllable or syllables is one of the most important pedagogical decisions that a conductor makes in preparing for the rehearsal.

WORKING WITH TEXT. Before a discussion of neutral syllables for rehearsal can take place, the conductor must understand why it is very inefficient to begin the rehearsal of a work with text. There are both vocal pedagogical reasons and learning efficiency reasons for using neutral syllables.

First, without entering into a lengthy discussion of the psychology of music learning, suffice it to say that to begin rehearsing with text confounds the music learning process for the choir. Research in the psychology of music has proven the value of neutral syllable teaching for children through adults. By using a neutral syllable, the conductor, in essence, limits the number of variables that may cause problems for the choir both musically and vocally. Moreover, the neutral syllable focuses the hearing of the choir on the basic elements of the music, i.e., rhythm, pitch, line, and finally, tone quality. Without the distraction of the text, it is possible for the choir to commit to their musical hearing memory those most basic elemental music ideas within the score. Perhaps an analogy will clarify this point. Have you ever asked a person with little music experience to sing the national anthem without words? In all likelihood, they cannot. The reason for this is because they learned the tune in association with the words. The tune is then forever bound to the words! The person is unable to separate the music from the words and focus upon the music. Amateurs believe that when they can sing a piece "with the words," they have learned the piece! Hence, adjustments in pitch, rhythm, and so on are almost impossible to make. An amateur choir that learns a piece immediately with text will find it difficult to separate out music elements for repair, such as accurate pitch and rhythm, because the notes and rhythms of the piece are psychologically married to the text. Teaching text too early also inhibits music expression and spontaneous music making. It also does not allow for accurate pitch and accurate rhythm in a consistent tempo to be "schooled in." Pitch, rhythm, and the stylistic colors of the piece must be in the choir's ear before text is added. To do otherwise is a serious oversight in rehearsal technique by the conductor in preparing for the rehearsal. Time spent at these early stages ensures good performance.

Second, there are compelling vocal pedagogy issues for delaying text as long as possible until the music elements of the score have been learned. The choice of learning a piece on one, two, or several vowels chosen for the pedagogically correct reasons is central to the rehearsal process. Neutral syllables chosen for the correct reasons can build a choral sound with the appropriate breath support from the initial stages of learning a piece. By using a few neutral syllables that relate to the textural color of the piece, the conductor can make sure that vowel verticality and forwardness of placement is maintained. Many amateur choirs sing many of their vowels in the jowls in performance because such a procedure has not been followed. If the choices are made correctly on one or two vowel sounds, when text is added, the conductor will find that a consistent "sound" has been built into the choir that transfers easily and immediately to other vowels. Rules to consider are as follows:

1. *Rehearse only on pure vowels—no diphthongs!* As stated earlier, a choir should always rehearse on pure vowels. Diphthongs, such as *doe,* or *tay,* will produce unclear sounds, many times manifested as pitch problems. It is a challenge to get a choir to sing a diphthong correctly: virtually each person in the choir places the second vowel at a different time; hence, the choral color and pitch problems. While diphthong execution must be taught to the choir, it is best handled after the music has been learned on a neutral syllable!

2. *Be careful with the choice of vowel sounds when all voice parts move into extreme high and low ranges.* No matter what pure vowel is chosen for rehearsing, caution must be used when those vowels move out of the middle register for each voice part. The conductor should give "helps" to the choir when the part moves into those extremes according to the suggestions below.

3. *Choose a consonant to precede the vowel that reflects the rhythmic spirit of the piece and that will assist with the correct vocal production of the sound for a particular music style period.* The choice of what consonant should precede the chosen vowel is also very important. The choice of the consonant can quickly establish the rhythmic style (legato, marcato, staccato, etc.) of the piece. The choice of the consonant can also "launch" the appropriate resonance (bright vs. dark) and maintain vocal placement for the style of the piece.

4. When in doubt about what vowel to choose, select oo, ee, *or the German* ü. The vowels which build a choral sound with head tone are *oo, ee,* and the German *ü.* The choir should be asked to perform these vowels with rounded lips, similar to a fish. This seemingly ridiculous analogy brings immediate focus to the vowel and also promotes frontal resonance!

5. Be vigilant about the tongue vowels, ee *and* eh. The vowels *ee* and *eh* are very hazardous for choral intonation. They are the vowels that tend to become "jowl vowels" in the amateur choir. Ask the choir to make sure that the side edges of their tongue are touching their upper side teeth as the vowel is being produced, and that the tip of their tongue is anchored against their lower front teeth. Also constantly reinforce that they should feel a great amount of vertical space above their tongue as they sing the vowel. By doing so, you insure appropriate high placement of the vowel and ensure accurate intonation!

6. Avoid the ah *vowel!* While the choir my have an easier time producing the *ah* vowel in various registers, the ease of execution does not outweigh the vocal problems it may foster. The vowel is a dangerous one to use because (1) it encourages the use of lower, or chest, register singing in amateurs; (2) it becomes flat easily because of the possible lack of head tone in the vowel by amateurs; (3) it requires a free and open vocal tract; (4) it requires consistently low breath support, which is difficult for amateurs; and (5) it is more difficult to adjust intonation with this vowel. Ask the choir to maintain very high vertical space with this vowel and to sing it toward their cheekbones.

CHOOSING A VOWEL FOR REHEARSING. Below are listed the possible vowels for rehearsing with explanations for choosing one vowel over another. (Note: vowels are spelled phonetically). The rule below should be observed for *all* vowels.

Basic Rule for All Vowels: Open the mouth like *ah* in the high range and ask the singers to bring their lips around the sound. In ascending, drop the jaw gradually; when descending, close the mouth gradually.

VOWEL   EXPLANATION FOR USE

oo   Is a healthy vowel for general vocalization because it fosters head tone for all voice parts. Should be performed with a slight rounding of the lips. In upper ranges, women should continue to sing *oo* with a rounded mouth position with the vertical space of *uh*, men should sing the *oo* vowel that is in the word *foot*.

ee   Is also a very good vowel for learning a piece. This vowel also fosters head tone for all voice parts and should be performed with a slight round mouth position. Remember that *ee* is a tongue vowel: for both men and women the tongue should contact upper side teeth and should be anchored against the lower front teeth, and singers should be asked to envision a great deal of space above their tongue. In upper ranges, women should continue to sing pure *ee* with a rounded mouth with the vertical space of *uh*. Men should sing the vowel that is in the word *him*. Use of this vowel fosters a brighter sound in the choir. If the vowel becomes too strident or pressed, ask the choir to think *oo* into the sound.

German ü   This vowel is the most desirable vowel for most circumstances because it combines the best qualities of both of the above vowels: the head quality of the *oo* vowel with the brightness of the *ee* vowel. This vowel is especially useful in initial readings of works sung with the beginning voiced consonant combination of *ny*. The use of the voiced *ny* demands the singer "connect" the vocal sound to the support mechanism. The *nyü* should be sung very bright so that the center of the pitches can be heard, and the choir can begin to hear and develop appropriate intonation. Once the accurate pitches have been "schooled in" through this brighter (almost French) vowel sound, rehearsal can progress to other vowel sounds. For both women and men, the jaw should be dropped when ascending. Maintain a round mouth position. Use of this vowel fosters a brighter sound in the choir. American choirs have difficulty producing this vowel. Simply tell them to sing *ee* and wrap their lips around the vowel in a very rounded mouth position. In effect, they are singing *ee* but their mouths look like *oo*.

o   Generally should be avoided because of its diphthong.

i
(as in   Generally should be avoided because of its diphthong.
night)

ah   While this vowel can be used, it should be used with caution. This vowel fosters chest quality in all voice parts and
is difficult to monitor in a choral situation. If it must be
used, it should be sung with a great deal of vertical space,
and with a rounded mouth position. The choir should also
be reminded that *ah* lives in the same "house" that *oo* does.
In upper ranges, the women should think *oo* into the
sound; men should sing the vowel that is in the word *but.*
This vowel is useful in building a darker choral sound.

CHOOSING A CONSONANT FOR REHEARSING. In
selecting a consonant or consonants to pair with vowels for rehearsing, the *style* of
the music is a major determining factor that helps to determine what consonant
or consonant combinations should be used. The conductor should choose a consonant which will most closely re-create the rhythmic style of the music.

NON-LEGATO CONSONANTS. A piece that is very rhythmic may require consonants such as *t, p, b,* and *d* could fit your needs. *The consonant* d *is most desirable
because it keeps the choir singing on the breath.* The other consonants tend to make the
choir unseat the breath. In any case, the choir should be instructed to spring
quickly into the vowel with the shortest possible consonant, thus creating a long
vowel.

LEGATO CONSONANTS. For works that are more legato and need a consistent
approach to continuous line and continuous sound, voiced consonants should be
used, such as *m, n, ny, v,* and *z.* The choir should be told to voice the consonant
and lengthen it so that it has time to sound the pitch before moving to the vowel
sound. The voiced consonants are also useful to build a connection between the
"support" and the voice. If conductors insist on the voicing of these consonants,
they will be insuring that support is connected to the following vowels. It is also
very helpful to intersperse humming and "chewing" a sustained sound between
long periods of rehearsing with the above consonants. "Humming and chewing"
with "thick lips" (lips that are slightly touching) helps bring continued relaxation
to the jaw and vocal mechanism, in addition to continuing to foster a healthy and
resonant forward placement.

TIP-OF-THE-TONGUE *L* CAUTIONS. If the consonant *l* is selected, care must be
taken to instruct the choir concerning the correct articulation of a "tip-of-the-
tongue *l*" Many American choirs articulate this consonant by humping the middle

of the tongue and touching the middle portion of the hard palate. This will immediately place the tone farther back than desired (jowl sound) and most likely produce a flatness of pitch, plus considerably slow the rhythm of the piece. The choir should be instructed to articulate the *l* with the portion of the tongue immediately behind the tip, touching that area to the gum line above the upper front teeth. This simple adjustment will insure that the sound maintains a forward placement, in addition to maintaining rhythmic integrity.

When working through the initial reading of a piece on a neutral syllable, it is possible to establish the texture of sections within the piece by alternating neutral syllables. For example, if one begins a work that has a rhythmic, marcato quality, *du* may be used. For a contrasting legato section, the choir could be asked to sing *noo*.

PROPER PRODUCTION OF THE VOWELS

A reminder once again about the tongue vowels, *ee* and *eh*. Ask the choir to make sure that the side edges of their tongue are touching their upper side teeth as the vowel is being produced and that the tip of their tongue remain anchored against their front teeth. Also constantly reinforce that they should feel a great amount of vertical space above their tongue as they sing the vowel. Proper production of all vowel sounds positively influences a choir's intonation.

THE INITIAL READING: CORRECTING PITCH AND RHYTHM PROBLEMS DURING REHEARSAL

The conductor should realize that when a mistake is sung by a choir, that mistake could be the result of one of two problems: either a pitch error or a rhythm error. Can you recall the times when sight reading that you made a mistake in pitch because you encountered a rhythmic problem, or vice versa? When you come upon a musical stumbling block, *always* rehearse the pitch aspects separately from the rhythm; that is, rehearse the "tune" or parts devoid of rhythm, and rehearse the rhythm devoid of the melodic materials. Isolation of the pitch and rhythm aspects will more effectively and efficiently correct the problem.

ADDING TEXT AFTER REHEARSING WITH NEUTRAL SYLLABLE

After correct pitches, rhythms, and overall color of the work have stabilized, introduce text. The point at which text is introduced is always a controversial one. It can be argued that it is more advantageous to introduce text soon after the work has been read. If the choir is fairly advanced, or if the rehearsal timetable is a short one, this can be very true. However, when it is possible, text should be delayed until the essential elements of the score have had a chance to "settle in." One will know that these elements have settled in because the works begins to "sing itself." Pitch becomes stable, as does the vocalism of the singers.

When text is introduced, it is important to follow a logical procedure that will teach the elements of diction quickly and efficiently.

1. *Speak the text slowly to make sure basic vowel sounds are in agreement.* This is a chance to show the singers how singing diction is very different from speaking diction. When speaking the text for the choir, speak the text as it would be sung. When done correctly, this spoken-chanting will sound like a "Julia Child" voice or heightened speech. *While modeling the text for the choir, much vertical spaciousness should be kept inside the mouth. Minimize the open vowel sounds in the text; it is those sounds that will tend to open and possess a spread tone quality in amateur singers.* The singers should speak the text back in an affected "Julia Child" voice, almost sung on a single pitch.

2. *Whisper the text in rhythm to make sure that consonants are of the desired length.* In a legato context, consonants should be as short as possible so that the singers get to the vowel as quickly as possible.

3. *Speak the text in an exaggerated "Julia Child" voice, or heightened speech, in the choir's middle to upper register.* Speaking the text in this fashion makes the transition for amateur singers between diction used for speaking and diction used for singing. By speaking in this style, the singers feel the internal height necessary to produced the vowels clearly and without pressure. Use of this technique usually transfers easily to singing.

4. *Speak the text with sustained speech.* Have the choir speak the text at a slower tempo so that you can hear the sustainment of the vowel sounds. Many times as the choir sings, they change quality of a vowel as they sustain it.

5. *Chant the text in a* regular metric style. Chant the text one syllable per pulse on a static whole tone chord, e.g., E-F♯-G♯-A♯, with basses on the E, tenors on the F♯, altos on the G♯ and sopranos on the A♯. By chanting on this static chord, the singers can hear which vowel sounds tend to go "out of tune" and make immedi-

ate adjustments to the color of the vowel. Remember that pitch problems are, for the most part, caused by vowel color problems and not "wrong pitches."

6. *Remind the choir to sing through each vowel sound.* Constantly encourage the choir to think forward to the next vowel sound. Often the choir sings vowels that seem to get stuck, or are stagnant and lack forward motion.

7. *Regardless of the style of the work, rehearse the work staccato.* Rehearsing a piece staccato is of great assistance to further tune the work and to align vowel sounds.

8. *Be certain to observe the schwa.* The schwa is the unstressed syllable in all languages. In English it is the final syllable in *garden, mother, father, sister, brother.* The entire word *the* functions like a schwa in the phrase "the moon." To produce a sung schwa, ask the choir to bring their lips around the sound. Improperly produced schwas will affect pitch.

9. *Sing the work as written.* Insist on the pure *oo* and *ee* vowels in the text. Then encourage the singers to sing the other vowels that follow the *oo* and the *ee* with the same purity as *oo* and *ee* and to stay "in the same house" as *oo* and *ee*. This procedure keeps the vowel sounds forward and high. Also eliminate all diphthongs. Be certain all schwas are sung correctly. Remove the *r*s in texts where necessary, and be certain that all *l*s are sung as "tip-of-the-tongue" *l*s and not American *l*s.

10. *Be aware of Americanisms.* Generally, Americanisms can be defined as diction problems that are peculiar to American English. Americans tend to speak with vowel sounds that are not high enough and forward enough in the mouth. They also tend to speak without the vertical spaciousness that is needed. By rehearsing with heightened speech, much can be done to correct this problem.

OPEN VERSUS CLOSED VOWELS FOR THE AMATEUR CHOIR

When teaching diction to amateur choirs, it is necessary to establish the importance of the closed vowel. The terms *open vowel* and *closed vowel* have to do with the opening of the mouth. They have nothing to do with the internal mouth space. That space is always tall and spacious. Amateur choirs tend to sing the way they speak. Their vowels generally lack vertical spaciousness and are generally spread. To bring focus to that sound, it is helpful to "close" the vowels that are spread, that is, ask the choir to bring their lips around the sound. By bringing their lips around the sound, they will bring more clarity to the sound, and hence improve pitch. Bringing their lips around the sound also mixes in the color of the vowel *oo* to the vowel being sung. By closing vowels that are spread, airy, or pinched, you will help pitch, diction, and the color of the sound.

SUMMARY OF REHEARSAL TECHNIQUE ISSUES

A chart of rehearsal problems and their possible causes and/or solutions can be found below. By no means is this chart all-inclusive; however, an attempt has been made to list the most commonly occurring problems with their solutions for novice conductors as they experience their first rehearsals. Do not try to listen for specific problems. Become very familiar with the list. If you are familiar with the list, as you listen to your choir sing, the "problem" with its solution will become apparent after the choir has completed its singing. If you try to think of these problems while the choir is singing, your ability to listen to the music in total will be greatly decreased.

PROBLEM	POSSIBLE SOLUTION
Tempo rushes	Conductor is not listening to breath of ensemble
	Choir does not possess a sense of consistent tempo
	Conductor is not breathing
	Choir is not breathing with the conductor
	Conductor does not provide impulse gesture for breath
	Conductor lacks internal subdivision of beat
	Choir needs to count sing more
Tempo slows	Conductor is not listening to breath of ensemble
	Choir does not possess a sense of consistent tempo
	Conductor's gesture does not stay ahead of sound
	Conductor's breath not taken in tempo of piece
	Conductor lacks internal subdivision of beat
	Conductor's rebound is a subdivision
	Consonants of the choir are too long
	Choir needs to count sing more
	Dotted rhythm needs to be impelled on the strong beat within the dotted values
Lack of musical line	Conductor's rebound is a subdivision
	Conductor's gesture and breath do not connect phrases
	Conductor is overconducting final consonants

Conductor's gesture is not expansive enough and does not utilize horizontal space

Conductor is not impelling line forward at essential points

Conductor's gesture is too weighted

Conductor's gesture always moves at same rate; no variance in velocity

Conductor does not allow choir to sing

Conductor does not trust choir to sing

Choir needs to count sing more

Have choir point with index finger each time either a long pitch is sung or a note associated with a textual stress is sung

Ask choir to think vowels constantly moving forward; ask them to make the vowel as long as possible

---

Initial "attack" tight and restricted and may be out of tune	Conductor needs to mirror the first vowel of the word that is sung
	Choir needs to breathe the vowel that starts their phrase
	Conducting gesture is causing the initial sound to be manufactured instead of spontaneously released as a natural outcome from rhythmic, deep seated breath
	The initial breath of the choir needs to rhythmically propel the choir into the phrase

---

Poor intonation	Color of vowel cannot maintain pitch; make sure vowels stay high and forward
	Use schwa on appropriate word endings
	Make more vertical space (drop jaw) as line ascends
	Conductor's gesture is too weighted
	Conductor is overconducting
	Singers are not using breath properly to sustain and move sound
	Conductor's gesture has too much muscular involvement
	Choir needs to count sing more
	Choir needs to rehearse on bright vowel, preferably

the German *ü*, so that the core of tone can
    clearly sound the pitch

Conductor's hand position adversely affecting pitch;
    make sure ictus is on the end of the third finger

Check diphthongs; tell the choir to sing only the
    first vowel

Piece keeps flatting or sharping	Raise or lower the key for performance one-half step Rehearse piece in a key a whole step or higher above original key, sotto voce; then return to original key

---

Texture too heavy, too thick	Ask choir to think all their vowels very tall but *very* narrow on their mouth, in addition to being high and forward

---

Alto section continually sings underpitch	Vowel color may be the problem: remind altos to keep vowels very vertical and forward Look for tongue vowels *ee, ih,* and *eh*: ask altos to think that there is space above their tongue when singing these vowels Make sure singers are seating breath low in the body

---

Unaccented syllables in text are heavily accented; no stressed and unstressed syllables	Use schwa; ask the choir to sing the vowel that is similar to the English word *learn* with very rounded lips Have choir speak text in a prolonged fashion using their fingers to press the corners of the mouth inward on every schwa

---

Same pitch or rhythm problem keeps occurring	Isolate part; rehearse the tones without rhythm; rehearse the rhythm without tone, then recombine Choir needs to hear piece played without them singing: harmonic changes not in ear Choir does not hear resting tone in that tonality

Musical style inappropriate	Conductor is not breathing and thinking color as he breathes Wrong neutral syllables chosen when choir began learning piece
Pressed vocal sound	Conductor does not believe that the choir will make a beautiful sound Choir learned piece at inappropriate dynamic Choir needs to count sing more Jaw rigidity Vowels not vertical and forward enough Choir does not make space as lines ascend
Poor legato	Conductor's gesture is causing consonants to be longer than necessary Choir needs to sing short consonants in order to get to vowel more quickly Conductor's gesture is causing accent Rehearse choir singing only vowel sounds of the text in order to make musical line continuous, add consonants
Rhythms written with dotted values inaccurate	Ask choir to place a space or daylight between the dotted note and the following note
Choir's breath not low enough in the body	Conductor's gesture too high Conductor does not breathe Conductor has not thought about the color of the sound he desires
Poor legato in Latin and Italian	Make certain no air or sibilant sound escapes on consonants such as *t*; in Latin and Italian you should never hear air—air should be made into tone
Vocal attack on open vowel (no consonant at beginning of word) has a glottal attack	Ask choir to move their jaw slightly before they start to sing

Piano dynamic lacks support and color	Ask choir to sing a forte on the passage in question; after they have sung the passage, ask them how their bodies felt; ask them to now have the same "body feeling" but sing piano
Ah vowel is sung flat	Color of vowel is causing the pitch problem: have choir think the vowel very high in their mouth and very forward—toward their cheekbones; think tall, vertical vowel with tongue flat in mouth
Ee vowel is sung flat	Color of vowel is causing the pitch problem: have choir think the vowel very high in their mouth and very forward—toward their cheekbones
Eh vowel, as in *let*, is sung flat	Color of vowel is causing the pitch problem: have choir think the vowel very high in their mouth and very forward—toward their cheekbones; raise tongue to close vowel and round lips
Ah vowel, as in *black*, is sung flat	Ask choir to think *eh* (as in *let*) into the sound
Women's (or trebles) sound on any pitch above third line treble clef note B-natural while singing the vowel *eh* as in *let* is spread, tight, pressed, thin, or out of tune	Ask women or trebles to (1) open the mouth like *ah* if the note is in their upper range, and (2) think a bit of the vowel *ee* into the sound and round the lips
Choir sounds out of tune when singing a diphthong such as *day, night,* etc.	Ask the choir to only sing the first vowel

Women's (or trebles) sound on any pitch above third line treble clef note B-natural while singing the vowel *ih* as in *with* is spread, tight, pressed, thin, or out of tune.	Ask women or trebles to (1) open the mouth like *ah* if the note is in their upper range, and (2) think a bit of the vowel *ee* into the sound and round the lips
Vowel sounds in general are spread, out of tune, or dull in sound	Consider closing the vowel; to close lip vowels (*oo, oh, ah*), narrow and round lips; to close tongue vowels (*ee, eh, ih*), raise the tongue position higher and forward
Women's (or trebles) sound on any pitch above third line treble clef note B-natural while singing the vowel *ah* as in father is spread, tight, pressed, thin, or out of tune.	Ask women or trebles to (1) open the mouth like *ah* if the note is in their upper range; and (2) think a bit of the vowel *oo* into the sound and round the lips
Women's (or trebles) sound on any pitch above third line treble clef note B-natural while singing the vowel *uh* as in *must* is spread, tight, pressed, thin, or out of tune.	Ask women or trebles to (1) open the mouth like *ah* if the note is in their upper range; and (2) think a bit of the vowel *oo* into the sound and round the lips; remind the choir to think ofthe vowel as very vertical
Women's (or trebles) sound on any pitch above third line treble clef note B-natural while singing the vowel *ee* is spread, tight, pressed, thin,or out of tune	Ask women or trebles to (1) open the mouth like ah if the note is in their upper range; and (2) think a bit of the vowel *oo* into the sound as in eat and round the lips; sing the German *ü* sound
Soprano sound in extremely high range is very piercing, tight, and pinched	First, have sopranos drop all consonants and just sing vowels; if the sound continues to be a problem because of extreme range, have the sopranos substitute a more neutral *uh* sound

	for all vowels, in addition to dropping the consonants that are giving them difficulties
Men's sound is out of tune, pressed, strident in their upper register	Have the men make more space similar to the vowel *ah*; ask them also to maintain a very round mouth position
Choral sound is out of tune, spread, on passages that leap	Ask the choir to (1) increase their support just prior to the leap, (2) drop the jaw as they leap upward, and (3) maintain a round mouth position on the leap upward
Choir is unable to perform either a crescendo or a decrescendo, or both	Ask the choir to (1) drop their jaw as they crescendo, and then to close it as they decrescendo, and (2) increase their support on the crescendo and maintain that level of support activity into the decrescendo, but reduce just the volume of the sound without losing intensity
Choral sound sounds weak and unsupported and thin	Rehearse the passage using one of the voiced consonants, *m, n, z,* or *v;* increase the dynamic one level while rehearsing with the voiced consonants.
When a particular voice part sings in their lower register, (especially alto or bass), the sound is spread and flat	Do not allow the choir to crescendo as they sing downward into their lower register; they should make sure that their two front teeth "feel" as if they are always "in" the sound no matter what the vowel
Choir consistently goes "out of tune," despite conductor's reexamination of gesture and vocal technique (specifically, vowel color)	Conductor should pay particular attention to those voice parts that have the third of the harmony to sing; choral intonation is "truer" when the third is sung high Have choir point with index finger as they sing every note of each passage

Vowel colors inconsistent; choir does not sing same vowel colors within each section or throughout choir between sections	Rehearse with singing text staccato in alternation with singing only vowels without consonants
Vowel sounds sound unclear, veiled, or foggy	Ask choir to bring lips around the sounds they sing Tongue vowels such as *eh* and *ih* (those sounds made with the tongue) are not pure; ask choir to bring lips around sound Pure lip vowels (*ee* and *oo*) are not pure; consequently, there is not enough head tone in sound to sing vowels clearly; ask choir to bring lips around sound Have choir point with index finger as they sing their part in the rhythm of their part; choir members should point with directness
Overall choral sound or a sectional sound is pressed	Work on inhalation and seating the breath Work to help choir maintain strength of support without excess "support pressure" by forcing air through the vocal chords
Vowels ee and oo not clear	Not enough vertical spaciousness for the sound; always fix the interior spaciousness of the vowel before adjusting the external lips shape; as a final step, ask choir to bring lips slightly around the sound and to think vowel high and forward Ask choir to breathe the vowel that they are about to sing: *oo* and *ee* are reciprocal vowels—both need a bit of the other mixed in in order to project; in the case of the *oo* vowel, mix *ee* into the *oo*; the pure *oo* vowel is unusable as a vowel in a choral texture—the vowel should sound as if the choir is singing the word *new*; in the case of the *ee* vowel, *oo* should be mixed in

Ee vowel has a pressed or overly bright sound	Ask choir to think *oo* into the sound Ask choir to bring lips around the sound Make sure that tongue vowel is being correctly produced, i.e., with the tip of the tongue anchored on the lower front teeth, and the tongue arched and long
Ah vowel is dull in color	Ask choir to have tall vertical space for vowel and to place vowel as high and forward as possible Ask choir to bring lips around the sound (in order to bring *oo* into the sound) Ask choir to sing the *ah* vowel in the *oo* register. Sing an exercise that has the *ah* vowel preceded by either the *oo* or *ee* vowels; ask choir to sing the *ah* vowel in the same register as the *oo* or *ee* Have choir place heel of hand on forehead while singing
Overall sound is thin, lacks color	Breath not properly seated at the start of the exercise or passage to better seat breath Vocalize choir on voiced consonants in order to better seat breath.
Clean vowel sounds absent	Listen for men's sound and women's sound; be certain all are singing the vowel that was requested Have choir sing exercise staccato to establish clean vowel sounds
Choral sound lacks sustainment and line	Choral breath not in rhythmic spirit of the passage Air flow (support) of choir interrupted Vocalize choir with voiced consonants to connect support to the voice
Pitch problems in legato passages	Ask choir to resing the vowel on each pitch. Check to see that jaw rigidity is absent Vowel modification may be needed in extremes of range Vowel color not unified; listen carefully to the tongue vowels and the *ah* vowel

	Check to make certain consonants are being properly executed; make sure consonants are not twisting into the vowel sounds that follow them
Crescendos in passages and exercises lack color	Ask singers to make more vertical space as crescendo occurs; bring lips around sound
Upward leaps sound pressed and tight	Ask choir to make more space as they ascend
Sound on sustained tones is pressed, almost strident	Air is "locked"; sustained sound being obtained by vocal pressure—"spin" of the tone is needed; have choir gesture fast circles with arms or hands as they sing longer tones
Texture in faster passages seems to be clouded; rhythm seems to be sluggish, even slow; singers are beginning to sing under the pitch	Rehearse the passage staccato; ask the choir to spring to the vowel as quickly as possible; you may also have the choir point in front of their face every time they sing a consonant or tap their forehead every time they speak a consonant
Sound is pressed and out of tune on downward leaps	Ask choir to sing in same register as they descend; bring *ee* into the sound and do not increase the dynamic

Appendix I

A Rhythm Syllable System Based on Beat Functions

$\mathbf{W}$hen learning music, many of us have been taught to first sing the music solfège syllables, i.e., do, re, mi, etc. But few of us were taught a system of rhythm solfège. If we were taught such a system, it was based upon the time values of individual notes such as 1-and-2-and-3-and-4-and, etc. *(The syllable system presented here is based on the relationships of the actual sounds among the rhythm patterns being heard or audiated.)* The syllable system that was introduced in this text can be a valuable tool for learning the rhythmic structure of a piece. The system presented below was developed by Edwin E. Gordon and is explained in detail on pages 266–287 in his book *Learning Sequences in Music: Skill, Content, and Patterns,* 1993 (Chicago: G.I.A. Publications, Inc.). By use of the table below, one can infer the syllables and the logic of the system. When learned, this system can be an invaluable tool in the score learning process and can contribute greatly to one's musical growth.

RHYTHM SYLLABLES BASED ON BEAT FUNCTION

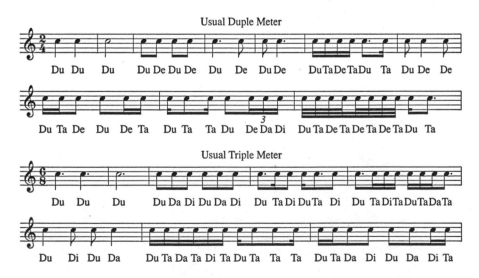

From Edwin E. Gordon, *Learning Sequences in Music: Skill, Content, and Patterns* (Chicago, 1993), 284–285, by permission of GIA Publications, Inc.

APPENDIX II

INNER GAME OF MUSIC: CONDUCTING

The *Inner Game of Music Solo Workbook for Voice* (GIA Publications, Inc., 1995) by Barry Green and Donna Hallen Loewy offers some valuable exercises for choral conductors concerning "awareness," "will," and "trust" that can contribute to one's understanding of the various components of focus. As an introduction to those concepts, several of the exercises are included below. The reader is referred to the complete volume for further exercises.

EXERCISE 1: AWARENESS—SIMULTANEOUS READING

Finding out if you really can listen and talk at the same time. You should do this exercise with your partner.

ACTIVITY:

Read a paragraph from a book or newspaper **out loud** to your partner, while he or she is reading a completely **different paragraph** to you. If you don't have a partner, then read out loud while listening to someone talking on the radio or TV.

Your task is to listen intently to everything that is being read to you at the same time that you carefully note what you are reading.

DIALOG:

Did you find this difficult? It should be!

Were you able to hear more of what you said and less of what the other person was saying? Or was it the other way around?

Were you unable to listen to either yourself or the other party?

It is very difficult to talk and listen at the same time. And in the same way, it is very difficult to 'listen' to the music you are playing—while 'talking' at the same time (I'm thinking of that little voice in your head that tells you, *get your fingers in the right place... don't rush... careful now, play the right notes... here comes the hard part...* and so on).

Since almost everyone agrees you need to listen to yourself when you're playing, it follows that you need to silence that little voice, if you are going to be able to hear yourself play...

EXERCISE 2:
AWARENESS—TENNIS BALL THROW 'B'

Awareness of feeling. This exercise can be done individually or with your partner.

ACTIVITY:

Stand approximately ten feet from your partner, and ask them to throw the tennis ball so that it hits either (a) a trash basket or (b) your left foot. Get them to **try as hard as possible** to hit the target. When they throw the ball, notice how close to the target they were.

Now ask them to repeat the task, but this time tell them to throw the ball at the target with their **eyes closed.** After they have thrown the ball, they are to keep their eyes closed until you have retrieved it.

Note: If you are alone, you can use a bean bag so it will remain at the spot it landed.

Now **change the game.**

While your partner's eyes are open, let them know that the object of the game has changed. The idea is no longer to hit your feet (or the trash basket) but for them to be able to tell you where they felt the ball went. Tell them they will find they can answer this question if they pay attention to what they can feel in their fingertips and arm. Then ask them to close their eyes, and tell them to throw the ball again as before.

Ask them where they felt the ball went.

If their guess is wide of the mark, tell them where the ball went, and ask them to repeat the exercise. Repeat the exercise until your partner begins to get a fairly good feel for where the ball goes when they throw it with their eyes closed.

DIALOG:

Did you find your partner actually got closer to the target with your partner's eyes closed (even though that wasn't what they were asked to do?)

Regardless of where the ball went, did you notice a shift in your partner's concentration when you asked your partner to perform the 'feeling' parts of the exercise as compared with the 'hitting the target' parts?

Did you notice whether your partner was more relaxed, or concentrated, or was throwing more naturally, when your partner's attention was on the 'feeling' parts of the exercise?

If your partner had difficulty with this exercise, can you find out why? Was the exercise too complicated? confusing? Was your partner trying to hit the target and tell you where the ball went in the 'feeling' steps? Or thinking of something else?

This exercise is designed to show that a shift occurs between the **trying** mode (trying to hit the ball) and the more natural **awareness** mode (feeling where it went). This shift may take the form of a more natural and unthinking motion while throwing the ball.

Now reverse the roles and repeat the exercise.

EXERCISE 3:
AWARENESS—INNER GAME OF RUNNING

This exercise can be done alone, with a partner or in a group. Wear appropriate shoes. This is about finding what works naturally for you when running.

ACTIVITY:

Run twenty-five yards—preferably on an oval track, but on any 25 yard segment of grass or other running surface as necessary.

Now express any thoughts that came into your head while you were running: *'I hate running...' 'Why am I doing this?' "I'm wearing the wrong clothes for this sort of thing... they make me look clumsy...' 'My back hurts...' 'I'll never be able to finish this class.' 'I already know how to run, and besides, it's music I'm interested in...'*

Did you let it all out?

Now run another 25 yards, and this time notice exactly how your feet are hitting the ground. Most people land with the heel of their foot, but do you?

DIALOG:

What part of your foot hits the ground first when you run?
Does the ball of the foot hit first? the toe? the heel? the entire foot?

Do you transfer your weight through the middle of your foot? outside or inside?

Do you push off with your toes? Do you lift your foot?

Does your shoe hit the ground differently when you are running slowly, or uphill, or downhill?

ACTIVITY:

Now put your right hand on the front of your right leg and your left hand behind your right leg. Flex the muscles in the front and back of you leg and *try* to walk.

Now, keeping your hands in the same positions on your legs, take a few slow steps, noticing *when* and *where* you can feel the muscles in your legs contracting.

DIALOG:

Was it difficult or impossible to walk when you had flexed your muscles that first time? Impossible?

When you held your leg while you walked, did you notice you used the muscles in front and back of your legs at different times?

If you flex your arm and feel the muscles in your upper arm (biceps and triceps), you will notice the same alternating activity.

While you are running, walking, or moving virtually any part of your body, half of your muscles are being used, and the other half are relaxing!

ACTIVITY:

Now run another 25 yard segment, and put your attention on your legs, noticing the muscles that are **relaxed** rather than those that are flexed.

DIALOG:

Was this a relaxing or a tense experience?

When you noticed which muscles were more relaxed, were you able to run more easily?

Any time you feel fatigue, you can either pay attention to the tired muscles that have been doing the work, or **switch your attention** consciously to the alternate muscles which have been relaxed. By doing this, you may eliminate some unnecessary tension and help **both** sets of muscles to relax.

ACTIVITY:

Choose a partner for the next part of this exercise.

If you can conveniently find a grassy area, do this part of the exercise on grass.

The idea here is to run about 15 yards with your upper body held perpendicular to the ground.

Your partner should run about 1 foot behind you, and very **gently** push with their open hand in your back several times, to gauge how much force it takes to push you.

The partners who are pushing need to make sure they don't push too hard.

Now reverse the roles, and do it again.

When you have both done this, do the same thing—but this time, the partner who is **running** should lean forward about 15 degrees, and the partner who is **pushing** should be extra careful not to push too hard, or the runner may take off in a hurry, and maybe not come back.

Note: if you are alone, you can be aware of the feeling of your body weight in your feet or legs as you run in the erect or leaning forward positions.

DIALOG:

Did you notice how much more energy it took to push your partner when they were running erect?

Did you notice how easy it was to push them when their body was already at an angle?

When you were running leaning slightly forward, did you notice how much lighter you were on your feet?

When you were running at an angle, were there times when you felt you were close to falling?

What else did you notice?

ACTIVITY:

Run another 25 yards, paying attention to the position of your arms and hands. First run with your hands at chest height, then around your stomach, then drop them to your waist.

DIALOG:

Where did your hands feel most comfortable?

Most people find their arms are most comfortable when they are at about stomach height. You can also notice what's a comfortable distance for your elbows to be from your body.

ACTIVITY:

Now run three more 25 yard segments, putting your attention on the position of your head. First run with your head up and eyesight parallel to the ground, then looking about 15 yards ahead, and then looking straight down at your feet.

DIALOG:

Where did your head feel most comfortable?
Most people find their head is most comfortable when it is aligned with the spine. If the body is leaning forward, the head probably feels comfortable looking only a little ahead. What was your experience?

ACTIVITY:

Run another 25 yard segment, and count the number of steps (each foot equals one step) that you take to breathe in and out. You should wind up with two numbers: 4 steps when I inhale and 3 on the exhale, or 3 and 5, or 4 and 4, or whatever.

DIALOG:

What is your breathing pattern?

When you run at a comfortable aerobic pace (i.e. at an exercise rate that's appropriate for your heart), your breathing should be fairly steady, at a level where you could still carry on a conversation with someone while running.

ACTIVITY:

Run another segment, but this time put one hand on your throat and breathe from there, again counting the number of steps that you take to breathe in and out.
Then lower your hand to your chest area, and repeat the exercise.
Finally, put your hand over your abdomen and count the number of steps per breath.

DIALOG:

Did you notice your breathing changing as you moved your hand down from your throat to your abdomen?

Did your breathing get slower or faster as it got lower?
Were you more comfortable with your breathing slower or faster?

Most wind players and singers are well aware that their best breathing comes from the lower part of the body, and the same holds true for running.

If you ever experience shortness of breath, you can **notice** where you are breathing from, and **regulate your breathing** by placing it lower (as in this part of the exercise).

EXERCISE 4: TRUST—INNER GAME OF RUNNING

This exercise should be done as indicated—with a partner and in a group. Wear appropriate shoes. This exercise is about letting go when running. Note: do not do this exercise until you have completed the Awareness—Inner Game of Running exercise.

THE ACTIVITY:

Choose a partner who is close to your own size and height.

While they run about 25 yards **at a steady pace,** you should run alongside them, **attempting to distract them** by running first faster, then slower than they are running. Make sure your arms are not coordinated with theirs

Note that your partner should run at a steady pace, but is intended to notice your attempts to distract them.

Now exchange roles, and do it again. Note: If you are alone, you can imagine someone running next to you.

THE DIALOG:

Did you notice how much energy it took to run 'against' your partner?
Was this difficult?
Was it hard to distract your partner?
When you were the one who was running at a steady pace, did you feel your partner's distracting behavior cost you any energy?
Was it difficult to ignore them?

It takes a lot of work to control the environment and run 'against' the speed of someone else.

The same is true with music. It is hard to play 'against' the rhythm of an ensemble.

It is also hard not to be affected by others around you who are themselves not coordinated with the ensemble.

ACTIVITY:

This time, one partner runs at a steady pace while the other partner allows their own body to simply *mimic their partner's rhythm's*—running alongside with the same hand, leg and body cadences, but *without making a huge effort* to do so.

Repeat the exercise with the roles reversed.

THE DIALOG:

Was this difficult?

Were you able to do it after just a few steps?

Did Self 1 come in and tell you you had to get your feet, arms, head and body position all perfect before you could relax?

If so, did you notice how tense and difficult the whole thing became?

Did you just finally give up and allow your body to let go and flow with the movements your partner was making?

Did you notice how much your success in letting go had to do with how much mental interference you experienced while running?

It is much easier to let go in this kind of way than it is to control your physical movements.

When you just notice what's happening while avoiding thinking, your body knows how to move—and it will show you, gracefully and efficiently.

ACTIVITY:

The whole group or class—3 or 4 people at least—should run, grouped closely together, with **everybody** stepping off at approximately the same moment.

Everybody should notice if their foot cadence is **ahead of** or **behind** the cadence of the bulk of the group, and then let go to the group sound, allowing their steps to match up naturally with those of the rest of the group.

You should just **listen** to the **sound** of the group's feet as you run.

Note: If you are alone, you can run with a Walkman radio, and run in time with the rhythm of some music. Notice if your feet are ahead of or behind the beat of the music.

DIALOG:

How long did it take for you to get into rhythm with the group? Did you find the cadence right away?

If so, did you do it without thinking? Was it easy?

If not, what were you thinking until you matched the sound of the group?

This is an exercise in both **awareness** of **sound** and **trust** (letting go to the rhythm of the group).

Notice that you first have to be aware of the sound outside you, before you can entrust yourself to the cadence and adjust your own steps to match it.

The same principle comes into play when two percussionists need to play together from opposite sides of a stage, or a string section has rhythmic eighth-notes that have to be played together as one.

❦

BIBLIOGRAPHY AND SUGGESTED

LIST FOR FURTHER READING

Abramson, Robert M. *Dalcroze Eurhythmics*. Chicago: G.I.A. Publications, Inc., 1992. Videocassette.

———. *Rhythm Games for Perception and Cognition*. Miami, Florida: C.P.P. Belwin, 1973.

Adler, Kurt. *Phonetics and Diction in Singing*. Minneapolis: University of Minnesota Press, 1967.

Agostini, Emilo. "Diaphragm Activity in Breath Holding: Factors Related to Onset." *Journal of Applied Physiology* 18 (1963): 30–36.

Alexander, F. Matthias. *Constructive Conscious Control of the Individual*. Downey, California: Centerline Press, 1985.

———. *The Use of the Self*. Long Beach, California: Centerline Press, 1989.

Appelman, D. Ralph. *The Science of Vocal Pedagogy*. Bloomington: Indiana University Press, 1967.

Bamberger, Carl, ed. *The Conductor's Art*. New York: Columbia University Press, 1965.

Bamberger, Jeanne. *The Mind behind the Musical Ear*. Cambridge: Harvard University Press, 1991.

Bandler, Grinder. *Frogs into Princes: Neuro-Linguistic Programming*. New York: Carl Fischer, 1988.

Barker, S. *The Alexander Technique: The Revolutionary Way to Use Your Body for Total Energy*. New York: Bantam Books, 1978.

Barlow, W. *The Alexander Technique*. New York: Alfred A. Knopf, 1973.

Bartenieff, Irmgard. *Body Movement: Coping with the Environment*. New York: Gordon and Breach, 1980.

Batstone, P. "Musical Analysis as Phenomenology." *Perspectives of New Music* 7, no. 6, (1969): 94.

Beach, David. "A Schenker Bibliography." *Journal of Music Theory* 17, no. 1 (spring 1969): 2–37.

Belan, William. "An Interview with Roger Wagner." *The Choral Journal* 32 (August 1991): 7–14.

Benjamin, Thomas. "Against Analysis." *Journal of the Liszt Society* (June 1984): 167.

———. "The Learning Process and Teaching." *College Music Symposium* 22, no. 2 (fall 1982): 120–132.

———. "On Teaching Composition." *Journal of Music Theory Pedagogy* (spring 1987): 57–76.

Bergman, Leola Nelson. *Music Master of the Middle West: The Story of F. Melius Christiansen and the St. Olaf Choir* 1944. Reprint, New York: Da Capo, 1968.

Bernstein, Leonard. *The Conductor's Art.*

————. *Findings.* New York: Doubleday, 1982.

————. *The Joy of Music.* New York: Simon and Schuster, 1959.

Bent, I. "Analysis." *The New Grove Dictionary of Music and Musicians.*

Berry, Wallace. *Music Structure and Performance.* New Haven: Yale University Press, 1989.

Bertalot, John. *Five Wheels of Successful Sightsinging.* Minneapolis: Augsburg, 1993.

Blum, David. *Casals and the Art of Interpretation.* Los Angeles: University of California Press, 1977.

Bouhuys, Arend. *The Physiology of Breathing.* London: Grune and Stratton, 1977.

Bouhuys, Arend, D. F. Proctor, and J. Mead. "Kinetic Aspects of Singing." *Journal of Applied Physiology* 21 (1966): 483–496.

Boulez, Pierre. *Orientations.* London: Faber and Faber, 1986.

Boult, Sir Adrian. *A Handbook on the Technique of Conducting.* London: Paterson's Publications, Ltd., 1968.

Brenan, F. "The Relation between Musical Capacity and Performance." *Psychological Review* 36 (1926): 249–262.

Brody, V. A. "An Experimental Study of the Emergence of the Process Involved with the Production of a Sound." Ph.D. diss., Michigan University, 1948. *Dissertation Abstracts* 15, no. 90 (1948). University Microfilms no. 13-1417.

Brown, Ralph Morse. *The Singing Voice.* New York: Macmillan Co., 1946.

Brown, William Earl. *Vocal Wisdom: Maxims of Giovanni Battista Lamperti.* Enlarged edition. Supplement edited by Lillian Strongin. Boston: Crescendo Publishers, 1973.

Buber, Martin. *Between Man and Man.* New York: Collier Books, 1965.

————. *I and Thou.* New York: Macmillian, 1958.

————. *The Knowledge of Man.* Atlantic Highlands, New Jersey: Humanities Press International, 1988.

Bunch, Meribeth. *Dynamics of the Singing Voice.* New York: Springer-Verlag, 1982.

Caldwell, J. Timothy. *Expressive Singing: Dalcroze Eurhythmics for Voice.* Englewoood Cliffs, New Jersey: Prentice-Hall, Inc., 1995.

Cameron, Julia. *The Artist's Way.* New York: G. P. Putman and Sons, 1992.

Campbell, Don G. *Master Teacher: Nadia Boulanger.* Washington, D.C.: The Pastoral Press, 1984.

Campbell, E. J. Moran. *The Respiratory Muscles and the Mechanics of Breathing.* Chicago: The Year Book Medical Publishers, Inc., 1958.

Caplan, Deborah. *Back Trouble.* Gainsville, Florida: Triad Publishing Company, 1987.

Card, R. E. *A Study of Clavicular, Intercostal, and Diaphragmatic Breathing in Relationship to the Control of the Breath in Expiration.* Ph.D. diss., Detroit Institute of Musical Art, 1942.

Chapman, Sara A. *Movement Education in the United States: Historical Developments and Theoretical Bases.* Philadelphia: Movement Education Publications, 1974.

Christiansen, F. Melius. "Ensemble Singing." *Yearbook of the Music Supervisors National Conference* (Chicago Music Supervisors National Council) 1932.

Christy, Van A. *Expressive Singing.* 3rd ed. Dubuque, Iowa: William C. Brown and Co., 1974.

———. *Foundations in Singing.* 3rd ed. Dubuque, Iowa: William C. Brown and Co., 1976.

Clark, Hiro, ed. *Picasso: In His Words.* San Fransisco: Collins Publishers, 1993.

Clifton, Thomas. *Music As Heard.* New Haven: Yale University Press, 1983.

Clippinger, David Alva. *The Head Voice and Other Problems.* Boston: Oliver Ditson, 1917.

———. *Systematic Voice Training.* Chicago: Gamble Hinged Music Co., ca. 1910

Coffin, Berton. "The Relationship of the Breath, Phonation and Resonance in Singing." *The NATS Bulletin* 31 (1975): 18–24.

Conable, Barbara, and William Conable. *How to Learn Alexander Technique: A Manual for Students.* Columbus, Ohio: Andover Road Press, 1992.

Cone, Edward T. "Music Form/Musical Performance Reconsidered." *Music Theory Society* (1985): 149–58.

———. *Musical Form and Musical Performance.* New York: W. W. Norton and Company, Inc., 1968.

———. "Three Ways of Reading a Detective Story—or a Brahms Intermezzo." *Georgia Review* (fall 1977): 544–77.

Copeman, Harold. *Singing in Latin.* Printed privately at 22 Tawney Street, Oxford 1NJ, United Kingdom, 1990.

Cooper, Grosvenor, and Leonard B. Meyer. *The Rhythmic Structure of Music.* Chicago: University of Chicago Press, 1960.

Copland, Aaron. *Music and Imagination.* New York: New American Library, 1952.

Corbin, Lynn A. "Practical Applications of Vocal Pedagogy for Choral Ensembles " *The Choral Journal* 26 (March 1986): 5–10.

Covey, Stephen R. *The Seven Habits of Highly Effective People.* New York: Simon and Schuster, 1990.

Coward, Henry. *Choral Technique and Interpretation* 1914. Reprint, Salem, New Hampshire: Ayer Co. Publishers, 1972.

Dart, Thurston. *The Interpretation of Music.* New York: Harper and Row, 1963.

Darrow, G. F. *Four Decades of Choral Training.* Metuchen, New Jersey: Scarecrow Press, Inc., 1975.

———. "The Nature of Choral Training as Revealed through an Analysis of Thirty-Three Years of Published Writings." Ed.D. thesis, Indiana University, 1965.

Davidson, Archibald T. *Choral Conducting.* Cambridge: Harvard University Press, 1940.

Davis, Martha. *Towards Understanding the Intrinsic in Body Motion.* New York: Arno Press, 1972.

———. *Understanding Movement: An Annotated Bibliography.* New York. Arno Press, 1972.

Decker, Harold A., and Julius Herford. *Choral Conducting Symposium* 2nd ed. Englewood Cliffs, New Jersey: Prentice-Hall, 1988.

Dell, Cecily *A Primer for Movement Description.* New York: Dance Notation Bureau, 1977

Donaldson, Robert P. "The Practice and Pedagogy of Vocal Legato." *NATS Bulletin* 29 (1973): 12–21.

Duckworth, William. *Talking Music: Conversations with Five Generations of American Composers.* New York: G. Schirmer, 1995.

Dwyer, Edward J. "Concepts of Breathing in Singing." *NATS Bulletin* 24 (1967): 40–43.

Ehmann, Wilhelm. *Choral Directing.* Minneapolis: Augsburg Publishing House, 1968.

Ehmann, Wilhelm, and Frauke Haasemann. *Voice Building for Choirs.* Chapel Hill, North Carolina: Hinshaw Music, Inc., 1982.

Epstein, David. *Beyond Orpheus.* Cambridge: MIT Press, 1979.

Ericson, Eric. *Choral Conducting.* New York: Walton Music Corporation, 1976.

Fellows, M. "The Young Conductor: An Interview with Thomas Schippers." *Etude* 70 (October 1952): 9.

Finn, William J. *The Art of the Choral Conductor.* 2 vols. Evanston, Illinois: Summy-Birchard Company, 1960.

————. *The Conductor Raises His Baton.* New York: Harper and Brothers, 1944.

Fowler, Charles, ed. *Conscience of a Profession: Howard Swan.* Chapel Hill, North Carolina: Hinshaw Music, Inc., 1987.

Franck, Frederick. *The Zen of Seeing.* New York: Vintage Books, 1973.

Fuchs, Peter Paul. *The Psychology of Conducting.* New York: MCA, 1969.

Fuchs, Viktor. *The Art of Singing and Voice Technique.* New York: London House and Maxwell, 1964.

Fulghum, Robert. *All I Really Need to Know I Learned in Kindergarten.* New York: Ivy Books, 1988.

Gajard, Dom Joseph. *The Solesmes Method.* Collegeville, Minnesota: Liturgical Press, 1960.

Gal, Hans, ed. *The Musician's World.* London: Thames and Hudson, 1965.

Gallwey, W. Timothy. *The Inner Game of Tennis* New York: Bantam Books, 1989.

Gardner, Howard. *Frames of Mind.* New York: Basic Books, 1983.

Garlinghouse, Burton. "Rhythm and Relaxation in Breathing." *NATS Bulletin* 7 (1951): 2.

Gelb, Michael. *Body Learning.* New York: Henry Holt and Company, 1987.

Glenn, Carole. *In Quest of Answers: Interviews with American Choral Conductors.* Chapel Hill, North Carolina: Hinshaw Music, Inc., 1991.

Gordon, Edwin E. *Learning Sequences in Music: Skill, Content, and Patterns.* 1988 ed. Chicago: G.I.A. Publications, Inc.

————. *Learning Sequences in Music: Skill, Content, and Patterns.* 1993 ed. Chicago: G.I.A. Publications, Inc.

————. *The Manifestation of Developmental Music Aptitude in the Audiation of "Same" and "Different" as Sound in Music.* Chicago: G.I.A. Publications, Inc., 1981.

————. *Manual for the Primary Measures of Music Audiation and the Intermediate Measures of Music Audiation.* Chicago: G.I.A. Publications, Inc., 1986.

————. *Manual for the Advanced Measures of Music Audiation.* Chicago: G.I.A. Publications, Inc., 1989.

————. *The Nature, Description, Measurement, and Evaluation of Music Aptitudes.* Chicago: G.I.A. Publications, Inc , 1987.

————. *Primary Measures of Music Audiation.* Chicago: G.I.A. Publications, Inc., 1979.

Green, Barry. *The Inner Game of Music.* New York: Doubleday, 1986.

Green, Barry, Donna Hallen Loewy, et al. *The Inner Game of Music Solo Workbook for Voice.* Chicago: G.I.A. Publications, Inc., 1995.

Green, Elizabeth A. *The Modern Conductor.* Englewood Cliffs, New Jersey: Prentice-Hall, 1969.

Grunow, Richard F., and Milford H. Fargo. *The Choral Score Reading Program.* Chicago: G.I.A. Publications, Inc., 1985.

Grunow, Richard F., and Edwin E. Gordon. *Jump Right In: The Instrumental Series.* Teacher's Guide: Book One. Chicago: G.I.A. Publications, 1989.

Haasemann, Frauke, and James M. Jordan. *Group Vocal Technique.* Chapel Hill, North Carolina: Hinshaw Music, Inc., 1991.

————. *Group Vocal Technique: A Video.* Chapel Hill, North Carolina: Hinshaw Music, Inc., 1989. Videocassette.

————. *Group Vocal Technique: The Vocalise Cards.* Chapel Hill, North Carolina: Hinshaw Music, Inc., 1990. Drill cards.

Haberlen, John. "Microrhythms: The Key to Vitalizing Renaissance Music," *The Choral Journal* 13 (November 1972): 11–14.

Hanslick, Eduard. *The Beautiful in Music.* New York: Bobbs-Merrill Company, Inc., 1957.

Harnoncourt, Nicholas. *Music Today: Music As Speech.* Portland, Oregon: Amadeus Press, 1982.

————. *The Musical Dialogue: Thoughts on Monteverdi, Bach and Mozart.* Portland, Oregon: Amadeus Press, 1984.

Hawking, Stephen W. *A Brief History of Time.* New York: Bantam Books, 1988.

Heffernen, Charles W. *Choral Music: Technique and Artistry.* Englewood Cliffs, New Jersey: Prentice-Hall, 1982.

Henke, Herbert H. "The Application of Emile Jaques-Dalcroze's Solfege-Rhythmique to the Choral Rehearsal." *The Choral Journal* 25 (December 1984): 11–17.

Herford, Julius. "The Conductor's Search." *The Choral Journal* 32, (December 1991): 23–26.

Heider, John. *The Tao of Leadership.* New York: Bantam Books, 1985.

Highwater, Jamake. *The Primal Mind.* New York: Meridan, 1981.

Hillman, James. *Re-Visioning Psychology.* New York: Harper Perennial Publishers, 1992.

————. *The Thought of the Heart and the Soul of the World.* Dallas: Spring Publications, 1982.

Hindemith, Paul. *Elementary Training for Musicians.* New York: Schott Music Corporation, 1974.

Houle, George. "Meter and Performance in the Seventeenth and Eighteenth Centuries," *The Journal of Early Music America* 2 (spring 1989).

————. *Meter in Music, 1600–1800.* Bloomington: Indiana University Press, 1987.

Jaques-Dalcroze, Emile. *Eurhythmics Art and Education.* New York: Benjamin Blom, Inc., 1972.

Jaynes, Julian. *The Origin of Consciousness in the Breakdown of the Bicameral Mind.* Boston: Houghton Mifflin Company, 1990.

Jeffers, Ron. *Translations and Annotations of Choral Repertoire.* Vol. 1, *Sacred Latin Texts.* Corvallis, Oregon: earthsongs, 1988.

———. *Translations and Annotations of Choral Repertoire.* Vol. 2, *German Texts.* Corvallis, Oregon: earthsongs. Forthcoming.

———. *Translations and Annotations of Choral Repertoire.* Vol. 3, *French and Italian Texts.* Corvallis, Oregon: earthsongs. Forthcoming.

———. *Translations and Annotations of Choral Repertoire.* Vol. 4, *Other Foreign Language Texts.* Corvallis, Oregon: earthsongs. Forthcoming.

Jones, A. J. "A Study of the Breathing Processes As They Relate to the Art of Singing" (Ph.D. diss., University of Missouri, Kansas City, 1970) *Dissertation Abstracts International,* 1971, 31/10A, 5447. University Microfilms no. 71-3693.

Jones, F. P. *Body Awareness in Action: A Study of Alexander Technique.* New York: Schocken Books, 1979.

Jordan, James M. "Audiation and Sequencing: An Approach to Score Preparation." *The Choral Journal* 21 (April 1981): 11–13.

———. "The Pedagogy of Choral Intonation: Efficient Pedagogy to Approach an Old Problem." *The Choral Journal* 27 (April, 1987): 9–16.

———. "False Blend: A Vocal Pedagogy Problem for the Choral Conductor." *The Choral Journal* 24 (June 1984): 25–26.

———. "Laban Movement Theory and How It Can Be Used with Music Learning Theory." In *Readings in Music Learning Theory.* Edited by Darrel Walters and Cynthia Crump Taggart, 316–333, Chicago: G.I.A. Publications, Inc., 1989.

———. "Music Learning Theory Applied to Choral Performance Groups." In *Readings in Music Learning Theory.* Edited by Darrel Walters and Cynthia Crump Taggart, 168–183, Chicago: G.I.A. Publications, Inc., 1989.

———. "Rhythm Learning Sequence." In *Readings in Music Learning Theory.* Edited by Darrel Walters and Cynthia Crump Taggart, 26–37, Chicago: G.I.A. Publications, Inc., 1989.

———. "Toward a Flexible Sound Ideal through Conducting: Some Reactions to Study with Wilhelm Ehmann." *The Choral Journal* 25 (November 1984): 5-6.

Jordan, James M., and Constantina, Tsolainou. *Ensemble Diction: Language and Style, Principles and Applications.* Chapel Hill, North Carolina: Hinshaw Music, Inc., 1995. Videocassette.

Jung, Carl G. *Man and His Symbols.* New York: Doubleday, 1988.

———. *Memories, Dreams and Reflections.* London: Collins and Routledge, 1963.

———. *The Undiscovered Self.* Princeton: Princeton University Press, 1990.

Kapit, Wynn. and Lawrence M. Elson. *The Anatomy Coloring Book.* New York: Harper Collins Publishers, 1977.

Keller, Hans. "Epilogue/Prologue: Criticism and Analysis." *Music Analysis I* (1982): 9.

———. "The Musical Analysis of Music." *The Listener* 58 (August 1975): 326.

———. "Wordless Analysis" *Musical Events* 12 (December 1957): 26.

Kemp, Helen. *Of Primary Importance.* Garland, Texas: Choristers Guild, 1989.

Kern, Jan, ed. *Jubilate Deo: Easy Latin Gregorian Chants for the Faithful.* Chicago: G.I.A. Publications, Inc., 1974.

Kohut, D. L. *Musical Performance: Learning Theory and Pedagogy.* Englewood Cliffs, New Jersey: Prentice-Hall, Inc., 1985.

Laban, Rudolf von. *Choreutics.* Edited by Lisa Ullman. London: MacDonald and Evans Ltd., 1966.

———. *A Life for Dance.* London: MacDonald and Evans Ltd., 1975.

———. *The Mastery of Movement.* Edited by Lisa Ullman. London: MacDonald and Evans Ltd., 1980.

———. *Modern Educational Dance.* Edited by Lisa Ullman. Boston: Plays Inc., 1980.

———. "Movement Concerns the Whole Man." *The Laban Art of Movement Guild Magazine* 21 (November 1958): 12–13.

Laban, Rudolf von, and F. C. Lawrence. *Effort.* London: MacDonald and Evans, 1947.

Lakeoff, George, and Mark Johnson. *Metaphors We Live By.* Chicago: University of Chicago Press, 1980.

Lamb, Warren. *Posture and Gesture.* London: Gerald Duckworth and Company, 1965.

Lamperti, Francesco. *The Technics of Bel Canto.* New York: G. Schirmer, 1905.

LaRue, Jan. *Guidelines for Style Analysis.* New York: W. W. Norton and Co., Inc., 1970.

Lautzenheiser, Tim. *The Joy of Inspired Teaching.* Chicago: G.I.A. Publications, Inc., 1993.

Le Hurray, Peter. *Authenticity in Performance: Eighteenth-Century Case Studies.* Cambridge: Cambridge University Press, 1990.

Leinsdorf, Erich. *The Composer's Advocate.* New Haven: Yale University Press, 1981.

Leyden, Norman Fowler. "A Study and Analyis of the Conducting Patterns of Arturo Toscanni as Demonstrated in Kinescope Films." Ph.D. diss., Columbia University, 1968. University Microfilms 69-10,546.

Lieberman, Philip. *Intonation, Perception and Language.* Cambridge: M.I.T. Press, 1967.

Little, Meredith, and Natalie Jenne. *Dance and the Music of J. S. Bach.* Bloomington: Indiana University Press, 1991.

Long, Dorothy. *The Original Art of Music.* Lanham, Maryland: The Aspen Institute and University Press of America, Inc., 1989.

Maisel, E., ed. *The Resurrection of the Body—The Essential Writings of F. M. Alexander.* Boston: Shambhala Inc., 1986.

Mark, C. "Simplicity in Early Britten." *Tempo* 147 (December 1983): 8–14.

Marshall, Madeleine. *The Singer's Manual of English Diction.* New York: G. Schirmer, Inc., 1953.

McElheran, Brock. *Conducting Technique for Beginners and Professionals.* New York: Oxford University Press, 1966.

Meyer, Leonard B. *Emotion and Meaning in Music.* Chicago: University of Chicago Press, 1956.

———. *Explaining Music: Essays and Explorations.* Los Angeles: University of California Press, 1973.

———. *Music, the Arts, and Ideas.* Chicago: University of Chicago Press, 1967.

Meyer, Leonard, and Grosvenor Cooper. *The Rhythmic Structure of Music.* Chicago: University of Chicago Press, 1960.

Moe, Daniel. *Problems in Conducting.* Minneapolis: Augsburg, 1968.

Molnár, Antal. *Classical Canons.* Budapest: Editio Musica Budapest, 1955.

Moore, Carol-Lynne and Kaoru Yamamoto. *Beyond Words: Movement Observation and Analysis.* New York: Gordon and Breach, 1988.

Moore, Thomas. *A Blue Fire: Selected Writings by James Hillman.* New York: Harper Collins Publishers, 1989.

———. *Care of the Soul.* New York: HarperCollins Publishers, 1992

Moriarty, John. *Diction.* Boston: E. C. Schirmer, 1975.

Mostovoy, Marc. "The Modern Orchestra and Period Performance Practice." *Journal of the Conductors' Guild* 10, nos. 3 and 4 (1989): 97–110.

Miller, Richard. "Diction in Relation to the Vocal Legato." *NATS Bulletin* 4 (1966): 12–23.

———. *English, French, German, and Italian Techniques of Singing: A Study in Tonal Preferences and How They Relate to Functional Efficiency.* Metuchen, New Jersey: Scarecrow Press, Inc., 1977.

———. *The Structure of Singing.* New York: Schirmer Books, 1986.

Monsaingeon, Bruno. *Mademoiselle.* Manchester, England: Carcanet Press Limited, 1985.

Persichetti, Vincent. *Twentieth-Century Harmony.* New York: W. W. Norton and Co., Inc.,1961.

Peter, Franklin. *The Idea of Music: Schoenberg and Others.* London: Macmillan, 1985.

Picasso, Pablo. *In His Words.*

Preston, Valerie. *A Handbook for Modern Educational Dance.* London: MacDonald and Evans, 1963.

Proctor, Donald F. *Breathing, Speech and Song.* New York: Springer-Verlag, 1980.

Proulx, Richard. *In Praise of Mary: Five Gregorian Chants in English and Latin.* Chicago: G.I.A. Publications, Inc., 1988.

Pullias, Earl V., and James D. Young. *A Teacher Is Many Things.* Bloomington: Indiana University Press, 1977, p. 90.

Reid, Cornelius L. *A Dictionary of Vocal Terminology.* New York: Joseph Patelson Music House, 1983.

———. *The Free Voice: A Guide to Natural Singing.* New York: Joseph Patelson Music House, 1965.

———. *Voice: Psyche and Soma.* New York: Joseph Patelson Music House, 1975.

Reiner, Fritz. "The Technique of Conducting." *Etude* 69 (October 1951): 164.

Reti, Rudolph. *The Thematic Process in Music.* London: Greenwood Press, 1978.

Richards, Mary Caroline. *Centering.* Middleton, Connecticut: Wesleyan University Press, 1989.

Rilke, Ranier Maria. *Letters to a Young Poet.* New York: W. W. Norton and Company, 1962

Robinson, Ray. "Wilhelm Ehmann: His Contributions to the Choral Art." *The Choral Journal* 25 (November 1984): 7–12

Robinson, Ray, and A. Winold. *The Choral Experience.* New York: Harper's College Press, 1976

Roe, P. F. *Choral Music Education.* Englewood Cliffs, New Jersey: Prentice-Hall, Inc., 1970.

Rorem, Ned. *Setting the Tone.* New York: Limelight Editions, 1983.

Rudolph, Max. *The Grammar of Conducting.* New York: G. Schirmer, 1950.

Sachs, Curt. *Rhythm and Tempo: A Study in Music History.* New York: W. W. Norton, 1953.

————. *World History of the Dance.* New York: W. W. Norton, 1937.

Sacks, Oliver. *An Anthropologist on Mars: Seven Paradoxical Tales.* New York: Alfred A. Knopf, 1995.

Schmalfeldt, Janet. "On the Relation of Analysis to Performance: Beethoven's Bagatelle Op. 126, Nos. 2 and 5." *Journal of Music Theory* 29, no. 1 (1985): 1–31.

Schopenhauer, Arthur. *The World as Will and Representation.* 2 vols. New York: Dover, 1966.

Sessions, Roger. *The Musical Experience of Composer, Performer and Listener.* New Jersey: Princeton University Press, 1950.

————. *The Musical Experience of Composer, Performer, Listener.* New York: Atheneum, 1965.

Shaw, Robert. "Letters to a Symphony Chorus." *The Choral Journal.* 26 (April 1986): 5–8.

————. *Preparing a Masterpiece: The Brahms Requiem.* Carnegie Hall. Videocassette.

Shrock, Dennis. "An Interview with Margaret Hillis on Score Study." *The Choral Journal* 31 (February 1991): 7–12.

————. "An Interview with Paul Salamunovich on Aspects of Communication." *The Choral Journal* 31 (October 1990): 9–18.

————. "An Interview with Weston Noble." *The Choral Journal* 32 (December 1991): 7–11.

Shuter-Dyson, Rosamund, and Gabriel Clive. *The Psychology of Musical Ability.* London: Methuen, 1981.

Spector, Irwin. *Rhythm and Life: The Work of Emile Jaques-Dalcroze.* Dance and Music Series, no. 3. Stuyvesant, New York: Pendragon Press, 1990.

Stevens, Chris. *Alexander Technique.* London: Macdonald and Co., 1987.

Storr, Anthony. *Music and the Mind.* New York: Ballatine Books, 1992.

————. *Solitude: A Return to the Self.* New York: Ballatine Books, 1988.

Stransky, J., and R. Stone. *The Alexander Technique: Joy in the Life of Your Body.* New York: Beaufort Books, 1981.

Stravinsky, Igor. *An Autobiography.* New York: M. and J. Steuer, 1958.

————. *Poetics of Music.* Cambridge: Harvard University Press, 1974.

Sunshine, Linda, ed. *A Teacher Affects Eternity.* Kansas City: Andrews and McMech, 1995.

Swan, Howard. *Conscience of a Profession.* Chapel Hill, North Carolina: Hinshaw Music, Inc.

————. "The Development of the Choral Instrument." In *Choral Conducting: A Symposium.* Edited by H. Decker and J. Herford. Englewood Cliffs: New Jersey: Prentice-Hall, Inc., 1973.

Szell, George. "Toscanini in the History of Orchestral Performance." *Saturday Review,* 25 March 1967, 53.

Szell, George, and Paul Henry Lang. "A Mixture of Instinct and Intellect." *High Fidelity* 15 (January 1965): 42–45, 110–112.

Tacka, Philip, and Michael Houlahan. *Sound Thinking: Developing Musical Literacy.* New York: Boosey and Hawkes, 1995.

Tagg, Barbara, and Dennis Shrock. "An Interview with Helen Kemp." *The Choral Journal* 30 (November 1989): 5–13.

Thakar, Markand. *Counterpoint: Fundamentals of Music-Making.* New Haven: Yale University Press, 1990.

———. "Principles of Conducting Technique." 1991.

Thomas, Kurt. *The Choral Conductor.* English adaptation by Alfred Mann and William H. Reese. [Published as a special issue of the *American Choral Review* 13, nos. 1 and 2.] New York: Associated Music Publishers, 1971.

Thornton, Samuel. *Laban's Theory of Movement: A New Perspective.* Boston: Plays, Inc., 1971.

Thurmond, James Morgan. *Note Grouping.* Ft. Lauderdale, Florida: Meredith Publications, 1980.

Toch, Ernst. *The Shaping Forces in Music.* New York: Criterion Music Corporation, 1948.

Tovey, Sir Donald Francis. *Essays in Musical Analysis.* London: Oxford University Press, 1941.

Trame, Richard H., SJ. "The Choral Accompanist and the Choral Director: An Interview with Robert D. Hunter." *The Choral Journal* 24 (December 1983): 19–20.

Treitler, Leo. "Structural and Critical Analysis." In *Musicology in the 1980's.* Edited by Holman and Palisca. 67–77. New York: Da Capo Press, 1982.

Uhlrich, Homer. *A Survey of Choral Music.* New York: Harcourt Brace Jovanovich, 1973.

Valentine, C. W. *The Experimental Psychology of Beauty.* London: Methuen, 1962.

Vinquist, Mary, and Neal Zaslaw, eds. *Performance Practice: A Bibliography.* New York: W. W. Norton and Co., Inc., 1971.

Wagner, Richard. *On Conducting.* London: William Reeves, 1919.

Walter, Bruno. *Theme and Variations.* New York: Alfred A. Knopf, 1947.

Webb, Guy B, ed. *Up Front.* Boston: ECS Publishing, 1993.

Wehr, David A. "John Finley Williamson (1887–1964): His Life and Contribution to Choral Music." Ph.D. diss., University of Miami, 1971. University Microfilms 72-12,878.

Weikart, Phyllis. *Teaching Movement and Dance: A Sequential Approach to Rhythmic Movement.* Ypsilanti, Michigan: High Scope Press, 1989.

Whitehead, Alfred North. *The Aims of Education and Other Essays.* New York: Mentor Books, 1957.

Willetts, Sandra. *Upbeat Downbeat: Basic Conducting Patterns and Techniques.* Nashville: Abingdon Press, 1993.

Williamson, John Finley. "Choral Singing: [articles individually titled]." Twelve articles in *Etude* 68 and 69 (April 1950–October 1951).

———. "The Conductor's Magic." *Etude* 69 (April 1951): 23.

———. "Training the Individual Voice through Choral Singing." *Proceedings of the Music Teachers National Association* 33 (1938): 52–59.

York, Wynn. "The Use of Imagery in Posture Training." *The NATS Bulletin,* 16 (1963: 34.

Zuckerkandl, Victor. *Sound and Symbol.* Translated by Willard R. Trask. New York: Pantheon, 1956.

————. *Man the Musician*. Translated by Norbert Guterman. Princeton: Princeton University Press, 1973.

————. *The Sense of Music*. Princeton: Princeton University Press, 1959.

Zukav, Gary. *The Dancing Wu Li Masters: An Overview of the New Physics*. New York: William Morrow, Inc., 1979.

INDEX OF QUOTED PERSONS

Topical Index

ABOUT THE AUTHOR

James Jordan is associate professor of conducting at Westminster Choir College in Princeton, New Jersey, one of the world's foremost centers for the study and performance of choral music. He is conductor of the Westminster Chapel Choir.

From 1986 to 1991 he was chair for music education at the Hartt School of Music of the University of Hartford in West Hartford, Connecticut. He also served on the faculty of the School of the Hartford Ballet. Dr. Jordan holds the bachelor of music degree from Susquehanna University; the master of music degree in choral conducting from Temple University, where he was a student of Elaine Brown; and the doctorate in music education with an emphasis on the psychology of music from Temple University, where he was a student of Edwin E. Gordon. Dr. Jordan has studied conducting with Wilhelm Ehmann, Frauke Haasemann, Volker Hempfling, and Gail B. Poch. Prior to his appointment at Hartt he taught at Pennsylvania State University and conducted The University Choir. From 1977 to 1985 Dr. Jordan developed the nationally recognized choral music program at Lewisburg (Pennsylvania) High School. Dr. Jordan is an authority concerning rhythm pedagogy, choral methods, and music learning theory applied to choral performing groups. His choirs have performed at numerous conventions of the Music Educators National Conference (MENC) and the American Choral Directors Association (ACDA).

Dr. Jordan enjoyed a professional collaboration with the late Frauke Haasemann. As a result of that collaboration, he coauthored with her three landmark publications concerning group vocal technique published by Hinshaw Music: *Group Vocal Technique* (book), *Group Vocal Technique* (vocalise cards), and *Group Vocal Technique* (video). He has coauthored with Constantina Tsolainou a video, *Ensemble Diction*, also published by Hinshaw Music. He was also a major contributor to the text *Up Front*, published by E. C. Schirmer, and to *Readings in Music Learning Theory*, published by GIA Publications.